CONFRONTATION: BLACK AND WHITE

Lerone Bennett, Jr.

Lerone Bennett, Jr., was born in Clarksdale, Mississippi, in 1928 and educated in the public schools of Jackson, Mississippi, where he worked on the local Negro weekly, *The Mississippi Enterprise*. He attended Morehouse College and was Editor of the student newspaper, *The Maroon Tiger*. Upon graduation he joined the staff of the *Atlanta Daily World*, first as a reporter and then as City Editor. In 1960 he became the first Senior Editor of *Ebony*. Among his other books are *What Manner of Man: A Biography of Martin Luther King, Jr.*; *The Negro Mood*; and *Before the Mayflower* (now published in a Pelican edition). Mr. Bennett is married and the father of four children.

CONFRONTATION

BLACK AND WHITE

By Lerone Bennett, Jr.

Foreword by A. Philip Randolph

PENGUIN BOOKS INC.

BALTIMORE · MARYLAND

Penguin Books Inc,
3300 Clipper Mill Road, Baltimore, Maryland 21211

First published 1965

Penguin edition published 1966 by arrangement with
Johnson Publishing Company, Inc., Chicago

Printed in the United States of America

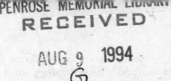
FOREWORD

THE civil rights revolution has been caught up in a crisis of victory; a crisis which may involve great opportunity or great danger to its future fulfillment. The victory consists in the winning of civil rights, through the enactment of the Civil Rights Act of 1964, for which Negroes have struggled for over a hundred years. There is, therefore, opportunity for the civil rights movement to mount and carry out a vigorous program of implementation of the Act, and also to look beyond to the larger goal of human freedom—political, social, industrial, and economic.

Negroes enjoy civil rights in the North, but they do not possess the basic freedoms. The socioethnic dynamism generated by the struggle for civil rights may be used to help attain the goal of full freedom as a way of life. The achievement of freedom from poverty, freedom from ignorance, freedom from disease, freedom from fear and war, freedom from racial bias and religious bigotry is far beyond the power of any single segment of our society. It is a fundamental challenge to the American Establishment.

Unless the fight is waged and won for the larger freedoms, civil rights, like civil liberties in time of war, may not be permanently secure. It is difficult to find a social group which has been in possession of civil rights and civil liberties for long, and yet has been without economic rights, economic freedom, economic citizenship, and public power. Negroes must therefore make a major objective the enlargement and broadening of the base of civil rights to involve the basic freedoms.

Inspiring the Negro masses to play a creative role in the civil rights revolution is extremely difficult without the development of massive demonstrations in which they can be involved easily, since all that is required is energy and the will to march. But the day of demonstrations of tremendous dimensions, such as the March on Washington in August 1963 [and

Extracted from "Opening Remarks" at the Conference of Negro Leaders, National Council of Churches in New York City, January 30-31, 1965.

the massive Selma to Montgomery March in March, 1965] are practically over, and a new strategy must be found to bring Negroes together. A transition from the politics of confrontation of civil rights forces with anti-Negro-freedom forces in the streets, to the politics of confrontation of ideas at the conference table is under way, and is our hope for the future. But there is a psychological and social gulf between the Negro masses and Negro classes—the teachers, students, doctors, lawyers, preachers, businessmen—it must and can be bridged. This gulf is real, and it is widening instead of narrowing. It can be seen in the scepticism and cynicism in many Negro workers, employed and unemployed, and also in the apathy of the middle classes when they are approached by the Negro leadership, unless as a rule the leaders are rabble rousers spitting the fire and brimstone of black nationalism and anti-whiteism. The climate of black racism, created though it is by white racism, presents a problem which must be overcome if the movement for freedom is to move forward to a productive and creative confrontation of ideas.

The Negro masses must be won to the struggle in the civil rights movement by Negro leadership. The strength and progress of the freedom movement depend upon the unity of these two forces. The manpower for mass activities in the streets must come from the masses, as importantly as the qualified and specialized talent needed at the conference table to find the complex remedies required to solve the problems of de facto ghetto schools and housing segregation must come from the leadership. Dedication, though indispensable, is not enough. In the socioethnic spectrum of our community life, more light and less heat is needed for racial progress.

A danger that must be guarded against is the state of psychological and emotional relaxation into which Negroes may sink after the crisis of victory. This could undermine the morale of civil rights activists and the rank-and-file workers, and could weaken the entire organizational structure of the civil rights movement. Any severe loss of public approval of the Negro Freedom movement could be a grave threat not only to the implementation of the Civil Rights Act of 1964, but to the struggle to improve and strengthen it—indeed, even to maintaining it without emasculating amendments.

The civil rights organizations, facing new and different tasks and problems incident to a great historic legislative victory, must undergo a basic and comprehensive reexamination, involving tactics and strategy as well as policies and objectives. The Freedom movement cannot any longer build strength around the traditional classical concept of civil rights which has been its major goal for a hundred years.

Even if all racial barriers are abolished, it is hardly possible for the Negro workforce to catch up with the white workforce and bridge the widening gap of the annual average median wage between the two groups. Automation may mean that Negro workers as young as thirty years of age may never work again, especially those without skills, training, and education. Negro civil rights organizations must lead the war on poverty in the interest of developing a socioeconomic order which will bring about the humanization of the revolution of automation. To this end, Negroes must take the leadership in building a coalition of conscience to include the black poor and the white poor, the black unemployed and the white unemployed, the black workers and the white workers, civil rights organizations and organized labor, Negroes and Jews, Catholics and Protestants, liberal intellectuals and progressive businessmen, to create a national consensus which will prod, persuade, and support the federal government to build decent, low-costing housing for all, integrated quality schools for all, and jobs or a guaranteed decent income for all.

Verily, with the pressure of history behind us and of the age of automation before us, Negroes must move ahead with the white poor and the citizens of goodwill, or history will again pass us by.

A. PHILIP RANDOLPH

CONTENTS

PROLOGUE

CONFRONTATION I

con·fron·ta·tion \ˈkän(ˌ)frən·ˈtāshən\ n -s [F, fr. ML *confrontation-*, *confrontatio* comparison, boundary, fr. *confrontatus* (past part. of *confrontare* to bound) + L *-ion-*, *-io* -ion]: the act of confronting: the state of being confronted: MEETING, OPPOSITION, COMPARISON; *specif*: the bringing face to face of an accused person and his accusing witnesses — used esp. in the phrase *right of confrontation.*

¹con·front\kən'frənt*vt*- ED/-ING/-s [MF *confronter* to confront, border on, fr. ML *confrontare* to bound, fr. L *com-* + ML *-frontare* (fr. L *front-*, *frons* forehead, front) — more at BRINK] **1 a**: to stand facing or opposing esp. in challenge, defiance, or accusation: FACE : stand up to (enemies ∼ *ing* one another) ⟨∼ an accuser in court⟩ **b** : to face (something dangerous or dreaded) without flinching or avoiding ⟨the test of a free society is its capacity to ∼, rather than evade, the vital questions of choice — J. M. Burns⟩ . . .

THE Negro rebellion is a classic example of the confrontment of black and white as symbols and as presences.

This epochal event, which is beginning not ending, is unfolding on several levels. Black man and white man are standing now forehead to forehead, spiritually and physically, but so also are black man and black man, white man and white man.

The Negro rebellion, in short, is a series of interlocking encounters in the community of men and in the minds of men; and these encounters are forcing an ultimate confrontation of America and America, of the Commonwealth of Absence that exists and the Commonwealth of Silence that was promised.

This is a descriptive analysis of that confrontation and its beginnings and implications.

Black man and white man, black man and black man, white man and white man, America and America have been approaching each other for hundreds of years. They stood face to face for the first time in August, 1619, when twenty black seeds were planted at Jamestown. They looked at each other again, without masks, in the 1780's, when the Founding Fathers made slavery and freedom lie down together in the Constitution. Again in 1820, with the Missouri Compromise, in 1860, with the Civil War, and in 1877, with the Bargain of 1877, black man and white man, black man and black man, white man and white man, America and America stood face to face. At each great turning of the fork, men turned from each other at the last moment and fled precipitately from truth. The Negro rebellion of 1960-65 is a continuation on a higher level of desperation of the evaded confrontations of the past. It is an attempt to force a truth men—black men and white men—have always avoided.

The concept of confrontation—the idea of forcing men to confront the gap between word and deed, promise and performance—has always been a key element in Negro strategy. The slave insurrectionists and the leaders of Freedom movement I, were motivated by the same vision that haunts the demonstrators of Freedom movement II. But since the migration and urbanization of the Negro folk, Negro leaders have demonstrated increasing audacity in the use of confrontment as an instrument of induced social change. With the beginning of Freedom movement II in 1960 and the institutionalization of the concept of confrontation, America entered a new stage of relation with itself and with its white and Negro citizens.

The roots of the rebellion (and of the white hysteria) lie deep. Hate and horror did not appear from nowhere in the summers of 1964-65. They were seeded hundreds of years ago in slavery and Reconstruction and manured by years of compromise and bad faith. Bryan Edwards said once that there was not "a real revolution in all human history which developed in less than three generations." In the age of Sputniks and supersonic aircrafts, Edwards' timetable is suspect. But his observation contains a great deal of truth. Revolutions cannot be created at will by agitators. A certain degree of social putrefaction is an indispensable prerequisite. Revolutions are usually the last link in a long chain of events, and they are usually preceded by a long period of social unrest. Most revolutions, moreover, are attempts to force recognition of a change that has already occurred. The Negro explosion falls into the classic pattern. There has been a basic shift in the power of Negroes, as expressed by the mounting population of every large metropolitan area, and that power has not been validated in the world of men. The Negro explosion of 1960-65 is an attempt to force Americans to face a palpable fact: the color of America and of the world has changed.

Although the Negro upheaval bears a superficial resemblance to a revolution, it is not a revolution—yet. Whether or not it becomes a revolution depends on us. A revolution is a rapid but not necessarily violent change through which the power relations and statuses of social groups are changed and a new social order created. The main criterion of a revolution is a desire and a will on the part of a group to force a fundamental change in the social order. Almost all American Negroes have a revolutionary desire but only a minority have a revolutionary will. To repeat: whether or not this will develops depends to a great extent on our responses in the next five or ten years.

Because of limitations of will and strategy, we have chosen here to call the emerging peak of the Negro upheaval a rebellion—a going out of, a becoming, an accession to being.

How did the rebellion come about and why?

There can be no easy answers to that question. The rebellion is a product of a plurality of causes linked to the Negro situation and to the Negro's perception of that situation. And what is the Negro situation? It is a situation defined by powerlessness in a context of broken community.

The basic fact of the Negro situation is shattered community. Negro and white Americans do not belong to the same social body. They do not share that body of consensus or common feeling that usually binds together people sharing a common land. The relation between equals in a community, as Abram Kardiner and Lionel Ovesey pointed out in *The Mark of Oppression*, "is characterized by complete emotional reciprocity. . . . In large groups of equals, the reciprocal influence is maintained by certain *conventions*. For example, property rights are largely a convention among equals; their force is maintained by mutual support of the conventions, and the invocation of commonly ordained agencies of enforcement, should one of the parties violate the convention. This is effected through police and courts of law. Reciprocity is also extended among equals to all forms of positive affects, such as love, sexual union, marriage, friendship, and the like. Reciprocity of feeling also involves the free convention of access to conviction. . . ."

The law of reciprocity does not reign between Negro and white Americans who do not share a common purpose or a common expectancy. Worse, they do not have a common image of man. And, as Camus said, "If men cannot refer to a common value, recognized by all as existing in each other, then man is incomprehensible to man."

Black man is incomprehensible to white man in America, and vice versa: this is the root cause of the rebellion—broken community and the failure of Americans to create a single social organization.

It is a matter of immense importance that Negro and white Americans began their journey as members of one community. In the beginning, Negro and white Americans confronted each other as brothers, brothers-in-law, and fellow passengers on a journey into the unknown. For a period of forty years or more, from 1619 to about 1660, Negro Americans accumulated property, participated in the public life of the community, and mingled and mated with whites on a basis of substantial equality. This racial Eden was destroyed in the 1660's by a decision that led step by step to the fateful confrontations of the 1860's and 1960's.

The breaking of the bond of community between Negro and white Americans began with a conscious decision by the power structures of Colonial America. In the 1660's, men of power in Colonial America decided that human slavery organized on the basis of skin color was to be the linchpin of the new society. It therefore became a matter of public policy to separate forcibly black and white immigrants who had little or no racial prejudice at that time. The evidence indicates that Negro and white Americans were taught to hate and fear each other by a pervasive process of persuasion that continued over a period of hundreds of years. During this epoch, the Negro or, rather, the African-American was shattered as a social being. Not only the Negro but America was degraded by slavery which disrupted the social fabric and stained the Declaration of Independence and the Constitution.

Freedom movement I, which began during the Revolutionary War and reached a peak in the antebellum abolitionist crusade, was an attempt on the part of Negro and white reformers to force Americans to face themselves. The movement reached a minor peak in the period between 1780 and 1830. The Negro church, from which came Freedom movement II, the first Negro newspaper, the first Negro mass meeting: all date from this pioneering period of self-discovery and self-naming.

The second peak of Freedom movement I was the abolitionist crusade which was a revolutionary attack on the fundamentals of the slave system. Many of the techniques of Freedom movement II (passive resistance, professional agents who live on subsistence wages, the use of melody and meter, and a revolutionary insistence on total change) were invented by the abolitionists. Freedom movement I triumphed apparently with enactment of the Thirteenth, Fourteenth, and Fifteenth Amendments. But success masked a fundamental failure. America emancipated the slave in 1865, not the Negro; it decided what it was not, not what it was. As a result of the failure to emancipate the Negro and to create a new social system in the South, Reconstruction was doomed from the start and the road was paved to our present conundrum.

In the post-Reconstruction world separatism again became a matter of public policy. A circle was drawn, nationally and locally, and Negroes were excluded. The net effect of all this was to make Negroes quasi-colonials in their native land. Worse, in many places, not all of them in the South, white Americans used the state police power to exclude Negroes and to grind them down. By law, vigilante action, and terror, the South created two worlds. In this same period, the North created separate communities by restrictive covenants and other "genteel" instruments of exclusion.

Legal fictions sanctified the break in community which was blessed by every agency of power including the Supreme Court. In the years between 1877 and 1946 the Court refused to take judicial notice of separatism. The justices and practically all other Americans hid behind the fictions of "separate but equal," "the police power of the state," and "states' rights."

The creation of two Americas had a disastrous effect on both Negroes and whites. Separated in ghettos in the North and South, Negro Americans were exploited economically, politically, and socially. With the help of the state, they were forced out of several occupations (building trades, catering, barbering, etc.) and deprived of rights and privileges most citizens take for granted. More ominous yet, Negroes were divested of power and deprived of the means of demanding public services and citizenship privileges as a matter of course and right.

Nor did white Americans escape. In the dry years of the "separate-but-equal" era, white Americans began to identify their social, psychological, and economic interests with the containment of Negroes who were seen as threats to their ego-structures. As the decades wore on, segregation became a social drug. The more men imbibed, the more they needed. As walls of hate and fear multiplied, negating what men said they believed and the America they said existed, men grew anxious, evasive, afraid.

The abrogation of the law of reciprocity in this period created a substructure of conflict that needed only a proper psychological moment and a tool of the right size and weight for proper expression.

For more than sixty years now, Negroes have been gathering fury against the system. The Negro rebellion grew out of internal and external migrations in the Negro community and the failure of white Americans to make viable responses to the changing situation and the changing consciousness of Negroes. The Great Negro Migration, which began in 1915-16 and continues today, changed the Negro's relation to himself and to America. Under the impact of urbanization, the Negro became more conscious of himself and of the totality of horror of his situation. The grand outcome was a profound change in Negro consciousness, which led, in turn, to three basic shifts in the Negro mode of being in America: a shift in sensibility, a shift in strategy, and a shift in timing. The demonstrations in the streets are reflections of these basic shifts and the deeper, more profound, shifts in the Negro mode of being a Negro and his mode of being an American.

The change in Negro consciousness was hastened by impersonal socioeconomic forces. The growth of the Negro middle class and Negro institutions (churches, mass media, fraternal organizations, reform organizations, etc.) based on the Negro middle class prepared a foundation for rebellion. So also did events in the world beyond the Pacific and Atlantic. The four-hundred-year expansion of the European ego came to an abrupt halt in the forties, and black and brown men all over the world began to stretch out their legs and their souls, with results that are still reverberating in the troubled streets.

The Negro rebellion, to sum up, is the product of a long process of disillusionment and re-education under the impact of events—favorable and unfavorable.

No group moves en masse to a predetermined goal.

There are advances and retreats, brilliant victories and stunning defeats. The battle goes on for decades against rain and fire and storm and hate. There are mountains to climb and rivers to cross and enemies on all sides—and within. Individuals rise from the masses; a group breaks through here and there, but the people flow on like a great, slow-moving river. Like a mass of sluggish hot lava, like a flock of sheep or a thundering herd of cattle, the people advance and retreat, advance and retreat, break through and are thrown back. Dark nights follow dark nights and the valley of the mind, where all great battles are fought, reverberates with the screams and groans of the dying and the defeated. The people halt on a dry level place and regroup; stragglers drop out; the timid go over to the enemy; straws are clutched, dope or drink or God or sex, each man or woman clutching according to different lights. In the rear, in a safe and elevated place, the leaders confer, posture, make speeches. New maps are drawn, new roads are made, and scouts are dispatched into the white no man's land. Following the scouts—"the first Negroes," "the only Negroes," "the token Negroes"—the group advances, losing many to mines and snipers, taking up a new position on a dry and level place. From millions of throats come cries of victory, from sociologists and priests and preachers come new myths. Men rest on their arms for a spell, drop their guards and are hurled back by a violent counterattack. The battle begins again and goes on, night and day alternating, men and women clutching straws, dope or drink or God or sex, each man or woman clutching according to different lights.

Like all groups, the Negro has come, advancing and retreating, across rivers and up mountains in the wind and the fire and the hate of a dream. Like all groups, the Negro has been seeking a dry level place. The key to his struggle, the key to all group struggle, is not race but conflict, not words but power.

In the black beginning, as I have said elsewhere, was not a word but a fact: white power.

White power is the ambience of black being. Negro responses on all levels are adaptations to the overwhelming reality of white power. This is the basic, the irreducible, fact of Negro-white relations in America.

The human, the natural response to arbitrarily imposed power is open and naked revolt. The Negro knows this, he feels it in the vitals of his being; yet he rejects it. Why? Because of a sophisticated analysis of the terrain. He knows that open revolt will not succeed for him in America. He knows that at the first sign of open revolt practically all white Americans will join hands and smite him down. The Negro, in a word, is faced with a brute fact: minority status in a situation maintained by the naked force of an overwhelming majority.

For some four hundred years now, the Negro has operated within the taut halters of a maddening dilemma. His situation beckons him to open revolt; but his situation is so structured in terms of material and men that open revolt is suicidal. Barred from the open road of revolt and adventure, the Negro postures, revolves, debates. He erupts from time to time in open revolt, but he holds deep within him, he fears, in fact, the volcanic impulses that push him toward the forbidden road of open and continuous self-assertion. The whole voluminous literature on the American Negro gives abundant evidence of a felt need to check responses—the first blind urge to curse, for example, or strike back in the face of constant provocations.

The Negro situation, which is tragic by any definition, has placed severe limits on the responses of Negro leaders. From a strategic standpoint, there can only be two basic postures vis-á-vis a state of oppression: revolt or accommodation. In practice, the middle ground is constantly being pushed toward one or other of the two extremes. The real weakness of the old protest tradition was its failure to confront that fact. Guy B. Johnson, a white sociologist, called attention to this in a brilliant essay published in 1937. "Paradoxically," he wrote, "if [the protest movement] leaves the attitudes and folkways of the white man out of its picture, it is doomed to fail, and if it takes those attitudes and folkways into account, it is either forced back to the gradualistic and conciliatory position of Booker Washington or forced forward into revolutionary tactics. . . ."

What this meant, as a practical matter, was that the Negro was faced with two choices, both of which were unacceptable. He could not accept his situation, for acceptance on any level was violation. But he could not revolt, for revolt was suicidal. The whole history of Negro resistance has been a quest for instruments, relations, and tools that would open a way out of this cruel dilemma. As we shall see, the migration and urbanization of the Negro folk opened new alternatives which became live options in the new climate of the post-World War II world.

Before Freedom movement II, which marked a new departure for the Negro, strategically and spiritually, almost all Negroes were enmeshed in different levels of collaboration. Some Negroes, to be sure, were more articulate in verbalizing via protest their nonacceptance of the system. But protest is one thing and revolt is another. The difference between the two words and the states of being they mediate is crucial to an understanding of the Negro rebellion. One *writes* a petition of protest, one *deplores,* one *sues,* one *appeals,* but one also waits and accepts, squirming, as it were, within the halter. Revolt, on the other hand, is not a posture or an attitude; it is an act, a refusal to accept. Before the Negro rebellion, most Negroes, however much they protested, accepted their situation. In one way or another, they made a separate peace with the system. The price of this peace was high. The Negro not only donned a mask; but he became a mask, a fact noted by poet Paul Laurence Dunbar.

> *We smile, but, O great Christ, our cries*
> *To thee from tortured souls arise.*
> *We sing but oh the clay is vile*
> *Beneath our feet, and long the mile;*
> *But let the world dream otherwise,*
> *We wear the mask.*

The theory of masks is basic to an understanding of the patterns of Negro resistance and revolt. Faced with the implacable hostility of a majority which controls all lines of power, Negro leaders have expressed themselves in two dominant patterns: protest and activism. Protest is an *attitude* of nonacceptance based on sustained contention via political and legal action within the system. Activism, on the other hand, is a program of direct *action* based on revolt on the edges or outside the system. To the right of these dominant patterns of resistance are programs of accommodation (acceptance of the system), black nationalism (separation from the system) and interracial conciliation ("goodwill efforts" to effect gradual changes in the system via education, research, exposure, etc.).

Since the beginning of the Negro Renaissance in the dawn years of the twentieth century, these approaches have been institutionalized in the Negro community and social types have emerged with life styles embodying the dominant patterns. The major social types are militants who rely on protest methods; accommodators who counsel acceptance and the proving of self and race by accumulation and good works; nationalists who call for the creation of Negro states; and moderates who articulate a *via media* between protest and accommodation.

The seeds of the current rebellion were sown in the first two decades of the twentieth century by Negro militants who opposed Booker T. Washington's program of accommodation and called for a remembrance of Freedom movement I. With the organization of the Niagara movement and the National Association for the Advancement of Colored People, the Negro protest movement became a powerful force in the Negro community. Relying on "respectable protest" and contention in the courts and the political arena, the NAACP gave Negroes a new vision of battle. But the NAACP and organizations like it were primarily middle-class reform agencies detached in vision and program from the Negro masses from whom came the first revolutionary impulse. The largely leaderless migration movement which sent Negroes in ever-increasing numbers to Northern cities changed the shape of race relations in America, destroying the old racial equilibrium which was a delicate balance of understanding between the white power structure and the Negro power structure.

In the twenties, thirties, and forties, great changes occurred in the modes of life of the newly urbanized Negro. This gave rise to changes in his ideas, emotions, and perceptions—to changes, in a word, in his consciousness.

The gradual alienation of the Negro from the unilaterally subjective "mainstream" tradition began in the post-Reconstruction period and reached new heights in the fifteen-year period between 1930 and 1945. In this period, the Negro became real to himself and gave notice that it would not be long before he became real to others. During these years, there was a steady growth in racial consciousness, a growth reflected, first of all, in increasing sophistication in the use of mass pressure techniques and, secondly, in the increasing effectiveness of Negro protest organizations.

Parallel with the growth in racial consciousness was a rise in Negro nationalism which should not be confused with specific nationalist movements. The key elements in the nationalist syndrome were: 1) a common sense of oppression, 2) pride in the achievement of Negroes, 3) extreme sensitivity to racial disparagement, 4) a belief in the manifest destiny of Negroes, 5) a feeling of identity with the nonwhite peoples of the world.

The internal migration in the Negro community released forces that put a severe strain on Negro leadership machinery. The Buying Power movement of the thirties and Asa Philip Randolph's attempt to create a national civil disobedience movement in the forties marked a basic shift in strategy and vision, a shift from the Talented Tenth to the masses, from the conference table to the streets. The Negro revolts of the thirties and forties reached peaks of unprecedented intensity but failed in their larger purposes. It is important to remember, however, that abortive revolts are often preludes to a later revolution. It can be said, I think, that the Negro revolts of the thirties and forties were rehearsals for the rebellion of the sixties.

Freedom movement II and the Rehearsal of the forties were bridged by a dull period which intensified Negro disillusionment. Stimulated by changes abroad and revolted by timid and inadequate attempts to force a basic social change at home, Negroes sprang forth once more into revolt. Montgomery and Martin Luther King, Jr., created a revolutionary point of departure which the sit-in students carried to a new stage of development.

In the hands of the student rebels and the leading organizations of Freedom movement II—CORE, SCLC, and SNCC—the concept of confrontation became a tool of real revolutionary ardor.

The series of confrontations in and around Selma in 1965 and the widening of the conflict—geographically (as in the call for an economic boycott of the *state* of Alabama) and strategically (as in the demands for the creation of a *national* movement via Selma-type demonstrations in the North)—were dramatizations at a new level of indignation of the Freedom movement's central demand that Americans, North and South, black and white, confront radically the implications of the Negro's position in American life.

As the movement rounded the curve of the summer of 1964 and headed into a backstretch of ominous questions, there was a charged atmosphere in the ghetto, a sense of coming storm and apocalyptic possibilities. A measure of the change in mood was the increasing harshness of Negro-white confrontation as evidenced by the riot season of 1964, and the 1965 skirmishes.

How did we come to this point? Where do we go from here?

For more than four hundred years, the Negro has looked out on America from the prison of a mask. He has manipulated the mask, dropping it suddenly, becoming refractory and threatening, putting it on again, becoming conciliatory and charming, pushing it to one side, trying on new hats and new roles, admiring himself in the mirror of tempting but forbidden self-conceptions. For more than four hundred years, the Negro has wavered between the hot poles of submission and revolt.

Has the Negro decided now to abandon the mask completely?

Let us search for the answer to these and other questions in the tangled roots of desire and hate and love, roots that impelled the Negro in 1963-64 to lower his mask and face the white man across a deep and ever-widening moat.

I. ROOTS

Something Old, Something Borrowed, Something Blue

THE BREAKING OF THE BOND

IT is about to begin.

Black men and white men are going to meet for the first time in the womb of an American setting.

Look:

Far off on the horizon is a tiny speck. The speck grows larger, turns, lists and bobbles on the Atlantic waves. There is a cry ("A ship! A ship!") on shore, and men dash to the waterfront and peer through the late summer haze. To the bored and homesick settlers of Jamestown, Virginia, the approaching ship is a godsend. Jamestown, the first English settlement in America, is a miserable little hole with a handful of huts and almost no diversion. The ship, heaving into view, promises excitement and adventure; but there is no way for the men on shore to know how much excitement the ship really contains. For in the hold of this ship, figuratively speaking, is the whole vibrant panorama of Negro America: the blues and the spirituals, Booker T. Washington and Martin Luther King, Jr., the Twist and the Charleston, the bloody anger of Gettysburg and the nagging promise of the Fourteenth Amendment.

The ship, as befitting a messenger of fate, is nameless. There is an air of intrigue, of danger even, about the captain, one Mr. Jope, who comes ashore with an elegant lie on his lips. He has just robbed a Spanish vessel of a cargo of Africans bound for the West Indies, but he does not mention that. He "ptends," John Rolfe notes with suspicion, that he is in great need of food and he offers to exchange his cargo for "victualle." The deal is arranged. Antonio, Isabella, Pedro and

*seventeen other Africans with Spanish names debark, and an
argument begins.*

*It is August, 1619: 245 years before Emancipation, 346 years
before the long hot summer of 1965.*

The question in August of 1619, as in August of 1965, was:
What shall we do *with, for, to* and *about* the black people? It
was a question that would be asked over and over again in the
years to come, and it would be answered over and over again
as it was answered in the beginning—with a compromise. It
was decided in the summer of 1619 to hand the black people
over to the colony instead of to individuals. The twenty black
seeds of Jamestown were farmed out to various officials of the
colony—and they were farmed out as servants and not slaves.
In court and church records, the first black Americans were
listed as "servants." This is a point of immense significance in
the history of America. The first black immigrants were not
slaves; nor were the first white immigrants free. Most of the
English colonists, in the beginning, were indentured servants:
that is, they were sold or they sold themselves to the colony or
to individual planters for a stipulated number of years (five
or seven or more) to pay the price of their passage.

In Virginia and other colonies, the first black immigrants
fell into a well-established socioeconomic pattern that carried
no implications of racial inferiority. During this transitional
period of 40 years or more, a period of primary importance in
the history of America, the first Negro immigrants mingled
with whites on a basis of substantial equality.

History masks the faces and emotions of the black men and
women who lived in this racial wonderland. The record burns
with their presence, but the record is strangely silent on their
reactions and the reactions of their white colleagues. The black
Founding Fathers enter history thus: faceless men uprooted
from the warm womb of "Mother Africa" and flung willy-nilly
into the wilderness of an outpost of Western civilization. Nothing on the record indicates that the shock was very great for
Negroes or whites. The men and women of the black yeast
soon dropped their entrancing Spanish names. Antonio and Isabella, who were drawn to each other on the trip over, married
and became parents of the first Negro child born in English
America. In 1625, the black boy was christened William
Tucker in a Jamestown church. Thus in the span of a few
years, the Negro soul moved from Africa to Spain to America
—from X to Antonio to William.

Within the next few years, scores of Africans made the leap. By 1649, there were three hundred black folk in a population of about fifteen thousand. Some came directly from England, where Negroes had lived since 1553. Others came from Spain, Portugal, and the West Indies. A large number of these pioneer migrants were Christians, baptized either in Spain or England. John Phillip, for example, testified in a Jamestown court in 1624 and his testimony against a white man was admitted because he had been "christened in England twelve years since. . . ."

Some, perhaps all, of the first group of African-Americans worked out their terms of servitude and were freed. Within a few years, the more energetic were accumulating property, pounds, and indentured servants. Anthony Johnson, America's first black capitalist, earned the dubious honor of being the first person in the colony to hold a Negro as a servant for life. Still another Negro, Richard Johnson, imported a white man and held him in servitude. This, apparently, was integration with a vengeance.

But let us take care not to exaggerate. It is as certain as death that there were racists then, but the record indicates that some Negroes were accorded social privileges about equal to those accorded to freed white servants. More importantly, Negro freedmen seem to have had the same industrial and economic opportunities as white servants.

Within the confines of this system, which can only be called equality of repression, Negroes fared about as well as whites. They held real property and transferred it, sued in court and were sued. Some Negroes voted and a few held the minor offices of beadle and surety. In a limited sense, then, the Jamestown experience was an open experience. Negroes were free to express themselves according to their personalities and their different lights. They could live with white people if they wanted to, or they could live without them; and some Negroes, interestingly enough, wanted to live without them. On the banks of the Pungoteague River in Northampton County, a handful of Negroes established America's first Harlem. In 1651, Anthony Johnson imported five servants and received headrights (a grant of so many acres per servant imported) of two hundred acres along the Pungoteague. Other Johnsons and other Negroes moved to the burgeoning development. The settlement throve, but not without a certain dissension. The Johnsons were a proud, contentious folk, and were soon in court, suing each other over infringements of contract or property.

The Johnson settlement at its height included no more than

a dozen or so Negroes with very large holdings. Other Negroes were scattered throughout the colony in integrated communities. In 1656, Benjamin Doyle received a patent for three hundred acres in Surrey County. John Harris in 1668 bought fifty acres in New Kent County. And Phillip Morgan, with great optimism, leased two hundred acres in York County for ninety-nine years.

Morgan's optimism was not entirely groundless. The bulk of the population at that time consisted of indentured servants who were remarkably free from racial prejudice. Whites and Negroes worked in the same fields, lived in the same huts and fraternized during off-duty hours. And, predictably, they mated and married. There was widespread intermingling between Negroes and whites throughout the Colonial period. "Colonial Virginia," Peter Fontaine said, "swarmed" with mulatto children.

In this period, little or no distinction was made between indentured servants and Negro slaves and servants. What little prejudice there was stemmed mostly from English class prejudice. White servants and Negro servants were assigned the same tasks and many masters held them in equal contempt. It was not unusual in those days for a master to force a white woman servant to marry a Negro; nor was it unusual for Negro servants to serve as overseers over Negro and white work forces. Of particular interest in this context of developing community is the fact that whites and Negroes of the working class made common cause against the master class. They often ran away together; and, in several communities, they staged interracial revolts.

Working together in the same fields, sharing the same huts, the same situation, and the same hope, the first Negro and white Americans, aristocrats excepted, developed strong bonds of sympathy and mutuality. There was no barrier, psychological or otherwise, between them; and circles of community and solidarity began to widen. Skin color had a meaning then but not the meaning it has now. The basic division was between servants and free people; and there were whites and Negroes on both sides of the line. One has to make an effort to grasp the contours of this world. It seems somehow un-American, as undoubtedly it was, since it has existed in America for only one brief spell and then by default. A Negro in this world could almost feel at home. There was not the fatal split between being an American, whatever that is, and being a Negro, whatever that is. If there was prejudice then, and there was, it was not organized and sustained by the intractable will of an entire community. There was not, in fact, an agreed-upon name for the phenomena to be excluded—and names are indispensable for good exclusion. The first Negroes were called Blackamoors, Moors, Negers, and Negars. The word "Negro," a derivative of Spanish and Portuguese forms, did not come into general use until later. By that time, the reality it was supposed to denote had assumed cancerous proportions in men's minds.

But, to repeat, one must be careful not to idealize. One suspects that even then Negroes asked themselves in the closeness of their hearts: Who am I, God? And what? One suspects that the first generation of black Americans remembered the old gods and the old ways and moaned the plaintive cry of the exiled Jew: "By the river of Jordan, they sat us down and said sing us a song. But how can I sing the Lord's song in a strange land."

How, indeed? And which Lord?

From the beginning, there was a tenuous, subtle pressure, more menacing perhaps because it was shapeless and nameless. The tension points, then and now, were sex and status. Then, as now, the thrust came from fear, fear of self, fear of the unknown, fear of the different—fear, and a monstrous fascination. In 1630, a white man was denounced for "lying with a Negro" woman which was said (by the governing class) to be an abuse "to the dishonor of God and the shame of Christians." He was ordered soundly whipped "before an assemblage of Negroes." It is a measure of the progress in civilization that ten years later the white man in a similar episode was ordered "to do penance in church" and the Negro woman was "soundly whipped."

Sex continued to be a problem in the early colonies, not to the servants, who got on famously, but to the aristocrats, who were scandalized by the broad tolerance of the first Englishwomen. A system of intimidation was organized which increased in severity. Forty years after the Jamestown landing, white women were being whipped and sold into slavery or extended servitude for showing open preference for Negro men.

The problem of sex was largely a problem of the Negro male, which is to say that it was a problem of power. In the 1640's and 1650's, which marked a slight shift in the relations between Negroes and whites, tentative restrictions were placed on the Negro males. In 1639, for example, all colonists except Negroes were required to arm themselves. This restriction and others of similar weight and meaning were reflections of a mounting fear in the world of men.

To grasp the significance of this development, one must first understand the world context in which it occurred. The planting of black folk on American soil and their subsequent degradation were episodes in a world-wide drama, the African slave trade. The detailed story of the slave trade does not concern us here. What does concern us is the extraordinary nature of the initial contacts between Europeans and Africans.

Africa and Europe in the fifteenth century were on the same level of Toynbee's vaunted precipice of glory. In fact, in some areas, Africans were a ledge or two ahead. The Sudanese empire with its world-famous showplace of Timbuctu had passed its peak, but it could still show Europe a thing or two—the University of Sankore, for example, and intellectuals like Es Sadi who owned a private library of sixteen hundred volumes at a time when the whole of America was a howling wilderness. Nor was that all. There were huge empires and populous cities —some as large as all but the largest European cities—along the coast.

Europeans, noting these things, greeted Africans as allies and partners in trade. The recorded reminiscences of traders show that down to the eighteenth century they had no conception of their victims as racial pariahs. On the contrary, many traders expressed a belief that Africans were their equals and the superiors of many back home.

If Europeans forgot their place, there were Africans in this period to remind them. The first Africans were rather contemptuous of European claims. They did not, in any wise, consider themselves inferior. If anything, they considered themselves superior to the odd-looking men with pale skins. The king of Dahomey seldom shook hands with white men and when he did it was a "very uncommon mark of royal condescension." A French trader complained in 1660 that the Fanti were "so proud and haughty that a European trader there must stand bare to them."

Standing up to each other, as men and as equals, both Africans and Europeans profited. Plenipotentiaries were exchanged, and bright young men of the ruling classes went to Lisbon and Rome to study and observe. Black and white kings exchanged letters filled with terms of royal endearment ("my fellow brother and my fellow queen"). They also exchanged gifts and mistresses of various hues and dispositions.

Shakespeare's laudatory phrase, "I speak of Africa and golden joys," was not conjured up out of the air. The phrase was solidly grounded in the realities of life in the first phase of the African-European dialogue, a dialogue consisting of trade in men *and* goods and ideas.

As in Jamestown, Africans speedily absorbed the fundamentals of the European way of life. On May 15, 1518, one hundred years before the Jamestown landing, Henry of the Congo led a mission to the Vatican, formally addressed the Pope in Latin and was appointed Bishop of the Congo. In Rome, Lisbon and other European control centers, Africans rose to high positions in church and state. And Negro gametes were scattered throughout the populations of Europe. By 1518, the southern portion of Portugal was predominantly Negro and as far north as Lisbon Negroes outnumbered whites.

Descendants of these Christianized Africans were among the first settlers of the New World. As slaves, servants, and scouts, they accompanied Spanish, French, and Portuguese explorers in the pioneer penetrations of North and South Africa. Thirty Negroes were with Balboa when he discovered the Pacific Ocean; three hundred went with Cortez into Mexico, and some of them planted and harvested the first wheat crop in the New World.

The shape of this period is summed up in an old saying: "The first white man to meet an Indian in America was a Negro." This was true in many areas of North and South America. A bold Negro explorer, Estevanico, opened up the Southwest for the Spaniards. Negroes helped to found St. Augustine in 1565 and made up a large proportion of its population during the Colonial period. Negroes were in Florida, Alabama, New Mexico, and California as early as 1527, 1540, 1542, and 1537, respectively.

Perhaps the first permanent settlers in America were the Africans who accompanied Lucas Vasquez de Ayllon, the Spanish explorer. In 1526, De Ayllon settled in the area of present-day South Carolina with five hundred white men, one hundred Africans and eighty-nine horses. A few months later, the Africans revolted, slew several whites and fled to the Indians.

In the fervor of world-wide exploration and the commingling of peoples from different lands and cultures, new vistas opened up for both Africans and Europeans. It seemed for a spell that Christianity would have the same fertilizing influence in Africa in the sixteenth century as Islam had had in the eleventh and twelfth centuries. But it was not to be. While the bright young black men were feasting in the courts of Lisbon, while the eager black priests were genuflecting in the courts of the Vatican, the dream was dissolving in granules of greed.

Ships were already plying the seas, men were already experimenting with sugar cane—it was not to be.

The opening of the New World and the introduction of sugar planting in the West Indies created a demand for men that casual kidnapping could not supply. Men's vision shifted now from the poor whites of Europe to the poor blacks of Africa, and the African-European dialogue became a monologue focused almost exclusively on a trade in men. In vain did some of the more far-sighted African monarchs plead for an extension of the old trade in goods and ideas. In 1526, Mani-Congo, the ruler of the Congo states, made a desperate attempt to end the slave trade. In a strong letter to John III of Portugal, Mani-Congo said: ". . . we need from [your] kingdoms no other than priests and people to teach in schools, and no other goods but wine and flour for the holy sacrament: that is why we beg of Your Highness to help and assist us in this matter, commanding the factors that they should send here neither merchants nor wares, because it is our will that in these kingdoms [of the Congo] there should not be any trade in slaves or markets for slaves."

We would be living in a different world today if Mani-Congo's plea for "Point IV aid" and "Peace Corps" personnel had been heeded in the sixteenth century. But Europe was impervious to such pleas. She was only interested in the gold of black bodies, and she forced that obsession on Africa—to the undoing of both Europe and Africa.

As a result of the slave trade, white Europe became a single group opposed to the rest of the world, and a new and terrifying idea was invented: the idea of subordination and superordination based on skin color.

Slavery, contrary to the general impression, did not spring from racism; racism sprang from slavery. The concept of race was a direct outgrowth of the slave trade. And it was deliberately invented by an exploiting group which needed a theology to maintain and defend privileges founded on naked force.

The first act of the slave trade, the exchange of men *and* goods and ideas, unfolded against the permissive backdrop of the medieval world which sanctioned Negro and white slavery. But the slave trade soon took a more ominous turn. Within a few years, fifty thousand or more black men and women were crossing the Atlantic each year, and the soil of Africa and America was drenched with their blood. In the wake of this development, a need arose for justification of that which could not be justified by any theory in Western thought. By this time, of course, the slave trade was the bulwark of the whole European economy, a fact which made the search for a theology more desperate.

Blessed are men who can steal without the need of theology. For when the need for justification arises, the thief and his cause are more than half-lost. As long as man-stealing and man-selling occasioned no public outcry, the slave trader could fight down his doubts. But when voices cried out in rebuke and remonstrance, men cast about for a reassuring straw. It was evil, of course, to ravage continents and exterminate hundreds of thousands of black and red men. But what if—what if Negroes and Indians were not men in the same sense that Europeans were? On this question—what if?—was raised a terrifying theology of guilt and fear.

Europe emerged now as the great white Subject in counterpoise to the nonwhite Other. The Europe of Plato and Socrates was invaded by a new spirit, a spirit born of the Renaissance and the Commercial Revolution. There was something amoral about this spirit, something demonic, Faustian, and recklessly individualistic. Stimulated by the invention of paper, gunpowder, and printing (the three often went together), and the opening of a whole new world beyond, Europe threw itself with a bloody spasm across the face of the Earth, ravaging, plundering, tearing down and, yes, building up.

This thunderous outer event, when fed into the stream of internal Colonial politics, produced explosive changes. Negroes and whites in the American colonies began to experience each other in different ways. They began to withdraw into themselves and to prepare, in their different lights, for the confrontation to come.

In the crucial period between 1640 and 1660, the furies began to gather in America for a portentous decision. Some Negroes in this period were servants, and some were free. But an increasingly large number of colonists were falling into the habit of regarding incoming Africans as servants for life.

This development, a reflection of eddies and currents in the outer world, was menacing but not conclusive. The Negro's status, until the latter part of the seventeenth century, was so amorphous that ultimately it could have been defined in any one of a number of ways. Slavery or modified slavery was a distinct possibility for all disadvantaged people—Indians as well as black and white immigrants. So was an open society. Socioeconomic forces—a world-wide demand for tobacco and the development of capitalist planting techniques based on the use of gang labor—tilted the structure in the direction of Negro slavery.

In the fateful sixties of the seventeenth century, men of power in the colonies, egged on by men of power in London, made a catastrophic decision that would lead step by step to the fateful sixties of the nineteenth century and the fateful sixties of the twentieth. It was decided in the 1660's to ground the American economic system on human slavery organized around the random distribution of melanin in men's skins. Beginning around 1660, the planter class drafted and passed laws that made Negroes servants for life. Intermarriage was interdicted, and children born of Negro women were ruled bond or free, according to the status of the mother.

This was a fatal and perhaps irreparable break in the sense of community between Negro and white Americans. It was the starting point, the first turn, on the road to the summer of 1964 and the dangers beyond.

Having made one step, the white power structure had to take another, more ominous, step. Nature does not prepare men for the roles of master and slave. It requires rigid training, long persisted in, to make a slave or a slaveholder. Men must be carefully taught, and the lessons taught one generation must be learned anew by the next.

The Negro and white working class of the 1660's, the bulk of the population, had not been prepared for the roles outlined in the new script of statutes. It was necessary, therefore, to teach Negroes and whites that they should not and could not deal with each other on the basis of reciprocity and emotion and relation. And this, remarkably enough, proved exceedingly difficult.

The forced breaking of the bond can be traced with precision in the emotionally-toned areas of love and sex—two constitutive factors in *communitas* which is, by definition, a state of organic wholeness between equals residing in a common territory, equals who extend to each other complete reciprocity or the possibility of complete reciprocity in positive affects (love, sexual union, marriage, friendship, social communion) and communal conventions (property, law, trade).

The complete severing of the fragile bonds of community in the areas of positive affects became the dominant note in planter strategy. Fearing a deterioration of slavery if the boundaries between white and black people were dissolved in the caldron of sexual intimacy, the planter class mobilized every unit of power for an assault on intermingling. Legislatures began to grind out laws of every imaginable description. Virginia legislated against intermingling in 1662, 1691, 1696, 1705, 1753, 1765. There were similar legislative paroxysms in other states. Maryland passed anti-amalgamation laws in 1664, 1681, 1715, 1717. The sentiment of the aristocratic lawmakers leaped out from the dry statutes in words like "spurious issue," "disgrace of the nation," "defiling."

Private vigilante associations and racial purists whipped the doubtful into line. Behind the purists and the good grey lawmakers stood God himself in the person of parsons who blessed the rupture in community with words from the Holy Bible. But, astoundingly, nothing worked. Against the law as revealed by the parson and the legislator, intermarriage and intermingling continued in America for more than one hundred years. Men would say later that there was a natural antipathy between Negores and whites that no law could mitigate. But the record belies them. Negroes and whites were taught hate and fear. They were driven apart by symbols, sermons, and signed papers. Every instrument of persuasion— law, religion, prison, banishment—was used to destroy the developing bonds of community between Negro and white Americans.

Who was responsible for this policy?

The planters, the aristocrats, the parsons, the lawyers, the Founding Fathers—*the good people:* they sowed the seeds of the bitter harvest.

James Hugo Johnston, who made a detailed study of this problem, placed the responsibility squarely on the shoulders of "the governing class." Johnston wrote: "The system of life built up in the agricultural colonies resulted in planter control. Both social and governmental institutions were devices wrought by the planters. The system of slavery may have been thrust upon them by England, but the problems arising from it were first of all the planters' problems; and on the governing class is the responsibility for the system worked out in the colonies." Planters were motivated primarily by economic considerations. But, Johnston added, "it is also to be believed that *the planters wished to develop an attitude of race superiority . . .* through a fear that at some future time the poor white might lead the mulatto and the Negro in revolt against the established order." [My emphasis.]

How was this policy justified?

At first the rationalization was religion. Negroes were condemned not because they were Negroes but because they were non-Christians. The limitations of this policy were glaringly apparent. It was not permanent: men could *become* Christians. As an increasingly large number of Negroes became Christians, planters cast about for a more enduring disability, something that could not be changed. But before this step could be made, it was necessary to clear up certain theological difficulties. A celebrated divine wrote a long book of two hundred or more pages to prove that it was not a sin to baptize slaves. With great seriousness, Puritans and planters debated this issue and decided that Christianity and slavery were not incompatible. It was decided, moreover, that it was a duty, a Christian duty, to bring "barbarians" into the folds of Christian civilization so their souls could be cleansed for the heavens beyond. Thus, in the end, God and profits were reconciled. Virginia, in 1667, clothed the ideological sleight-of-hand in legal language: ". . . the conferring of baptisme doth not alter the condition of the person as to his bondage or freedom." After that, it was easy. The Negro population, which had grown slowly during the twilight interim of freedom, lunged forward. By 1710, the number had increased to fifty thousand. When the Declaration of Independence was signed, there were five hundred thousand Negroes in America.

Not all Negroes were reduced to slavery. Remnants of a free Negro class survived and grew by natural additions, manumissions, and escapes. The status of free Negroes during the early part of the eighteenth century was relatively high. But as slavery fastened itself on the minds of men, free Negroes were pushed down to a status that was almost indistinguishable from bondage.

What happened now dwarfed everything that had happened before. The Jamestown experience, the early African experience, Antonio, Isabella, Mani-Congo: all were forgotten. There emerged an image of the Negro as a person who was powerless not because he lacked power but because of some inherent defect in his character, a defect related in some mysterious way to the packets of melanin in his skin. The Negro became in Lewis C. Copeland's phrase "a contrast conception." He was *black* to the white man's *white*. He was the *devil* to the white man's *god*. He was *dark* to the white man's *light*. It was not necessary, within this conceptual framework, for men to *do* anything. One was born white and in this aspect one inherited the earth. Propelled by this psychic dynamism, the white ego expanded, puffed up, exploded and rolled across the face of the earth, absorbing the consciousness and the souls of men born black, red, and brown.

The effect of all this, whatever the intention (and the intention was not far removed from the effect) was to deprive the Negro of legal force and standing in the community of men. It was to make him a person outside the protection of law, an exile, a stranger, and an outcast. This, as Thomas Jefferson pointed out in a rejected draft of the Declaration of Independence, was war against human nature or at least against that part of human nature enshrined in black skins. For more than four hundred years this war continued. Before it was over, one hundred million black people had perished and twenty million more had been scattered over the Western Hemisphere.

When the war started, there was no mask between black men and white men—there was no screen between insult and retaliation, stimulus and response, blow and retort. Black men and white men, therefore, stood toe to toe, hacking, burning, and slashing. Murder piled on murder, and a red ribbon of violence enclosed black people and white people in a circle of fate.

Direct, violent resistance: this was the black man's first response to white power. Resistance began with sit-downs and hunger strikes on the slave ships. Although every precaution was taken, although the males were shackled together and guards walked the decks with drawn cutlasses day and night, there were repeated uprisings on the slave ships—at least fifty-five documented mutinies between 1699 and 1845, not to mention fragmentary references to two hundred more. The struggle continued on land. There was a slave revolt in Hispaniola as early as 1502. The governor immediately asked for a temporary suspension of the slave trade because "the Negroes encouraged the Indians to rebellion." Twenty-four years later, the struggle moved to the American mainland with the revolt of the one hundred Africans who accompanied Lucas de Ayllon.

Direct, violent resistance continued and reached a peak in the nineteenth century. Herbert Aptheker, the authority on American Negro slave revolts, has documented at least 250 insurrections and conspiracies in continental America. Although some of his sources have been questioned, there can be little doubt that revenge and revolt were dominant motifs in the reaction-patterns of the first African-Americans.

The Negroes who came to America in the eighteenth century were strikingly different from those conditioned by one hundred years of bondage. The first African-Americans saw themselves through the prism of the old gods. They did not feel inferior to white men and, what is more to the point, white men were not so sure that they were superior to them.

There were, accordingly, repeated revolts. In 1712, slaves in New York City revolted and killed at least nine whites. And a Virginia plot of 1730 prompted the lieutenant governor to order white men to take their pistols to church with them.

The first Negro leader to emerge with any clarity from the anonymity of the masses, Cato of Stono, was an advocate of direct, violent resistance. In 1739, Cato led a slave revolt near Stono, South Carolina. The black rebels, under Cato's leadership, killed several whites, fired a number of buildings and set out for Florida, which was held then by Spain. They "called out Liberty," a contemporary account said, "marched on with Colours displayed, and two drums beating." Some twenty-five whites were killed before Cato and his group were subdued.

Before anything else could be done, before the fields could be tilled, before Monticello and Mount Vernon could be built, the first generation of African-Americans, men made in the image of Cato, had to be mastered. The breaking of the slave, the destruction of the African as an individual—this was the first task before the pioneer white Americans. In order for slavery to succeed, it was necessary to annihilate the thinking processes of slaves. Naked power was not enough; the white man's power had to be internalized. The slave, in other words, had to be robbed of his self-conception and self-respect. He had to become someone else or pretend he was someone else.

Much has been said, and rightly, about the physical violence of slavery. Equally harsh, and far crueler, was the mental violence, the wrenching of minds out of cerebral sockets and the crushing of bones of belief and habit.

In order to control people, as we learned from Europeans in German concentration camps and Americans in Chinese concentration camps, it is necessary to subject them to constant fatigue, constant insecurity, and overwhelming power in a closed system. Long before Hilter, long before Mao Tse-tung, Southern planters had mastered these elementary techniques. Anticipating the devious tactics of the modern police state, masters laid hands on the minds of their chattel. By the old method of the carrot and the stick, by terror and by smiles, by whips, chains, words, symbols, prayers, and curses, the Negro was taught to "stand in fear" of white power.

In some such manner, Africans were given a new conception of themselves, a conception that carried as core-elements guilt, anxiety, and inferiority. The laying of hands on the mind of a whole people, the pulling out by the roots of old customs and habits, continued for hundreds of years. Hundreds of thousands died in the process, and hundreds of thousands went insane. But millions survived, maimed, to be sure, shrunken, shriven, *diminué* but, withal, alive and breathing, with enough fragmentary memories of the past to give them a mooring in the present and hope for the future. The terms of that survival were harsh and self-enforcing. In order to survive, the slave had to give up or pretend to give up that which makes man human—hope, ambition, responsibility, and will. No slave could stand up to life as a human being. To live, for a slave, especially a male slave, was to renounce, to renounce anger and love and indignation, to renounce hate and human hurt, to renounce the claims, and the rewards, of love, the responsibilities of parenthood and the pride of ownership—to renounce these things not voluntarily in the service of a higher ideal but at the command of another human will arbitrarily imposed by society. Millions learned to wear masks of renunciation in the inferno of slavery, but few adjusted to their situation. James Redpath and others who called slavery a state of perpetual war between master and slave cut to the bone of the problem. That which was human in the slave was always at war with that in the master which breached the bounds of the human.

Far from being a humane institution, American slavery was diabolically cruel in that it robbed the Negro of that sense of human dignity which underlies all social intercourse. Slavery destroyed the Negro's family, emptied his mind, and impoverished his soul. More than that: it made him doubt himself. Nor did the master escape. Unlimited power over men—and especially women—is debasing—one pays a price for it. In the attempted absorption and destruction of Negro consciousness, the white man remoulded himself and involved himself, catastrophically, with an image that was both loved and hated. White men entered into Negro, as W. J. Cash said, but Negro also entered into white man, subtly influencing every thought, every gesture, every desire. And the two groups, thus impaled, thrashed about, reciprocally making and destroying each other, in an embrace until death or salvation.

Between the master and the slave, between the white man who approached the Negro in the aspect of a master and the Negro who responded in the aspect of a slave, there was absolute silence. It was impossible for the two to communicate because the ground of communication—equality, responsibility, and mutual trust—had been destroyed.

Beyond that was the obvious fascination of black skin for

white men and women. The master opened his eyes on a soft black mother surrogate who ever afterwards held him in the lap of a monstrous and forbidden dream. The black mammy who extended the breast he sucked as a child, the black mammy who mashed with her own hands the food he ate, who sang to him strange lullabies and led him, smiling, into sleep: this image colored his dreaming and his desiring. And later, of course, it was this woman's daughter or, in many cases what turned out to be the same thing, his father's daughter who initiated him into the mysteries of love.

Incest piled on incest behind the Cotton Curtain of slavery, and the whole Faulknerian drama turned in on itself in an orgy of oblique fears. Men asked themselves, other men asked them: What have you become? *What, in the name of God, have you made yourself?* And, of course, there could be no answer, short of the grave, for master or slave.

White man and Negro were estranged, perhaps beyond reconciliation. But so were the Negro and the white state. Slavery was aggression against the Negro personality by individual masters, but it was also aggression by the state which gave to a surrogate power to hold, restrain, work, whip, convey, and sell human beings.

With the backing or, at least, the silence of every structure of power in America, Negroes were stripped of those rights of personality that are usually considered sacred between men. Vice, immorality, and brutality were institutionalized and given names. The sanctity of the family was violated: children were sold from mothers, and fatherhood was abolished.

It is not generally recognized that American slavery was significantly different and vastly more oppressive than slavery in other areas. In South America and the Caribbean, there was a margin of personality that the master could not violate. In America, the slave belonged to the master absolutely. It was true, literally true, that the slave had no rights that white men were bound to respect.

The Old South was a totalitarian system dominated by one party—the party of planters. The party line was cotton and human slavery. No deviation from this point of view was permitted, either in the church, school, or legislature. Nor was silence enough. Men were required to say often and loud that slavery was good and that freedom was bad. Things reached such a pass that the Declaration of Independence was repudiated and Thomas Jefferson was denounced as an unstable reformer infected by un-American ideas. In the end, Southern newspapers and Southern intellectuals demanded that the North endorse a crusade for the permanent enslavement of free Negroes and poor white immigrants.

In the South, planter strategy was based on the old maxim: *divide et impera* (divide and rule). Planters learned early to hide behind the images of the overseers (who were usually poor whites) and the drivers (who were members of the oppressed class). Thus there grew up the myth of "the good white folk" who were supposed to be above the crudities of the poor white class. On large plantations, most slaves never came into contact with the real power. Only a crisis would reveal the true nature of the system. Most slaves, therefore, did not focus their resentment against their real enemy, the planter, but against the poor whites who furnished most of the overseers.

And who were the poor whites?

They were white people who happened to be poor. They lived on the poor land planters did not want. Like slaves, they hated not planters, who were the real authors of their ills, but Negroes, whom they saw as threats to their social, economic, and psychological well-being. All this was pure windfall to the planter class which consciously and unconsciously fanned the flames of hate between poor whites and Negroes—fanned the flames and thereby controlled both classes utterly.

Not only poor whites, but, astoundingly, free Negroes (in the South) accepted the planter's definition of the situation. This is not to say that there were no brilliant and dedicated free Negroes. But the great majority of free Negroes in the South accepted the planter-inspired myth that the basic division in America was not between Negroes and whites but between free people (Negroes and whites) and slaves. Having accepted this definition, free Negroes in the South were leisurely pushed down to a position that was not radically different from slavery.

Having divided free Negroes and slaves, and whites and Negroes, planters turned now to a destruction of the community of victims. In a desperate attempt to prevent the growth of solidarity and racial pride, the only qualities on which a mass movement could base itself, planters exerted constant pressure from without and fostered internal divisions within.

Throughout the slave period, as Abraham Lincoln pointed out, there were packets of explosive material on every plantation. What was lacking was the indispensable connecting train: agitators, organizers, leaders.

To prevent the necessary connection between agitation and explosive packets, planters concentrated on three key elements—freedom of assembly, freedom of movement, and privacy of the home (where arms could be hidden). The slave codes, the crystallization of planter strategy, forbade slaves to assemble in groups of more than five or seven away from their home plantation. Slaves were forbidden to leave plantations without passes and they could not blow horns, beat drums, or read books. Slave patrols or "paderollers," as the slaves called them, were authorized to make periodic searches of slave cabins.

The whole complex apparatus of control was designed to isolate the slave and to cut him away from social moorings. But external control was not enough. Slavery could not succeed without the complicity of the enslaved. To oppress Negroes more effectively, masters made use of selected slaves as agents, spies, and bellwethers. This ancient technique was facilitated because of the differing relations of slaves to the center of power. The basic division, a division with implications and ramifications that color contemporary Negro life, was between house slaves and field slaves. In the context of current realities, it is definitely a hostile act to call a man a house Negro or a descendant of house slaves. The house slave syndrome (a certain servility before white power and a fawning imitation of white models) is used repeatedly today as a weapon of attack in the struggles for power within the Negro community.

Who were house slaves? How did they come by their low repute?

House slaves were defined spatially and psychologically, by their physical and mental proximity to the master class and their relative isolation from the great mass of Negroes who were field slaves. House slaves worked in and around the house (maids, butlers, gardeners) or performed special services as artisans and technicians. As a group, house slaves were exceptionally useful to masters who told them they were different, who urged them and, in some cases, commanded them to keep their distance from the masses.

At the apex of the slave elite was the driver who maintained order in the quarters and bossed the slaves in the fields. The driver was the archetype of the Negro leader, and his image would exert an enormous influence on the expectations and attitudes of both Negroes and whites after slavery. Like practically all Negro leaders until modern times, the driver was an agent—of the master class. It was his duty to restrain Negroes, to pacify them, and to see that they worked hard. His relationship to Negroes was anomalous, to say the least. Having no power of his own, existing at the sufferance of the planter, and receiving minor perquisites so long as he supported the planter's interest, the driver operated in a twilight world between the oppressed and the oppressor.

That some Negroes cooperated with masters and helped to make the slave system work should occasion no surprise. It has been so among all people at all times. The iron law of power is that most men, of whatever color, of whatever tongue, will accommodate themselves to their situation, and that a small minority on the left will protest while another minority on the right will seek to capitalize on the situation by ingratiating themselves with the powers that be. It was so with the Negro in slavery; it was so with Americans in Chinese concentration camps; it will be so as long as power is power and men are men.

What surprises, above all, in the slave experience is the amount of slave cohesiveness. Despite strong centrifugal forces, there was a bond of sympathy between slave groups. One discerns in the literature a systematic attempt to overemphasize the degree of intragroup conflict. One student said there was little cohesion among slaves because there was not enough counterpressure to prevent collaboration. This is an oversimplification of a complex problem. There is never enough counterpressure to prevent collaboration in a totalitarian system. France and other countries had a fair amount of social cohesion in World War II, but there was a bumper crop of collaborators. In the slave quarters, as in France, collaboration evoked the ire of the community of victims. In Tennessee, for example, a slave named Jim killed a slave named Isaac for helping to catch him after his escape. At the trial, the judge observed that "Isaac seems to have lost caste. . . . He had combined with the white folks . . . no slight offense in their eyes: that one of their own color, subject to a like servitude, should abandon the interests of his caste, and . . . betray black folks to the white people, rendered him an object of general aversion."

Subject to a like servitude, sharing the same interests, excluded from the general community, and proscribed by law, slaves of all ranks developed their own society which differed in many ways from the society of masters. The locus of this community was the slave quarters, the embryo of the Harlems of today.

All slaves—house and field—were members of the community of victims. There were, as we have noted, chasms between slave groups; but there were also bridges. The basic fact in plantation life was race. And slaves, no matter how high they rose or how light their skin, were black—and they knew it. The basic psychological fact is that the slave elite needed the field slaves, if only to have someone to look down on.

In the quarters, slaves of all ranks could drop their masks. In the circle of suffering, they could stretch out their legs and their souls. Paradoxically, the slaves who lived in closest proximity to white influence were the slaves most maimed. Those furthest removed from white influence, on the other hand, were the freest. In the Harlems of the plantations, field hands had a small, but nonetheless important, area of freedom. For a small part of the day, they were not under the thumbs and feet of white people. Thus a man or woman could build a fragile windbreak against white power. It is not at all surprising that the deep and brooding spirituals and the embryonic blues came not from the house but from the field.

Between the society of masters and the society of victims there was little interaction. Conflict did not grow out of their situation; it was inherent in that situation. The attempt to deny Negroes even a minimum of social life involved Negro slaves and masters in a web of espionage, a web of waiting and watching, of measuring and spying and maneuvering. In this web it was every slave against every white man, and every triumph over the master, no matter how petty, was recognized as a triumph for the cause.

Jean-Paul Sartre's description of resistance in occupied France illuminates the nature of the struggle between master and slave in the Old South. "Everywhere," he wrote, "on billboards, in the newspapers, on the screen, we encountered the revolting and insipid picture of ourselves that our oppressors wanted us to accept . . . Because the Nazi venom seeped even into our thoughts, every accurate thought was a conquest. Because an all-powerful police tried to force us to hold our tongues, every word took on the value of a declaration of principles. Because we were hunted down, every one of our gestures had the weight of a solemn commitment." There were no billboards in slavery, but there were tyrants— and there were men who stood up to tyrants. Every slave protest, direct or subtle, was a step in the development of new forms of life organization. Every slave protest was a choice made in the face of death for life.

A slave underground crystallized around the stealing of goods, the trading of information on the intentions and state of mind of the enemy, and the hiding and passing on of fugitive slaves. All slaves did not participate in the underground. Some

—a definite minority—had been so crushed by slavery that they were timid and afraid. Others—mainly house servants—had been so conditioned by the cast-off clothes and cast-off ideas of their masters that they kissed their chains. Still others —a definite majority—maintained a sense of expectancy and hope that is one of the most memorable tributes to the indomitable tenacity of the human spirit.

The dominant responses of the vast majority of slaves were discontent, unrest, and protest. There were repeated insurrections, and there is solid evidence that the South lived in constant fear of the "docile" slaves. The most dramatic form of resistance was terrorism (arson, murder, sabotage) carried out, for the most part, by the so-called "bad Negro," a germinal figure in Negro folklore.

Slaves also used a variety of techniques in undramatic, day-to-day resistance to slavery. On occasions, they staged sit-downs and slow-downs in the cotton fields. On impulse sometimes and sometimes on plan, they sat down and refused to move until work loads were lightened. Some groups fled to the forests at the height of the cotton-picking season and sent emissaries to negotiate with "old master."

Quieter still and equally effective was the day-to-day sabotage, the gate left open for cattle to escape, the expensive tool or implement "accidentally" dropped or broken.

At one time or another, almost all slaves dropped their masks—a little. The dissatisfied look, the slow unwilling movement, the labored stroke of the hoe, "the drawling tone, the slow hearing, the feigned stupidity, the sham pains and sickness, the short memory," and always, the mocking smile and the accusing laugh: these were the tactics of the undramatic slave.

Despite, or perhaps because of, all attempts to crush it, the rebellious will of the slave endured. There was something tragic about this stubborn will, but there was also something heroic about it. By escaping or helping others to escape, by reading and teaching others to read, by stealing and helping others to steal, by homicide, suicide, and infanticide, the slave opposed his will to his master's.

The unpleasant fact is that slaves did not feel that they had unqualified moral obligations to white people—and white people knew it. It was considered right and proper to steal from white people and to lie to them. In an odd reversal of the Taney dictum, slaves acted as though white people had no rights they were bound to respect—if they were clever enough, and quick enough.

Frederick Douglass, the great ex-slave, put his pen on the heart of the matter—the break in community. He was, he said, a "slave of society which has, in fact, in form and substance, bound itself to assist the white man in robbing me of my rightful liberty and the just rewards of my labor." As a result, Douglass said, "Whatever rights I have against the master, I have equally against those confederated with him in robbing me of my liberty. Since society has marked me out as privileged plunder, on the principle of self-preservation, I am justified in plundering in turn."

This attitude of defiance and protest flows out of the bottomless well of the Negro folk tradition. Few slaves wrote books, but almost all of them sang songs and told stories. It is to these stories and songs we must go for the slave's comment on his condition.

The spirituals, the best-known of Negro folk products, speak of exile and homelessness, of wandering in some lonesome valley or down some unknown road, a long way from home, without father or mother or sister or brother. The spirituals speak of sorrow and despair, but there is something else, a cosmic discontent, a discontent so deep and pervasive that only the blind or hard of hearing can miss it.

In these songs, the slave commented on a world composed of masters and slaves—commented and analyzed and judged. He also used song as a means of communication. The whoops, hollers, and field calls contained secret messages about meeting places, intentions, and dangers. As a matter of fact, double meanings permeate the whole fabric of Negro sacred and secular music. Consider, for example, the symbols of release ("de walls come tumblin' down"), of battle ("Joshua fit de battle of Jericho"), the judgment ("Pharaoh's army got drowned"). Consider also the obvious fact that the slaves identified with the Hebrew children and projected their hostility and hate onto Pharaoh, the slave symbol for the white master.

The biblical symbols did not appeal to all slaves. Scholarly interest in the spirituals has obscured the fact that the great majority of slaves were non- if not anti-Christian. The secular songs of this group were irreverent and impudent; some, which later metamorphosed into the blues, were existentially absurd.

The Negro slave also protested obliquely in story and folklore. A deep and bitter strain of hostility runs through the cycle of animal stories, particularly the Brer Rabbit series which a Southern newspaperman collected from ex-slaves and put into the mouth of a stereotype, Uncle Remus.

Uncle Remus was Joel Chandler Harris' creation, but the hostility and the "Malevolent Rabbit," in Bernard Wolfe's phrase, came from the Negro's heart. The central theme of the stories is the defeat of a powerful and wicked animal (the white man) by a weak and clever animal (the Negro). In the animal cycle, the weak prevails over the strong and evil meets an avenger. For the slave, the stories of rabbits outwitting and eventually leading foxes to death were a psychological release and a creative self-projection.

This image of revolt and revenge became flesh in the leaders of the three great slave revolts and conspiracies: Gabriel Prosser, Richmond, Virginia, 1800; Denmark Vesey, Charleston, South Carolina, 1822; Nat Turner, Southampton County, Virginia, 1831.

Though separated by time and space, Prosser, Vesey, and Turner were of a piece. Prosser and Turner were field slaves: Turner was a preacher and Prosser was a biblical student who found food for insurrection in the blood and doom passages of the Old Testament. Vesey, on the other hand, was a free man, a well-to-do carpenter. He was, by his own admission, satisfied with his condition; yet he risked his life and paid the supreme price in a bold effort to free his brothers. Vesey was relatively old, about fifty-four. Turner and Prosser were young, thirty-one and twenty-four, respectively.

The three men were obsessed by one dominant idea: the destruction of all white people. In their view, the enemy was society. The only solution, they believed, was a war of immediate and total extermination.

Nat Turner was moved by a mystical obsession that God had called him to rise up and "slay my enemies with their own weapons." Like Joan of Arc, he had provocative visions of the impending doom of his adversaries. Gabriel and Vesey, on the other hand, were motivated by the revolutionary concepts of the American, Haitian, and French revolutions. Gabriel and his men, in fact, had purchased a white silk flag on which were inscribed the words: *"Liberté ou Mort."*

Of the three men, Nat Turner came closest to succeeding. For forty-eight hours, he held Southampton County in a black embrace of death. With a long, bloody sprawl, he threw himself on his masters and slew sixty men, women, and children before he was defeated. Nat was hanged finally, but his spirit lived on. His career, it has been said, made an impact upon the South as great as the careers of John C. Calhoun or

Thomas Jefferson. After Nat, it was no longer possible for men to pretend. There were men in the slave quarters. One could not always depend on their masks. At any moment, the mask could turn into a horrid face of blood and vengeance.

Gabriel Prosser and Denmark Vesey did not succeed. They were thwarted at the last moment by the treachery of house slaves. But the record shows that they were leaders of large-scale liberation movements. Both men laid their plans with great care, storing weapons and disguises and creating huge organizations under the eyes and noses of the masters. Gabriel worked underground for four or five months, holding meetings at fish fries and barbecues, stealing into Richmond once a week to study the terrain. He had enlisted, according to contemporary estimates, from two thousand to fifty thousand slaves.

Vesey, who was by far the most astute of the slave rebels, demonstrated a talent bordering on genius. He worked undercover in Charleston and environs for more than five years, signing up whole plantations, perfecting a cell-like organization that was never cracked. It has been estimated that more than nine thousand slaves were involved in his attempt to destroy slavery.

The three great slave revolts were, in essence, attempts to re-create community. In rebellion, Turner, Prosser, and Vesey illuminated the chasm between man and man, and man and state. Throwing their bodies across the great divide, these three created "a boundary situation," a limiting moment of lucidity in which the master confronted traumatically the boundaries of freedom between man and man.

The implications of all this were clear enough, and bad enough. Fearing a total conflagration, men grew anxious and a language or, rather, a nonlanguage was invented to hold the terror that lived in men's hearts.

As the Civil War approached, slavery became, to appropriate Melville's arresting metaphor, a great white whale which threatened to devour both Negroes and whites. The long arm of slavery reached out and compromised the Constitution (which contained three proslavery clauses). It blunted the force of Jefferson and Washington and twisted Lincoln's words in his mouth.

The slave experience is basic to an understanding of current racial realities. It is the substructure of both segregation, *de facto* and *de jure*, and movements against segregation. As a result of slavery, whites were overwhelmed by a guilt so monstrous and pervading that it poisoned thought at its very roots. Another legacy of this period is a deep fear of the Negro, not a physical fear, but something deeper and more menacing, a fear of losing grip on life, a fear of losing control. And to this must be added the immense counterweight of Negro embitterment.

The habit of regarding the state as an expression of the white personality; the perfervid fascination with Negro sex life; the polarization of the North and South; the *noblesse oblige* approach to Negroes as suppliants seeking hand-outs rather than citizens with inalienable rights no man can bestow or withhold; and, above all, the rupture in community between black man and white man and black man and the state—all these are legacies of the slave substructure.

Slavery, in sum, was a seed experience. The significant dimensions of the race problem, the special dynamism that gave the summers of 1963 and 1964 their special harshness, are reflections of eddies that lie deep in the mind and deep in the past. The Negro is what he is today because he was once held in slavery by white people. And white people are what they are today because they cannot forget, because Negroes will not let them forget, what they did yesterday.

The most dramatic link with this substructure of remembered wrong is the image of the young student, sitting-in at a lunch counter, reading Hegel or Aristotle, and singing the same song that sustained his great-grandmother in the slave cabins.

> *Oh, freedom; oh, freedom;*
> *Oh, Lord, freedom over me,*
> *And before I'd be a slave*
> *I'd be buried in my grave*
> *An' go home to my Lord and be free.*

The song and the student's use of it tell us how much things have changed and how much they have remained the same. Even more significant is the fact that the song invokes something that transcends time and slaves and masters, something that was honored in Rome and Athens and will be honored as long as man breathes—something in man that does not love walls and chains.

THE FIRST FREEDOM MOVEMENT

THE Patriot, attended by a "faithful" Negro slave, climbed a steep mountain and tempted fate with a cry for FREEDOM! The word bounced off the craggy rocks and came back in a resounding echo: FREEDOM! FREEDOM! The echo was so close, so menacing, that the Patriot turned quickly to see if the slave had spoken. But the slave was silent or seemed to be silent. The Patriot lifted his head and shouted again: FREEDOM! And an echo came back: FREEDOM! FREEDOM! The Patriot drew back in fear. Was he imagining things? Or did the slave speak? In desperation, the Patriot railed at the rocks and commanded the words to stop. But the words echoed and re-echoed in the mountain air. The words swelled and swallowed the original sound, assuming a texture and a life of their own, reverberating from peak to peak in a continuous curtain of sound. In mounting fear, the Patriot shut his ears against the words of his own mouth. He stood thus, ears stopped and eyes closed, unable to climb to the peak or go down to the valley, a tragic figure paralyzed by the cry he had raised and the reality he had made. Shadows gathered in the crevices and, at length, darkness fell on the high and dangerous ledge where two men—one white and one colored, one slave and one free—stood face to face, uneasily watching and measuring each other, listening with bated breath to the sounds of freedom reverberating in the thin dry air.

Like a huge sounding board, the Negro Freedom movement reflects, amplifies and hurls back into the mainstream impulses activated by the germinal American Revolution. The first Freedom movement, the Civil War, the Niagara movement, the sit-ins, the Freedom Rides, the Bastilles of Birmingham and Selma: all were contained in a seed state in the internal contradictions of America's freedom movement.

Out of the blood and strife of the American Revolution came a new nation, and Negro and white groups irrevocably wedded to each other and to conflict by the terms of their common birth—terms that involved a contradiction between affirmation (equality) and reality (inequality), a contradiction that made conflict not only likely but, given the phrases of the Revolutionary ideology, inevitable.

It was the tragedy of American Patriots to reach for freedom on a platform that condemned them utterly; it was their tragedy to say words and to write words that, paradoxically, invited, nay, demanded revolt against them. In 1776, American Patriots held some five hundred thousand human beings, some of them white, in servitude. And yet they chose to make a revolution in support of human equality. By this incredible act, the Patriots sowed the seeds of continuous conflict. The friction generated by recurring clashes between the words of affirmation and the deeds of reality has powered every Negro resistance movement, and every Negro resistant, from Nat Turner to Martin Luther King, Jr., has taken his stand on the rock of the American Revolution which scattered four revolutionary premises to the four corners of the world. In rebellion, America said:

1) That all men are created equal and are endowed by their Creator with natural and inalienable rights no man or government can bestow or take away.

2) That to secure these rights men create civil communities and civil authorities who derive their just power from the consent of the governed.

3) That members of the community are colleagues and not subjects and that legitimate government consists in the dominion of equal laws applied equally—in the dominion, in short, of men over themselves and not in the dominion of communities over communities or of any men over any other men.

4) That when governments are destructive of these ends as evidenced by bad faith ("a long train of abuses and usurpations pursuing invariably the same object") it is the duty of men to alter or to abolish the government.

The crystallization of these ideas in the Declaration of Independence enclosed the colonists in a net of their own making and made Negro freedom an inevitable corollary of white freedom. Caught in the echo of their own cry, the colonists writhed in the uneasy knowledge that they could not condemn the Negro echo without also condemning themselves. There thus began a triple struggle, a struggle in the minds and hearts of men which reflected the external struggles against the Negro rebels within and the white tyrants without.

The irony of this situation was not lost on the more enlightened colonists. Thomas Paine and James Otis, the great yeasayers of the Revolution, thundered against English tyranny *and* slaveowner tyranny. Paine said slavery was no less immoral than "murder, robbery, lewdness and barbarity" and urged Americans to "discontinue and renounce it, with grief and abhorrence." More persuasive was Abigail Adams' hint to her husband, John: "It always appeared a most iniquitous scheme to me to fight ourselves for what we are daily robbing and plundering from those who have as good a right to freedom as we have."

So it seemed also to Negroes. Under the impact of the Revolutionary ideology, the Negro soul expanded and made its first tentative probes into enemy territory. Stimulated by the white cry for freedom, Negroes developed a concept of themselves as deprived citizens and dishonored native sons. Proceeding from a new self-conception, they invented techniques for demanding their rights within the bounds of the state, using the state, in fact, as a point of leverage.

For the first time in America, for the first time anywhere, city Negroes found a voice and a technique. Slave revolts and underground resistance had taken place outside the system. Free Negroes proposed now to use the ideology and instruments of the system to smash the system. They proposed to bore from within and destroy legal forms with legal forms. Their first technique, one that would reach full flower 194 years later, was legal contention. As early as 1766, Boston Negroes filed a test case against slavery. The movement later spread to Connecticut and other states. Under the leadership of men whose names were not recorded, Negroes collected money, hired lawyers and filed suits, asking for freedom and damages for unlawful detention.

Black Patriots also experimented with mass pressure. Meetings were held, petitions were circulated, and legislatures were bombarded with pleas. Ingenious men found other ways to turn the Revolutionary turmoil to their advantage. Some Negroes, like Crispus Attucks, the leader of the American crowd in the Boston Massacre, appropriated American slogans and assumed leadership in the street riots in Boston and other cities. Still others, more cynical, sided with the British. As the agitation intensified, the number of slave escapes increased sharply and the number of incidents multiplied.

In the Revolutionary War, as in every other war, Negroes used crisis points as levers to extract basic constitutional rights; and the Revolutionary War, like every other American war, advanced the Negro's cause. The key to this paradox is that war is a crisis, the maximum crisis. And crises shake people up, disarrange their institutions, and open their minds. The Negro, no more bloodthirsty than others, perhaps less so, has always perceived that his case bears most weight when he is needed most. War, accordingly, has been a key instrument of Negro protests, not in the narrow sense of promoting or even supporting war but in the larger sense of urging men to occupy high ground paid for by blood and pain. It has been America's fortune to fight always for freedom, and Negro leaders have always made America pay for that privilege.

Every American war, as far as the Negro is concerned, has resolved itself into two phases: a fight to fight on the same terms as others and a fight to make America flesh out the words on which the war was based. The Revolutionary War established the pattern for future conflicts. An attempt was made at the beginning of the war to bar Negroes from the American Army. The free Negroes of New England refused to take this blow without protest. And American officers, fearing large-scale defections to the British, reversed themselves. As a result, some five thousand Negro soldiers, slaves and free men, struck blows for American freedom.

Slavery died in the North as a direct result of forces loosed by the war. By legislative decrees and by court orders, Negro slaves in the North were freed. In the first flush of freedom, thousands of slaves were manumitted by slaveholders infected by the germinal ideas of the Declaration of Independence. And abolitionist societies sprang up in the North and South to remind Patriots of the universality of their creed.

There was no consensus, at this point, on the place of the Negro in a Commonwealth founded on the inalienable rights of all men. It was apparent to most men that the Declaration of Independence had created a new situation in America, but few men were willing to apply the rules of equality in their personal relations with Negroes and Indians. It can be said, I think, that most men avoided a personal confrontation between the words they espoused and the deeds they lived by. Insofar as possible, American Patriots tried not to think of nonwhites and the Declaration of Independence at the same time.

There was, as a result, a certain fluidity to postwar life. Negroes like Joshua Bishop of Virginia and Lemuel Haynes of New England pastored white churches in the North and South, and the Baptists and Methodists strongly condemned slavery. During this same period, Benjamin Banneker, the eminent astronomer and surveyor, helped to lay out the city of Washington, D.C., and Phillis Wheatley became an internationally known poet.

Banneker, Wheatley, and other prominent Negroes demonstrated latent possibilities in the developing American Dream. To be sure, things were not rosy in this period. But some Negroes, a very few Negroes, had room to dream and dare and hope.

Then the curtain dropped. Caste lines hardened; racial hostility increased. Free Negroes were insulted and driven off streets, and slaves were hemmed in by restrictions designed to deny them even the rudiments of human personality.

In the background of the big change was a machine, the cotton gin, which cooled the ardor of Patriots and made slave-grown cotton a national mania. No less persuasive as a proslavery prop was a wave of reaction that rolled over America after Shays's Rebellion in Massachusetts, the French Revolution in Europe, and the Haitian Revolution in the Caribbean.

Another factor in the changing climate of race relations was the rapid increase in the number of free Negroes. Above all else, poor whites feared and resented the economic threat of colonies of hungry and desperately insecure freedmen. As early as 1722 a petition hostile to Negro workers was presented to the General Assembly by the white laborers of Philadelphia who said that "the practice of the blacks being employed was a great disadvantage to them who had emigrated from Europe for the purpose of obtaining a livelihood."

Revolts at home and abroad, the increase in the number of free Negroes, the invention of the cotton gin, fear, frustration and hostility: these gave birth to a new phenomenon in the history of man: the American Negro.

Negroes, as a group, did not exist before the Revolution. The development of a national Negro group with a common viewpoint and a consciousness of a common fate was a product of a syndrome that recurs repeatedly in the history of the American Negro—the sudden dilation of the Negro mood under the impact of a war for freedom and the sudden contraction of the mood in the wake of postwar reaction. In the Revolutionary War, Negro individuals were lifted up and exalted by the declared war aims. Then from this great height they were suddenly dashed down. After the great hope, after the great dream, Negroes awoke to find themselves bilked. It would happen again—many times. But they had no experience then of betrayal. They saw suddenly with terrible lucidity that it was not going to happen to them. The shouting and hurrahs were not for them—not for them were the cries and hosannas of the brave tomorrows. Who was the shouting for? Americans.

And were they not Americans, too? And if they were not Americans, then who, in God's name, were they?

These questions gave rise to thought and to the American Negro, or, to be more precise, the African-American, for all of the first Negro institutions bore the interesting prefix—African. Rebuffed by white men, pulled off their knees in white churches, ridiculed and derided, Negroes went out into the alleys and fields and formed their own institutions and, in the process, invented themselves. The Negro church, from which came the current Freedom movement, the first Negro newspaper, the first Negro mass meeting, the first Negro convention: all date from the pioneer period between 1780 and 1830.

It is impossible to overestimate the importance of this movement, which marked a fundamental turning point in the Negro's relations with white America. Institutions are great social pools in which men see themselves and their ideals reflected. They are instruments with which men come to grips with the questions: Who am I? Where do I belong? Without meetings, without rituals, without ceremonies, myths and symbols, men cannot define themselves or enter into real relations with others. American Negroes, recognizing this, attempted first to enter institutions formed for Americans—and were rebuffed. They then embarked on a perilous journey of self-naming, self-legitimization, and self-discovery.

The quest began with a revolt in white churches. Negroes, as a rule, were required to sit in separate pews or in the galleries of white churches—"Nigger Heaven," the more irreverent called it. In the wake of the postwar reaction, attempts were made to limit the number of Negro parishioners and to confine them to the back of galleries or to benches in the rear of the hall. To the surprise of white pastors and parishioners, Negroes resisted the policy of containment and raised new demands for more humane treatment in the house of the Lord. In some cases, as tension rose, Negroes were asked to leave white churches. In other cases, Negroes walked out on their own initiative.

The separate church struggle began in the late 1770's with the founding of African Baptist Churches in South Carolina, Virginia, and Georgia. In the postwar period, the struggle assumed the shape of a national movement. Suddenly, without conscious planning, the free Negro class erupted in a frenzy of organizational activity. The climax of the movement came in Philadelphia with one of the first public demonstrations against Jim Crow. On a Sunday in November, 1786, a group of Negro worshippers were pulled from their knees during prayer at St. George's Methodist Episcopal Church. Without a word, the Negro worshippers filed out of the church. Under the leadership of two ex-slaves, Richard Allen and Absalom Jones, the disenchanted Methodists organized the Free African Society which was, as Du Bois pointed out, "the first wavering step of a people toward organized social life."

By withdrawing from the white Methodist church, the little band of Negro protestants affirmed the new image they had of themselves as human beings who demanded certain minimum concessions to their humanity. But the withdrawal raised large questions of identity. The members of the Free African Society discussed these questions at several heated meetings. Some members suggested an affiliation with the Quakers, others suggested an entente with the Episcopalians or the Methodists. Behind the debate was another question: What relation, if any, should Negroes have with white power?

After a long and bitter debate, the Free African Society split into two groups. The larger group followed Absalom Jones, an affable, easygoing ex-slave, into the Episcopal Church. In 1791, the African Church of St. Thomas was erected in Philadelphia and eleven words were engraved in the vestibule: "The People Who Walked in Darkness Have Seen a Great Light."

Or had they—really?

Richard Allen did not think so. The new Negro communicants were not given full status in the Episcopal Church, and they were barred from annual conferences and governing boards. To Allen, this was rank discrimination. He demanded first-class rights in an integrated church, if possible, and in a separate church, if necessary. In his mind, at that early date, was an image of the Negro as a leader and creator of institutions. In his mind, in an unmanifested seed state, was the idea of a Negro personality.

Who was this man?

Richard Allen was an ex-slave who began his career with an act of extraordinary symbolic significance: the conversion of his master. Shrewd and hardworking, Allen accumulated enough money to buy his freedom and migrated to Philadelphia. After the split in the Free African Society, he formed an independent Negro Methodist church. In 1816, he became the first bishop of the African Methodist Episcopal Church, the first interstate organization created by American Negroes.

Allen's point—and it is still revolutionary—was a point of power. He not only demanded the right of participation in American institutions, but he also demanded the right of sharing in the governing of those institutions. There is some exaggeration in Vernon Loggins' nomination of Allen for the title, "Father of the Negro"; but the exaggeration contains a core of truth. The blunt-spoken Allen was the first national Negro leader, a pioneer Negro abolitionist, and the organizer and president of the first Negro convention held in the Western world.

Men made in Allen's image dominated the second phase of the Negro freedom movement. In 1787, Prince Hall, a Boston protest leader, formed the first Negro Masonic lodge, African Lodge No. 45. In New York in this same period, James Varick and other Negro leaders organized the African Methodist Episcopal Zion Church. By 1830, there were Negro churches and organizations of almost every conceivable kind in America, including an Ethiopian Church of Jesus Christ in Savannah, Georgia, and a Negro Dutch Reformed Church in New York City.

The leaders of these institutions were vigorous defenders of Negro interests. Taking their stand on the Declaration of Independence, the pioneer Negro leaders attacked slavery and its Northern twin, bigotry. Richard Allen and Absalom Jones argued in a 1794 pamphlet that the social characteristics of Negroes were the direct result of enforced segregation and degradation. They also warned of the perils of slavery, telling Americans: "If you love your country, if you love the God of love, clear your hands from slaves, burden not your children or your country with them." Six years later, Jones and other Philadelphians sent an antislavery petition to Congress. Allied with Jones and Allen in the Philadelphia protest movement was James Forten, a Revolutionary War veteran who accumulated a $100,000 fortune as a sailmaker and employed Negro and white artisans. Forten attracted national attention with a series of letters that demolished the arguments of whites who wanted to limit the number of free Negroes entering Pennsylvania.

Another pioneer protest leader was Benjamin Banneker who reminded Americans of the pledges of their birth in a famous 1791 letter to Thomas Jefferson. "Sir," Banneker wrote, "suffer me to recall to your mind that time, in which the arms and tyranny of the British crown were exerted, with every powerful effort, in order to reduce you to a state of servitude: look back, I entreat you, on the variety of dangers to which you were exposed . . . you were then impressed with proper ideas of the great violation of liberty, and the free possession of those blessings, to which you were entitled by nature; but, sir, how pitiable is it to reflect, that although you were so fully convinced of the benevolence of the Father of Mankind, and of his equal and impartial distribution of those rights and privileges, which He hath conferred upon them that you should at the same time counteract his mercies, in detaining by fraud and violence, so numerous a part of my brethren under groaning captivity, and cruel oppression, that you should at the same time be found guilty of that most criminal act, which you professedly detested in others, with respect to yourselves."

Similar appeals came from Prince Hall, the Boston leader. In 1787, he filed one of the first public petitions on the perennial issue, equal education. Hall later asked the selectmen of Boston to establish a public school for Negro children. Also active during this period was Hall's contemporary, Paul Cuffe, a wealthy captain who sailed his own ships to Europe and Africa. Barred from the ballot box in Dartmouth, Massachusetts, Cuffe refused to pay taxes and filed a defiant petition of protest. After a long controversy, it was decided that taxation without representation in America was tyranny. The case was widely regarded as establishing a precedent for Negro suffrage.

For obvious reasons, the leaders of the second phase of the first Freedom movement muted their protests. They were a small and powerless group in a turbulent and threatening sea. They could issue no serious threats; nor could they make thunderous demands. With consummate skill, they picked their way through the field of battle, fighting here, retreating there, donning and dropping the inevitable mask.

The third phase of the first freedom struggle began with the colonization movement which called for the removal of free Negroes ("a dangerous and useless element") to Africa. Colonization was not an entirely new issue to Negro Americans. The Negro Union of Newport, Rhode Island, had suggested an exodus of free Negroes in 1788. This suggestion, the first Negro nationalist note in American history, was vetoed by the Philadelphia Free African Society which answered: "With regard to the emigration to Africa you mention we have at present but little to communicate on that head, apprehending that every pious man is a good citizen of the whole world."

Not all Negroes shared this viewpoint. Some Negroes, despairing of the good faith of white Americans, championed a return to Africa. Daniel Coker, Richard Allen's great rival, and John B. Russwurm, the first Negro college graduate, were among the first converts to the colonization cause. But the vast majority held fast, contending that the colonizationists were anti-Negro and proslavery. Thoroughly alarmed by the climate of repression stimulated by the colonizationists, free Negroes struck back, utilizing mass pressure techniques. The first widespread use of mass meetings by American Negroes occurred in 1817 in Richmond, New York, and Philadelphia. In state and local meetings, in pamphlets, papers and books, free Negroes told white America that the Negro was here and that he was here to stay. "This is our home," a Negro convention said, "and this is our country. Beneath its soil lie the bones of our fathers; for it, some of them fought, bled, and died. Here we were born; and here we will die." Free Negroes also affirmed their identity of interests with slaves. Migration to Africa, they said, would be a betrayal of their brothers in bondage.

Fighting with their backs to the waiting ships, free Negroes in the North developed a sense of solidarity and mutuality. Out of the ferment of the defensive anticolonization movement came the first militant abolitionists and the first Negro newspaper, *Freedom's Journal,* which was published for the first time on March 16, 1827, by Samuel E. Cornish and John B. Russwurm. In its first issue, the paper struck a note of militant protest: "We wish to plead our own cause. Too long have others spoken for us."

Another sign of internal stirring was the Negro convention movement which began in 1830, three years before the founding of the American Antislavery Society. Richard Allen was elected president of this convention which met in Philadelphia's Bethel Church. Periodically, after 1830, Northern Negroes met in convention and hammered out pleas and admonitions to their white brothers. Using a new technique, the "address to the nation," they condemned slavery and colonization, recommended the establishment of Tuskegee-type schools and set aside July 4 as a day of mourning and prayer.

The Negro convention movement and the establishment of the first Negro newspaper were tremendous leaps forward in Negro group consciousness. For the first time in America, Negro agitators from all sections of the country came together to define their situation and to seek common solutions. For the first time, Negroes saw themselves reflected in the pages of journals dedicated to their interests. Negro conventions and Negro newspapers welded Negroes into a common unit and served as sounding boards and mirrors. They were also instru-

ments of internal control, defining with increasing rigorous-
ness the bounds of permissible dissent from group values.

This phase of the protest movement was almost entirely defensive in nature. Even so, Negro leaders were a great deal
more militant than their white allies, whose efforts were
largely confined to innocuous humanitarianism. The pioneer
white abolitionists, with few exceptions, were gradualists who
believed that something should be done but not too soon and,
if possible, not here.

Beginning around 1829, the Freedom movement started to
move in a different direction. Two thunderous notes—the
words of a free Negro and the acts of a slave—marked the
change in tempo. David Walker, the free Negro, was a product
of the emerging group consciousness of American Negroes.
Born free in Wilmington, North Carolina, in 1785, Walker
moved to Boston and opened a secondhand clothes store. In
1828, he appeared on the Boston scene as a radical agitator;
the next year, on September 29, he published *Walker's Appeal
to the Colored Citizens of the World.* Into seventy-six closely-
printed pages, the forty-four-year-old author poured the accumulated disgust of his people. He lashed out at white people
whom he called "devils" and excoriated the slaveholding
Christians of "this Republican land of Liberty ! ! ! ! ! !"
The Negro's situation, he said, was abominable. "Can it be
more mean and abject? If there are any changes, will they not
be for the better, though they may appear for the worse
at first?" Rebellion, he said, was a religious duty. "Colored
brethren all over the world," he concluded, should revolt and
slit their oppressors' throats from ear to ear. "Kill," Walker
said—"Kill or be killed." Like a fire bell in the night, Walker's
pamphlet constricted men's hearts. The governors of several
Southern states called their assemblies into secret session to
discuss the pamphlet. And Southern mayors asked the mayor
of Boston to lock Walker up and burn his books.

Consternation turned to fear two years later when Nat
Turner added a bloody exclamation point to Walker's *Appeal.*
Turner's revolt and Walker's appeal were the opening shots
in the fourth and final phase of the first Freedom movement.
In rebellion, the two Negro activists created a climate of crisis
and paved the way for the militant abolitionists, America's
first radical sect.

Like Nat Turner, like David Walker, like Richard Allen,
militant abolitionists echoed the words of Thomas Jefferson's

Declaration. In a fierce struggle to complete what they called "the unfinished revolution," abolitionists created a revolutionary movement which attempted to smash the slave system and establish a new social order. They demanded the complete and immediate abolition of slavery without compensation to slaveholders. They not only demanded; they also went out into the streets and highways and acted. Like the sit-in students, the abolitionists goaded and provoked a slumbering people into facing the greatest problem of the age. And the people, so goaded and so provoked, have never forgiven them.

Although the abolitionist movement was America's greatest reform effort, it survives today more as a museum piece than a tradition. The lessons learned by the abolitionists and the techniques they used lay dormant for more than one hundred years. During this period, moderation became the accepted value in American race relations and historians vied with each other in vilifying the brave men and women who shaped the emotional climate that led to the Civil War. Not until the one hundredth anniversary of the Emancipation Proclamation would a movement achieve the force and passion of the nineteenth-century nay-sayers.

The nineteenth-century movement was remarkably similar to the contemporary Freedom movement. The abolitionists pioneered in the use of nonviolent direct action. Abolitionists, like contemporary rebels, held mass meetings, sang freedom songs, and staged sit-ins and freedom rides. They marched, demonstrated, and picketed. They were often in jail, where they sang freedom songs at all hours of the night and day. Like modern rebels, like every rebel in the history of man, abolitionists were witnesses who placed in question every value that impeded dialogue between man and man.

The nineteenth-century rebels were, for the most part, middle- and upper-middle-income people: doctors, lawyers, teachers, ministers. But some were in the upper strata of society. The Tappan brothers were New York merchant princes; Gerrit Smith was the largest landowner in New York state; the Grimké sisters, Sarah and Angelina, were South Carolina bluebloods who were hounded out of Charleston.

William Lloyd Garrison, the great symbol of the movement, was an editor and propagandist. Like Martin Luther King, Jr., he preached the virtues of love, passive resistance, and moral force. Garrison, like King, attracted devoted disciples and served as a rallying force for men of varying viewpoints and visions. Although Garrison was white, he threw himself into the struggle with so much determination that many people assumed that he was colored. "I never rise before a colored audience," he said, "without feeling ashamed of my race."

Born poor in Newburyport, Massachusetts, in 1805, Garrison educated himself and became a talented writer and propagandist. He began his antislavery career as a gradualist but soon switched to a more radical posture. Heavily influenced and subsidized by Negro abolitionists, he opened his famous paper, the *Liberator,* in Boston on January 1, 1831. His first editorial sang with indignation.

> I will be as harsh as truth, and as uncompromising as justice. On this subject [slavery], I do not wish to think, to speak, or write, with moderation. No! No! Tell a man whose house is on fire to give a moderate alarm; tell him to moderately rescue his wife from the hands of the ravisher; tell the mother to gradually extricate her babe from the fire into which it is fallen; but urge me not to use moderation in a cause like the present! I am in earnest—I will not equivocate—I will not excuse—I will not retreat a single inch—AND I WILL BE HEARD!

It was a magnificent manifesto, and Garrison, to his credit, lived up to it—at least until the Civil War. With other abolitionists—Negro and white—he organized the American Antislavery Society which served as an instrument for men who eschewed equivocation, moderation, and gradualism. Among the other leaders of the movement were Theodore Weld, the great lecturer and organizer; Wendell Phillips, "the golden voice" of abolitionism; Theodore Parker, the Unitarian minister; and Frederick Douglass, the ex-slave.

Repeated attempts have been made to portray the abolitionist movement as a white man's improvement association—attempts, as one writer put it, to stage Othello without Othello. The attempts fail, of course, for Othello was at the heart of the drama. In the early days of the struggle, Samuel E. Cornish, James Forten, and Charles Lenox Remond fought shoulder to shoulder with Garrison and Weld. In the forties and fifties, Frederick Douglass, Samuel R. Ward, Sojourner Truth, Harriet Tubman, and Henry Highland Garnet were in the forefront of the movement.

Of whatever color, of whatever rank, the abolitionists were revolutionaries who gave themselves heart and soul to the struggle. In the name of a higher law, they openly resisted state and federal authority and used force, when necessary, to prevent the recapture of fugitive slaves. In the name of the revolution of 1776, they hammered away at the national conscience, goading, prodding, shocking, startling.

Like Old Testament prophets, abolitionists preached sin, guilt, and purification. Their major theme was the complicity of good men in systems of evil. Slavery existed, the abolitionists said, because it was reputable and because it was sanctioned by structures of power in the North. Proceeding on this assumption, abolitionists tried to alter public opinion and isolate slaveholders. Their main aim was "to blister the conscience" of the good, the silent, and the indifferent. Their targets were the American government, the church, the business establishment—everyone, in fact, who supported the status quo. Abolitionists attacked the "sectarian organizations known as churches" as "combinations of thieves, robbers, adulterers, pirates and murderers." Equally harsh was Garrison's denunciation of the Constitution as "a covenant with death and an agreement with hell." After passage of the Fugitive Slave Law of 1850, Garrison tore up a copy of the Constitution, put a match to the fragments and shouted, dramatically, "And let the people say, Amen." The people said: "Amen."

With missionary fervor, abolitionists waged "a holy war" against American society. Wendell Phillips and several other abolitionists refused to vote, practice law, or exercise any function under the Constitution until slavery was abolished. Several preachers willingly gave up large churches and devoted all their time to the ministry of agitation.

For Phillips, Garrison, and other agitators, abolitionism was a way of life involving a total response to a total challenge. Abandoning father, mother, and brother, abolitionists spent hundreds of hours in mass meetings. They traveled thousands of miles on horses, distributing literature and organizing antislavery societies. Most abolitionists made a practice of sitting in "Negro sections" of public conveyances, if they were white, and in "white sections," if they were Negroes.

Some of the more eccentric abolitionists expressed their defiance in novel ways. The Rev. Henry C. Wright, a Congregational minister, shocked his parishioners by shedding his clothes in daylight and swimming the Merrimack River "for the cause." Some of his colleagues adopted the allegedly modern posture of growing a beard of defiance. Still others advocated free love, plural marriages, and improvements in women's underwear (bloomers). Thomas Wentworth Higginson, the great Unitarian preacher, looked on these eccentricities with a kindly eye. "Without a little crack somewhere," he said, "a man could hardly do his duty to his times."

Higginson's contemporaries did not share his broad-mindedness. The abolitionists were reviled and persecuted. But they throve on persecution; some of them even welcomed it. Frederick Douglass began his career as an antislavery advocate by accompanying Stephen Foster who said, according to Douglass, that his mission was to make converts or mobs. "If neither came," Douglass wrote, "he charged it to his want of skill or his unfaithfulness."

In mastery of propaganda, the abolitionists excelled. They used every technique (direct action and political action) and every instrument (platform, pulpit, pamphlet, and press). Some of the more imaginative made a practice of invading churches on Sundays and making impromptu speeches.

Abolitionists shared a common hope, but they were bitterly divided over strategy and tactics. One group, led by Garrison, championed moral force and passive resistance. Another wing, led by militant New Yorkers, advocated political action. Still another group, led by John Brown, championed direct revolutionary action.

The shock troops of this ardent army were agents (men and women) who lived on subsistence wages and went from town to town speaking against slavery and organizing antislavery groups. Some of these agents, incidentally, were college students from the same mould as the contemporary followers of the Student Nonviolent Coordinating Committee.

Abolitionists also organized vigilance committees which specialized in the dangerous work of harboring and transporting fugitive slaves. White men and women and gentle Quakers were brilliant as undercover agents who hid slaves and slipped them through to the next Underground Railroad station. No less brilliant were scores of Negro agents who did the same thing at far greater risks. James G. Birney, the white abolitionist, said the Underground Railroad in his area was "almost uniformly managed by the colored people. I know nothing of them generally till they are past."

Abolitionists did not always wait for "freight" or "bales of cotton," as fugitive slaves were called. Some slipped into the South to drum up business. Harriet Tubman, the short black ex-slave, was the greatest of these daring agents. After her escape from Maryland, she made nineteen forays into the South and led out more than three hundred slaves.

The Negro abolitionists were an elite group who dramatized the knotty problems of a difficult and despairing age. We are a long way now from the muted protest of the Allens and the Fortens. The Negro abolitionists were angry men, bitterly so in some cases. In books and pamphlets, in the press and pulpit, they articulated their agony with a harshness of tone and a richness of invective that has not yet been surpassed in America. Not until the middle of the twentieth century would so many men and women appear with so much indignation— and then it would be neither safe nor wise to say all that was said then. The Douglass of that period was very probably the most radical Negro national leader in American history—and Douglass was neither the most radical nor the angriest leader of his period.

In the forties and fifties, the angry black abolitionists came to grips with the central problems of a Negro protest movement.

What relation, if any, should Negro leadership have with white liberal leadership?

What was the key instrument?

Should Negroes integrate or separate?

How, precisely, could one sing the Lord's song in a strange land?

The answers revolved around the traditional weapons of agitation: the platform, the pulpit, and the press. But a surprisingly large number of Negro leaders championed direct action—violent and nonviolent. Nor were more traditional techniques ignored. Garnet and Ward were pioneer leaders in the Liberty and Free Soil parties that laid the foundation for the Republican party.

Litigation, the Negro's perennial tool, was also used. In 1849, Benjamin F. Roberts filed a suit in Boston on behalf of his daughter, Sarah, who had been barred from several white schools near their home. Boston abolitionists, led by historian William C. Nell, collected money and employed Charles Sumner as attorney. The Boston court discounted Sumner's eloquence and enunciated for the first time the "separate but equal" theory. Disappointed by the legal decision, abolitionists appealed to the bar of public opinion. They organized a school committee which led a vigorous propaganda campaign which included sit-ins and stand-ins. On one occasion, Negro parents and students massed in front of a white school and refused to let anyone enter. Finally, after a long campaign, the state legislature passed a law banning school segregation.

Frederick Douglass led a similar fight in Rochester, New

York. When his children were barred from P. S. 15, Douglass staged a one-parent boycott. "I hardly need say," he explained, "that I was not prepared to submit tamely to this proscription any more than I had been to submit to slavery, so I had them taught at home for a while. . . . Meanwhile, I went to the people with the question and created considerable agitation. I sought to obtain a hearing before the Board of Education, and after repeated efforts with voice and pen the doors of the public schools were opened and Negro children were permitted to attend them in common with others."

Black abolitionists also made pioneer explorations in the field of Negro culture. During this period, William C. Nell produced the first extended work on Negro history. William Wells Brown wrote a novel, *Clotel*, and a play. And Frederick Douglass became the first American to recognize the significance of Negro folk songs.

As a result of the essays and lectures of abolitionists, Negroes discovered that they had a past, a culture, and a tradition in which they could take pride. Benjamin Banneker, Phillis Wheatley, Toussaint L'Ouverture and other great Negroes were spiritually exhumed. Negro scholars and orators also revived the ancient glories of Africa and disputed the contention of whites that the Egyptians were not Africans.

Although black abolitionists were united in their support of Negro achievement, they were divided over matters of doctrine and strategy. Separate churchmen, for example, did not work well with integrated churchmen; and there was continuing friction between churchmen like Henry Highland Garnet and no-churchmen like Frederick Douglass.

Another problem in that age, as in this one, was passive resistance. Negro leaders in Philadelphia and Boston stressed the regenerative powers of love and passive resistance. New York Negro leaders, however, said passive resistance would never end slavery. The tough-minded New Yorkers also favored independent Negro action which the Philadelphians and the Bostonians condemned.

The issue here was a bitter controversy over white leadership. Douglass, Garnet and other New Yorkers were independent men who demanded a share in the "generalship" of the movement. Douglass broke with the Garrisonians on this issue, demanding the right to think his own thoughts and articulate his own vision. "We may fight," Douglass said, "but we must fight like the Sepoys of India, under white officers. [Some] Abolitionists don't like colored celebrations, they don't like colored conventions, they don't like colored Anti-slavery fairs for the support of colored newspapers. They don't like any demonstrations whatever in which colored men take a leading part. . . . I hold it to be no part of gratitude to allow our white friends to do all the work, while we merely hold their coats."

Black abolitionists were also divided over the crucial problem of identity. Early Negro leaders, as we have seen, identified themselves in African terms. In the 1830's, when the campaign to send Negroes back to Africa moved into high gear, a Negro convention, dominated by Philadelphians, urged Negroes "to abandon use of the word 'colored,' [and] especially to remove the title of African from . . . institutions." Philadelphia leaders urged Negroes to identify themselves as "Oppressed Americans."

Crucial questions of whoness and whatness plagued the Negro community throughout the antebellum period. Perhaps the most eloquent explorer of the no man's land of Negro identity was Alexander Crummell, a thin, intense Episcopalian priest who fled the narrowness of the American church, earned a degree at Cambridge and preached in Liberia before returning to America as rector of a Washington church. Crummell was probably the first apostle of African identity. In his sermons, lectures, and addresses, he explored some of the territory covered by the modern exponents of *Negritude*. There was a void, he said, an abyss in the breast of the African-American. "For the truth must needs be confessed by us all, that our natures have been dwarfed and our souls shriveled by the dread ordeal of caste and oppression through which our fathers, and some of ourselves, have passed." Crummell said that "our very speech" indicts us. He looked to a future, however, that would bring about "such an expansion of mind and such a development of character, that the report thereof shall bring to Africa curious travellers to behold here the nature, outgrowth and the grateful vision of a manly, noble, and complete African personality."

Crummell propagated the doctrine of challenge. American Negroes, he said, were a race God had preserved "to do something with." In an eloquent sermon, "The Destined Superiority of the Negro," Crummell argued that the Negro would probably emerge as a superior being endowed with the best qualities of other races.

Further to the right of Crummell was Martin R. Delany, who was perhaps the first major American Negro nationalist. "I thank God for making me a man simply," Douglass said, "but Delany always thanks him for making him a black man."

A short, brilliant man of a "most defiant blackness," Delany gave his children African names and organized a Negro nationalist convention which made the surprisingly modern prediction that "the question of black and white" would one day decide the future of the world.

The swirling currents of this age—separation vs. integration, direct action vs. political action—reached full tide in the career of Delany's colleague and adversary, Frederick Douglass, who was the noblest of all Negro abolitionists and one of the noblest of all Americans. Douglass came from a mould made in a bygone age. From this mould was made a Paine, a Jefferson, and a Darrow; from this mould finally was made a King.

With Douglass, the Negro came of age.

In the speeches and books of this archetypal figure can be found analyses of every facet of the American race problem. A man with a copy of Douglass' collected speeches, Du Bois' manifestos, Wright's novels, and Baldwin's essays would not be far from the agony and the pain and the joy of the American Negro soul.

For fifty years, from 1845 to 1895, Douglass' voice commanded the public ear. During this period, he laid the foundation and roughed out the boundaries and limits of the freedom fight, thereby earning the title, "Father of the Protest Movement." Although Douglass did not always counsel men to take arms against a sea of troubles, he always told them it was their duty to cry out. Men who accepted oppression, he said, would never want for oppressors.

Douglass essayed a program of continuous contention. Every Negro, he said, should challenge every case of bias he encountered. The great abolitionist practiced what he preached. He was perhaps the first systematic "sit-inner." He always assumed that every door open to a human being was open to him and, if turned away, he made an issue of it. Whenever he was asked to leave a "white" restaurant or a "white" railroad car, he would refuse. The conductors of Jim Crow cars usually responded by calling several burly assistants who would drag Douglass out of the car along with several seats he always managed to hold onto. Always, everywhere, Frederick Douglass was challenging the Jim Crow system.

Struggle—struggle and strife and pain: these three, Douglass said, were prerequisites for progress. Speaking at the West India Emancipation Celebration at Canandaigua, New York, on

August 4, 1857, Douglass gave a definitive analysis of one of his favorite subjects, the philosophy of reform.

"The whole history of the progress of human liberty," he said, "shows that all concessions yet made to her august claims, have been born of earnest struggle. . . . If there is no struggle, there is no progress. Those who profess to favor freedom and yet deprecate agitation are men who want crops without plowing up the ground, they want rain without thunder and lightning. They want the ocean without the awful roar of its many waters. This struggle may be a moral one, or it may be a physical one, and it may be both moral and physical, but it must be a struggle. Power concedes nothing without a demand. It never did and it never will. . . . Men may not get all they pay for in this world, but they must certainly pay for all they get. If we ever get free from the oppressions and wrongs heaped upon us, we must pay for their removal. We must do this by labor, by suffering, by sacrifice, and if needs be, by our lives and the lives of others."

What distinguished Douglass, above all, was his spaciousness of hope. It can be said of Booker T. Washington what a conservative French historian said of Louis XIV: "He did not know how to wish." Frederick Douglass knew how to wish. He wished for the immediate, total and complete integration of the Negro into the mainstream of American life.

Since the prize was glittering, Douglass demanded men worthy of the prize. No other Negro, with the exceptions of Martin Luther King, Jr., and A. Philip Randolph, has asked so insistently for so much from Negro men. Freedom, Douglass said, could not be granted; it was necessary to take it. And what was required for successful taking? Unity, Douglass said —unity, organization, and sacrifice.

Douglass' career fell into three great periods: the abolitionist era, the Reconstruction period, and the post-Reconstruction period. In the first period, he championed direct action and continuous agitation. As the Civil War approached, he became increasingly militant and advocated ballots, if possible, and bullets, if necessary. After leading a brilliant campaign for the Fourteenth and Fifteenth Amendments, he became, in the post-Reconstruction era, an advocate of political action and protest within the system.

Reformer, agitator, orator, author, abolitionist, philosopher, editor, social engineer: this was the man who went forth in the dangerous years to do battle with the Goliath of American prejudice. His background had prepared him for a long and hard fight. He was born Frederick Augustus Washington Bailey (he assumed the name Douglass later) in February, 1817, on the Eastern Shore of Maryland. For the first twenty-one years of his life, he worked as a slave in and around Baltimore. Two events during this period changed the contours of his life. When he was a boy of ten or eleven his mistress taught him a few words of the alphabet. But his master objected, saying that "learning would spoil the best nigger in the world." Douglass, who wanted to be spoiled, became his own teacher, hiding dirty pages in his pockets and painfully spelling out the words in dark corners of the attic.

Later, while still a slave, Douglass learned that power has its limitations. This was an extraordinary discovery and it opened his mind to a whole new vista of struggle. It happened this way. He refused to buckle down to the slave regime and was sent to Edward Covey, a "professional Negro-breaker" who specialized in annihilating the spirit of troublesome slaves. Covey worked Douglass until he was ready to drop from exhaustion and whipped him until he bowed and smiled. One day, Douglass tells us, he turned and made a desperate last stand. The two men grappled to an indecisive draw. Covey stalked off and never afterwards touched Douglass. From this incident, Douglass drew a moral which he applied to many situations after he gained his freedom. "He is whipped oftenest who is whipped easiest."

Four years later, at the age of twenty-one, Douglass escaped from slavery and joined the phalanx of Negro and white men who were waging a moral war against slavery. Douglass, on the platform in the years of the abolitionist crusade, was an arresting figure. He was a good-looking man, tall, well-made, with olive skin and a halo of hair worn long and *au naturel* in the African style. His physical presence moved people; so did the rolling thunder of his voice. "White men and black men," William Wells Brown wrote, "had talked against slavery, but none had ever spoken like Frederick Douglass." Within a few years, Douglass was known on both sides of the Atlantic. In 1847, after a triumphant tour of England, he stepped out on his own, opening his famous paper, the *North Star*, in Rochester, New York. From that year until the abolition of slavery, he was in the forefront of the Freedom movement.

Douglass' famous Fourth of July speech is a good example of the passion and brilliance he brought to the movement. Speaking at Rochester on July 5, 1852, he indicted every structure of power in America. "What," he asked, "to the American slave, is your 4th of July? I answer: a day that reveals to him, more

than all other days in the year, the gross injustice and cruelty
to which he is the constant victim. To him, your celebration is
a sham; your boasted liberty, an unholy license; your national
greatness, swelling vanity; your sounds of rejoicing are empty
and heartless; your denunciation of tyrants, brass fronted im-
pudence; your shouts of liberty and equality, hollow mockery;
your prayers and hymns, your sermons and thanksgivings, with
all your religious parade and solemnity, are, to him, mere
bombast, fraud, deception, impiety, and hypocrisy—a thin veil
to cover up crimes which would disgrace a nation of savages. . . ."

Then in symbols that are current today, Douglass pointed to
the mote in America's eye. "You boast of your love of liberty,
your superior civilization, and your pure Christianity. . . .
You hurl anathemas at the crowned headed tyrants of Russia
and Austria and pride yourselves on your Democratic institutions, while you yourselves consent to be mere tools and body-
guards of the tyrants of Virginia and Carolina. You invite to
your shores fugitives of oppression from abroad, honor them
with banquets, greet them with ovations, cheer them, toast
them, salute them, protect them, and pour out your money to
them like water; but the fugitives from your own land you ad-
vertise, hunt, arrest, shoot, and kill. You glory in your refine-
ment and your universal education; yet you maintain a system
as barbarous and dreadful as ever stained the character of a
nation—a system begun in avarice, supported in pride, and
perpetuated in cruelty. You shed tears over fallen Hungary,
and make the sad story of her wrongs the theme of your poets,
statesmen, and orators, till your gallant sons are ready to fly to
arms to vindicate her cause against the oppressor; but, in regard to the ten thousand wrongs of the American slave, you
would enforce the strictest silence and would hail him as an
enemy of the nation who dares to make those wrongs the subject of public discourse!"

Douglass dared to make "the ten thousand wrongs" the subject of public discourse. Week after week, year after year, in
the crucial decade before the Civil War, Douglass went up and
down the North, warning, pleading, rebuking. In the process,
he re-interpreted the Negro's role in America, establishing a
policy of unceasing agitation for integration and assimilation.

The 1850's—the famous white fifties—were a severe test for
Douglass and other Negro leaders. It seemed then that all was

lost and that there was no hope for the Negro in America. In this decade the Negro was slammed down by three impaling blows: a fugitive slave law which endangered the security of every Negro in America; the Kansas-Nebraska bill which opened Northern territory to slavery; and the Dred Scott decision which denied citizenship to men with black skin.

Worse still was the lengthening shadow of want. A potato famine in Ireland and political complications on the continent sent millions of white immigrants to America. Many of the immigrants settled in the big cities and fought Negroes for elbow room in the slums and working space in kitchens and on docks. In some cases, this contest approached an open war.

In the late fifties, white immigrants depressed wages and eliminated Negroes as competitors in several fields. Hundreds of Negroes were stoned in anti-Negro riots; thousands more fled America in panic. Those who remained dug in for a bloody fight. A mood of bitterness and hostility moved over the ghetto which trembled on the brink of a suicidal revolt. The mask came off completely. Never before, never since, has Negro leadership spoken with such defiance and bitterness.

Black nationalism reached such a peak in these years that no Negro leader could denounce it outright. Martin Delany, H. Ford Douglass and other Negro leaders repudiated "American hypocrisy" and called for the establishment of a Negro state in Central America, Africa, or the Wild West. Delany and other Negro leaders also recommended the establishment of a separate Negro economy in America.

Despairing of justice in the courts and legislative assemblies, Negro leaders sang the praises of bowie knives and rifles. In February, 1851, Negroes raided a federal courtroom in Boston and rescued a fugitive slave. In September, Negroes fought a pitched battle against slave catchers and U.S. marshals in Christiana, Pennsylvania. The next month, in Syracuse, New York, Negro rebels smashed into a courtroom and rescued another fugitive slave.

The Negro rebels of Christiana, Boston, and Syracuse were mirrored images of the American Revolution. *John Brown was revolution itself.* A great gaunt man with a noble head, the look of a hawk and the intensity of a saint, John Brown lived and breathed vengeance. More than Garnet, more even than Douglass, this extraordinary white man suffered for the slave. "His zeal in the cause of freedom," Frederick Douglass said, "was infinitely superior to mine. Mine was as the taper light; his was as the burning sun. Mine was bounded by time; his stretched away to the silent shores of eternity. I could speak for the slave; John Brown could fight for the slave. I could live for the slave; John Brown could die for the slave."

As a New England businessman, John Brown sacrificed profits by using his warehouse as a station on the Underground Railroad. In the fifties, he became a full-time revolutionary, fighting small wars in Kansas and leading a group of Negro slaves out of Missouri. During this period, he became a counselor to radical Negro leaders. He told Douglass, Garnet and others that the peaceful annihilation of slavery was impossible. Slavery, according to him, was a system of brute force which could only be destroyed by brute force. Brown's faith in the fighting ability of Negroes was not shared by all. A white reporter told Brown that "Negroes were a peaceful, domestic inoffensive race [who] seemed to be incapable of reprisal." Brown replied: "You have not studied them right and you have not studied them long enough. Human nature is the same everywhere."

Holding this idea in the center of his mind, Brown laid plans for a revolutionary attack on the government arsenal at Harpers Ferry. He hoped thereby to create a revolutionary situation in which slaves from all over the South would flock to him. In the early months of 1857, the blunt old rebel recruited a small interracial army and solicited support from Negro and white abolitionists. He begged Douglass to accompany him, but the Negro leader insisted that the plan was premature and ill-laid. The old white man and the young Negro leader argued for several hours at a deserted quarry near Chambersburg, Pennsylvania. While they argued, Douglass' friend, Shields Green, listened. After the discussion, Douglass rose and asked Green if he were ready to go. Green thought for a moment and then said: "I believe I go wid de old man." Green and four other Negro revolutionaries accompanied Brown to Harpers Ferry. When Brown was surrounded by federal troops, Green was in the mountains and could have escaped. Osborne Anderson, another Brown aide, suggested flight, but Green said: "I believe I go down wid de old man." And he did—all the way to the gallows.

In death, Brown was far more victorious than in life. He did not create a revolutionary situation in Virginia—but in death he created a revolutionary situation in America that pushed men to the edge of a civil war. The hanging of John Brown, the election of Abraham Lincoln, the words of Frederick Douglass and William Lloyd Garrison, and the acts of Nat Turner: all were links in the long chain of events that led to the emancipation of the Negro slave.

In the Civil War, as in the Revolutionary War, Negro leaders and their white allies had to force the issue of Negro freedom, an issue Abraham Lincoln and Northern moderates tried desperately to avoid. For almost two years, Lincoln appeased the slaveholding Border States (a current witticism said: "Lincoln would like to have God on his side, but he must have Kentucky"). Lincoln, it should be noted, was not an abolitionist. He was, in fact, an extremist-on-both-sides man. His plan was based on the gradual emancipation of the slaves over a thirty-seven-year period (up to 1900), compensation to slaveholders and deportation (voluntary) of the freedmen. On August 14, 1862, he called a group of hand-picked Negroes to the White House and sent up a trial balloon. American Negroes and American white people, Lincoln said, would be better off if they were separated—with a large body of water between them.

Not only Lincoln but significant sections of the abolitionist movement backed away from the radical implications of Negro emancipation. At this crucial juncture, William Lloyd Garrison urged a moratorium on protest and agitation. The great abolitionist also shied away from the burning issue of Negro suffrage. Wendell Phillips and Frederick Douglass plucked the torch of abolitionism from the hands of the faltering Garrison and crisscrossed the country, denouncing the "tardy, hesitating, vacillating policy of the President of the United States." Their objectives were, first, the freeing of the slaves as a war measure and, secondly, the use of slaves and free Negroes in an army of liberation.

Douglass saw the war as a struggle to complete the American Revolution. Legal emancipation alone, he said, would not free the slaves. It would be necessary to train new leaders, reknit shattered Negro family life and instill in the hearts of Southerners a respect for democratic processes. The task before America, Douglass said, was "nothing less than radical revolution in all modes of thought which have flourished under the blighting slave system." The great Negro abolitionist was openly contemptuous of men who placed the Union above freedom. The old Union, he said was dead. "We are fighting for something incomparably better than the old Union. We are fighting for unity; unity of idea, unity of sentiment, unity of object, unity of institutions, in which there shall be no North, no South, no East, no West, no black, no white, but a solidarity of the nation, making every slave free, and every free man a voter." There was poetry in this audacious conception and Douglass pushed it for all it was worth. Month in and month out, he demanded total war. With one eye on the famous "slow coach in Washington," he urged Negro and white agitators to "keep pounding on the rock."

As the war progressed and as defeat piled on defeat, Douglass and other agitators picked up powerful allies in Congress. Radical Republicans denounced the moderate Lincoln program and insisted that the North hit the South where it would hurt most: free the slaves and give them guns. Some Radical Republicans, speaking for the rising industrial capitalism of the North, championed Negro freedom as the best way to win the war. Others, like Charles Sumner and Thaddeus Stevens, saw the war as an excellent opportunity to smash the power of Southern planters and establish a new social order based on the political and economic emancipation of Negroes and poor whites.

Congressional Radicals seized the gauntlet in the early part of 1862 and passed a series of measures that undermined the foundations of the slave system. Military officers were forbidden to return fugitive slaves to rebel masters. Slavery was abolished in the territories and in Washington, D.C. Finally, in July, 1862, Congress passed a sweeping Confiscation Act which, in effect, freed the slaves of every rebel.

Prodded by the revolt of Congressional Radicals and repeated reverses on the battlefield, not to mention the threatened intervention of European powers, Lincoln changed his policy, saying with great honesty that he had not controlled events but had been controlled by them. Finally, on Thursday, January 1, 1863, he issued the celebrated Emancipation Proclamation.

The Emancipation Proclamation was a master stroke of international diplomacy, and it had enormous military and propaganda value at home—but it freed very few slaves. Lincoln "freed" slaves where he had no power (in the Confederacy) and left them slaves where he had power (in the Border States and in sections under federal control in the South). Still, there was something about the piece of paper. As a symbol, it changed the course of the war and outlined a future policy of liberation. But it is an error to suggest, even by implication, that Negroes were freed by a stroke of the pen. The emancipation of the Negro was a long and painful process that extended over many years—and it was never completed. The Emancipation Proclamation was only one link—and by no means the most important link—in a whole chain of events that stretched from Nat Turner's "dark arm of vengeance" to the Palm Sunday Scene at Appomattox Courthouse, a chain of events that included the hard fight waged by Negro and white abolitionists, the sacrificial death of John Brown and his Negro and white followers and the persistent devotion of Radical Republicans like Thaddeus Stevens and Charles Sumner.

The Negro slaves were freed finally by the hard logic of events and the continuous agitation of Negro and white leaders. After issuance of the Emancipation Proclamation and the arming of 186,000 Negro soldiers, without whose help the victory could not have been won, abolitionists and Radical Republicans mobilized a national campaign for a "complete emancipation." They insisted on political and civic freedom for the freedmen, the allocation of land to freedmen and poor whites and a crash program of education.

Negro leaders, acting independently, played a large role in this agitation. Meeting in Syracuse, New York, in October, 1864, Negro leaders organized the National Equal Rights League and issued an address to the nation. "Fellow-citizens," they said, "let us entreat you, have faith in your own principles. If freedom is good for any, it is good for all." The address called for "the complete abolition of slavery" and the granting of the ballot, "the keystone to the arch of human liberty."

An extraordinary convergence of forces gave Negroes their first national victory and insured passage of the Fourteenth and Fifteenth Amendments. At war's end, the North needed the Negro almost as much as the Negro needed the North. The freeing of the slaves was, paradoxically, a boon to the South. Under the old system, each slave counted as three-fifths of a person in apportioning representation. Now each slave counted as a full person, whether he voted or not. If the South took advantage of this situation, it would return to the national fold with increased political power and additional seats in the Congress. More than anything else, the industrial North feared the resurgence of hostile, agrarian-minded Southerners. There were, to be sure, idealists like Charles Sumner and Thaddeus Stevens who said the slaves should be given land and ballots because it was just. But most Americans were not willing to go that far. While men debated, while public opinion was congealing, the South, for the second time in this troubled decade, played into the hands of Northern agitators and politicians. Having been whipped by the Yankees, the South vented its wrath by whipping Negroes. A brutal reign of terror swept the South. The bodies of dead Negroes littered the roads, and hundreds of freedmen were massacred in "riots" staged by policemen and other public officials. Nor was this all. The new Southern legislatures refused to make even a token gesture toward Negro liberation. Harsh black codes were enacted that virtually re-enslaved Negroes. To make matters worse, the South flaunted its defiance by sending numbers of ex-Confederate generals and colonels to Congress.

The North, still reeling under the emotional sting of Lincoln's assassination, was enraged; and wily old Thad Stevens, who was virtually the boss of Congress, moved swiftly, organizing a Joint Congressional Committee which seized control of Reconstruction. The congressional committee put the South under military rule and ordered new elections in which all males over eighteen—Negro and white—could vote. About a million Negroes, of whom perhaps three-fourths were illiterate, and about one million whites, of whom at least one-third were illiterate, were thus enfranchised. As it turned out Negro voters outnumbered white voters in five Southern states. Here at last was a real revolution and freedmen greeted the new age with a slogan: "The bottom rail is on top."

With the passage of the Fourteenth and Fifteenth Amendments and enabling legislation which sent federal troops into the South to protect the rights of freedmen, Reconstruction reached a climax. The final touch came later, in 1875, with passage of a Civil Rights Bill which gave Negroes the right to equal enjoyment of the accommodations, facilities and advantages of public conveyances, inns, theaters, and places of public amusement.

It seemed then that the Freedom movement's triumph was complete. Some Negroes said, "All distinctions founded upon race or color have been forever abolished in the United States." And one man announced, prematurely: "There are no colored people in this country."

THE REVOLUTION THAT FAILED

IT was coming true at last, and men and women burst into song.

> *Free at last!*
> *Free at last!*
> *Thank God Almighty,*
> *We're free at last!*

So ran the hymns of hope in the summer when red violets bloomed and black women sang.

But what is freedom?

Can you spend it?

Is it negotiable in the social world of status and the political world of power?

What precisely can you do with the *word* freedom?

Behind these questions, which were asked on almost every plantation in the summer of 1865, was a deep and gnawing fear. Cut adrift suddenly without food, money, or land, the four million freedmen perceived, almost from the beginning, that the house of freedom was built on wind and words and sand. Unlike the emancipated serfs of Russia, they received no interest in the land they were tilling. They were free—free to the wind and to the rain, free to the wrath and hostility of their ex-masters. They had no tools, they had no shelter, they had no cooking utensils; and they were surrounded by hostile men who were determined to prove that the whole thing was a gigantic mistake.

In this hostile atmosphere, with nothing working for them but hope and faith and a certain tenacity of spirit, Negroes began their odyssey as quasi-free men.

In the first years of freedom, Negro leaders and the Negro masses raised a clamorous cry for land. So did Charles Sumner, Thaddeus Stevens, and other Radical Republicans. The original cry of "forty acres and a mule" seems to have come from Stevens who suggested the breaking up of large plantations and the distribution of land to freedmen in forty-acre lots. But Stevens' program was too radical for most Americans who tried, as usual, to do too much with too little.

For fifty years or more, freedmen chased the pipe dream of

"forty acres and a mule." Thousands of freedmen were defrauded by operators who sold them colored pegs which, they said, could be used to mark off the cherished forty acres. Thousands more bought halters for mules that were never given. It is fashionable in some circles to sneer at the "stupidity" of slaves who clung to the "forty acres and a mule" myth for so long. But theirs was a just and a brave dream. That they held onto it for so long and that no one heeded the cry of their hearts is cause not for sneering but for weeping.

Land reform, as Myrdal and other modern scholars have pointed out, was an indispensable prerequisite for a lasting peace. The failure of abolitionists and Radical Republicans to achieve this basic objective doomed Reconstruction from the start and paved the way for our present conundrum.

This tragic period of aborted hope began with a promising political revolution. Negroes were elected to the legislatures of every Southern state. Lieutenant governors were elected in Mississippi, Louisiana, and South Carolina. Twenty Negroes were sent to the House of Representatives, two Negroes were elected to the Senate by the Mississippi legislature, and a prominent Negro politician, P. B. S. Pinchback, served briefly as governor of Louisiana.

During the heyday of Reconstruction, in the years between 1867 and 1877, Negroes made provocative steps toward groupness. A series of political gatherings of a frequency and intensity unparalleled in American political history were held in the old slave states. Contemporaries said there was a "camp meeting excitement" and "a religious intensity" about the huge alfresco political meetings held by ex-slaves in Black Belt areas. On registration days, freedmen thronged the courthouses and virtually mobbed the registrars in frantic efforts to get their names on the books. "After their names [were] taken," a South Carolina paper said, "they went on their way rejoicing."

Negro political power was based in the areas of contemporary conflict, the Black Belt counties of central Georgia, northern Florida, western Mississippi, south central Alabama, east central Louisiana, eastern North Carolina, southeastern Virginia, and central South Carolina. In these areas, strong political organizations emerged. The Union League and the Loyal League, the major Negro political organizations, came in time to rival the Negro church as centers of community life.

Southerners would say later that Negroes were disfranchised because they did not understand the duties of citizenship. The trouble was that they understand their duties too well. If politics is the science of "who gets what, when, and why," as the CIO Political Action Committee said, then the Negro masses demonstrated a genius for the essence of the game.

Most writers have accepted too readily the myth that the Negro masses were passive. On the contrary, the Negro masses knew they were menaced. They had a tremulous, almost hysterical, fear of being re-enslaved. And they knew, better than some of their leaders, who the enemy was. Governor Lindsay of Alabama, who cannot be suspected of pro-Negro views, said: "They [Negroes] were disposed to get into a drunken disposition—I use that expression not in the literal sense—to assert their rights, thinking that such assertion was necessary to their maintenance. . . . [They] would rush right into church, without any change having taken place, where the white people were sitting; not that they had no place to sit [i.e., the Negro pews] but simply to show their equality."

The revolutionary mood of the Negro masses changed the shape of race relations in the South. Men are not wanting who insist that there was very little integration during this period and that Negroes knew their place and stayed in it. But the evidence—most of which these same men cite in disapproval and disdain—is against them. There *was* a revolution in America in 1867-77, and it poked black-white fingers into every area of Southern life, except the most vital—land. And poor whites, surprisingly, did not prove as intractable as aristocrats hoped they would be. The much-maligned Scalawags were, in many instances, leaders of poor whites who entered into a shaky alliance with Negroes. For this, the South has never forgiven them.

Negroes moved in and out of the glittering social worlds of Jackson, Columbus, and New Orleans. Crinoline rustled at gay South Carolina balls attended by black and white belles and black and white officers. Official receptions and dinners brought together Negro and white legislators and their wives and sweethearts. The old aristocrats shut themselves up in their homes and pretended that the brave new world did not exist; but poor whites, believing the new order was permanent, leaped over the barriers of caste and married and mingled with Negroes.

The leaders of this revolution were typical American political types. Some, like Robert Brown Elliott of Eton, were handsomely educated; others, like Beverly Nash, pulled themselves up by their bootstraps. Most were educators, lawyers, and preachers; but some, like Blanche K. Bruce and James R. Napier, were well-to-do planters.

We need not concern ourselves here with the myths of corruption and ignorance that men used to overthrow the Reconstruction governments. The wild charges are ex parte accounts from men who murdered and stole in order to regain power, men who found it necessary to believe their enemies were subhuman in order to believe that they themselves were human. The fact is that practically all of the Negro leaders of Reconstruction had more formal education than Abraham Lincoln. Nor should we concern ourselves overly with the myth of corruption. There was, undoubtedly, some corruption; but it has been magnified out of all proportion. None of the Reconstruction governments reached the scale of stealth of the Ferguson regime of Texas, the Huey Long regime of Louisiana, and some of the more picturesque Chicago and New York administrations.

The basic problem of Reconstruction was not graft or education—the basic problem was power and color. A Southern historian has said as much. "The worst crime of which [Reconstruction leaders] have been adjudged guilty," F. B. Simkins said, "was the violation of the American caste system. The crime of crimes was to encourage Negroes in voting, office-holding, and other functions of social equality. . . ."

It is enormously important to a power structure that its rituals, so to speak, remain inviolate. And it seems, in retrospect, that Negro leaders offended the power structure most by exposing the shams of government. A great deal of nonsense is written about the intricacies of Western government; but actually it is quite simple: one learns to rule by ruling, and ruling is the same everywhere—the manipulation of emotions and myths and paper.

It was said rather freely in the beginning that "Sambo" would make a fool of himself in the complicated world of foolscap. But a conservative South Carolina senator told James S. Pike that Negroes learned the rules and methods "like a flash." Charles Nordhoff, another hostile witness, said after a visit to the South that Negroes "have among them not a few shrewd and calculating demagogues who know as well how to 'run the machine,' to fix a ring, and to excite the voters to their duty, as any New York City politicians."

What Nordhoff was saying, in a backhanded way, was that Negroes showed a real talent for politics—so much so that the ruling class was alarmed and moved quickly before they got used to it.

The constitutions drafted by Negro leaders and their white allies, the Carpetbaggers and Scalawags, were excellent documents which dragged the South, screaming and crying, into the modern world. Slavery and servitude were abolished; so was the ancient custom of imprisonment for debt. The property rights of women were protected and divorce laws were written. Negro politicians were largely responsible for the most important innovation in Reconstruction governments—the establishment of a public school system for poor and rich, black and white. The constitutions of Mississippi, South Carolina, and Louisiana, incidentally, called for integrated school systems.

Largely at the insistence of the Negro masses, school systems in the old South opened their doors to the sons and daughters of ex-slaves. In 1873, the University of South Carolina was integrated. The institution had an integrated board of trustees, an integrated faculty, and an integrated student body. Despite strong opposition from racists, school systems in Louisiana and other states were integrated.

During this troubled period of conflict and decision, the Negro protest moved into state houses and city halls. Having established beachheads of power *within* the community, Negro leaders used their influence to force concessions in the areas of public accommodation and school integration. Speaking in the South Carolina legislature, F. L. Cardozo told his colleagues that "the most natural method of removing racial distinctions would be to allow children, when five or six years of age, to mingle in school together. . . . Under such training prejudices will die out." Cardozo added: "We are laying the foundation of a new structure here. . . . We must decide whether we shall live together or not."

Although Negro Republicans relied on political tactics, direct action was not neglected. Strikes in which Negro women played crucial roles were staged in rice fields and cotton fields. In New Orleans, Charleston, and several Northern cities, Negro leaders organized ride-ins, sit-ins, and walk-ins to force implementation of federal and state laws. In May, 1871, Negro leaders in Louisville, Kentucky, organized a ride-in campaign that attracted national attention. The campaign began on May 12 with Negroes boarding horse-drawn streetcars and sitting in the "white" section. Louisville whites counterattacked by overturning streetcars and smashing windows, but the campaign continued until the company instituted a new policy of integrated seating.

Reconstruction in all its various facets was a supreme lesson for America, the right reading of which might still mark a turning point in our history. For ten years in these United States, for one hundred and twenty months, America tried democracy. Negro and white people married each other in the South—and the world did not end. Little black boys and little white girls went to school together—and the Confederate dead did not rise, did not, in fact, make a sound at all, though the Klan said they were turning over in the grave. All over the South, in these years, Negroes and whites shared streetcars, restaurants, hotels, honors, dreams. The sun rose and the sun set, and the Constitution of the United States had meaning from Maine to Mississippi—for ten years.

Reconstruction was overthrown finally by a violent counter-revolution led by the Klan, the Red Shirts and other terrorist groups. The key elements in this counterrevolution were not the South but the North, not terrorists but businessmen. It was impossible for Reconstruction to succeed if it were not backed up by force. The North used force in the first years of Reconstruction because its interests—solidification of national unity, supremacy of Northern financial policy, high tariffs—paralleled the interests of Negroes—the supremacy of the Republican party and the consolidation of the party's Reconstruction program.

Faced, in the beginning, with what seemed to be the implacable will of America, Southerners accommodated themselves to Negro freedom. In fact, Southerners seemed a trifle overwhelmed. James Pike made an extraordinary observation on his trip to South Carolina. There was, he noted, "an air of mastery among the colored people"; he expressed surprise at "how reticent the whites are in their dealings with the blacks, and how entirely self-contained and self-assertive, the blacks appear to be."

Southerners remained relatively quiescent until the early 1870's when the climate of Northern opinion changed. As soon as the Northern victory was solidified beyond recall, beyond the power of the South to alter or disturb, voices of compromise and conciliation emerged. There were demands for a political settlement from Northern business interests who said the political troubles in the South were impeding the establishment of a national domestic market. Northern sentiment crystallized in 1874-75, and newspapers and periodicals started hammering away at "Negroism" and "corruption." The conservative Northern press said the South was "tumbling and rolling about in the Black Sea of Negroism." A new slogan came into being: "Emancipate the whites."

Perceiving the drift of the age, which was made flesh in the creeping power of the Democratic party, Southerners became increasingly bold. Large groups of whites who had been thoroughly subdued at the end of the war regained their courage. Convinced that the North would not put up a real fight for democracy, Southerners emerged from their integrated cocoon and staged a violent counterrevolution.

The counterrevolution came to a head in 1876, the centennial of the Declaration of Independence. Small wars were fought in 1876 by white men and black men in South Carolina, Louisiana, and Florida. In these states, both Republicans and Democrats claimed victory and established governments; and both sides, incredibly, invoked the words of the Declaration of Independence.

As it happened, the Presidential race between Republican Rutherford B. Hayes and Democrat Samuel J. Tilden hinged on the disputed electoral votes from South Carolina, Louisiana, and Florida. Hayes claimed these states and the Presidency, and an Electoral Commission sustained him. But it was necessary for both houses of Congress to certify the results and Democrats had a majority in the House of Representatives. As inauguration day approached, a group of Southerners in the House launched a filibuster which prevented the orderly counting of the electoral votes. If the Democrats could hold out until inauguration day, America would not have a President. And disorder, perhaps war, would be inevitable.

From the packers of pork and beef, from the makers of boots and shoes, from the manufacturers of iron and steel, from the sellers of dry goods and cordage and shot, from the boards of trade and the chambers of commerce of Pittsburgh, Chicago, and New York came one unanimous cry: "Peace, peace at any price." Congressman Lucien Bonaparte Caswell of Wisconsin limned the spirit of the age. "The members of Congress," he said, "are of the impression that the people wish to revive business at any political sacrifice."

At the sacrifice, in short, of the Negro.

Representatives of Rutherford B. Hayes and representatives of the South huddled in plush rooms in Georgetown and garish bars in downtown Washington and negotiated the sacrifice. The climax of the bargaining sessions came on Monday and Tuesday, February 26-27, 1877, at the Wormley House, a fashionable hotel owned by a Negro businessman. An agreement was reached which gave the South "home rule" and Hayes the Presidency. The essence of the Bargain of 1877 was a *de facto* suspension of constitutional safeguards that protected the rights of Negro citizens in the South. The bargain was signed and delivered. The South called off the filibuster, and Hayes was elected. On April 10, 1877, federal troops were withdrawn from Columbia, South Carolina, and the white minority took over the state government. Ten days later, the guard changed in New Orleans. It was over, the dream was stillborn. Eighty years and five months would pass before federal troops would enter the South again to uphold the dignity and majesty of the United States Constitution.

This was a new situation and it required a new response. But the trumpet of leadership gave an uncertain sound. There were two moments of truth in this tragic era when institutional arrangements had hung in the balance and concerted action on the part of Negroes and their white allies might have made a difference. The first point came in November, 1875, when the Republican governor of Mississippi appealed for federal troops to protect Negro voters. Grant, who owed his election to Negroes, refused to send the troops and his attorney general replied flippantly that "the whole public was tired of these annual autumnal outbursts."

It is possible—though by no means certain—that a concerted and vigorous protest by Negro leadership and white liberals could have plugged the dike at this point. The failure to do so was disastrous, for after the Mississippi Revolution of 1875, the stream became a flood.

The second moment of destiny came in January and February of 1877 when Hayes was formulating his Southern policy. There were seven Negroes in the House of Representatives at this time and one Negro in the Senate. The two national Negro leaders, Frederick Douglass and John Mercer Langston, were in and about Washington. And yet there was a curious silence. Worse still were implications that some Negro leaders supported the compromise. James Poindexter, a Negro leader from Hayes's home state of Ohio, openly supported the new departure. So did several other Negro leaders. John Langston, who was then acting president of Howard University, called the new policy a wise departure, saying that federal troops in the South were an unnecessary irritant. Langston was in favor of something he called "Pacific Reconstruction." Frederick Douglass denied later that he was silent at the Commonwealth's moment of truth; but his protest, if he protested, was muted—and muted protest was not in Douglass' style.

Some Negro leaders supported Hayes's policy because they

believed it was an experiment that could be abandoned if it failed to produce results. Hayes told various Negro delegations that he would change his strategy if Southerners curtailed the rights of Negroes. When it became clear that the South was not going to live up to its part of the "bargain" and that the Republican party and the North would not or could not force the issue, Negro leaders protested bitterly. But it was too late then to turn the tide.

Negro leaders, at this fateful turning, seem to have suffered a fatal failure of nerve. They had, it seems, no heart for a fight to the finish. Moreover, they seemed to feel guilty about the new situation, as though the successful counterrevolution proved something against Negroes, when, in fact, it only proved that Negroes failed to win a war they were neither equipped nor organized to fight.

There is an air of unreality about most discussions of the power realities of this period. Long discussions about the morals and educational qualifications of Negro leaders obscure the main point—power or the lack of power. The worst thing that can be said about Negro leaders in this period is that they did not seem to understand that the only issue was power—that, and the obvious fact that many of them did not know what time it was.

Reconstruction was a revolution, and a revolution can only be accomplished by overwhelming force overwhelmingly applied. What was required at the crucial turning points in the drama was quick, drastic, and decisive action; but at each turning point Negro leaders and their white allies hesitated and the moment passed.

Not stupidity but gentility doomed these men. They were idealist, in the main—men who placed, as Robert E. Park said, "too high an estimate upon their respectability" and were too ambitious to behave in "an Anglo-Saxon manner." The tragedy of the Negro leaders of Reconstruction, and it was a tragedy, was that they were too polite. A revolution was going on; and revolutions are fought nowhere by *Robert's Rules of Order*.

Nothing in the literature covered this situation. Not until the rise of the Afro-Asian states would there be a body of knowledge about the action required in a post-colonial situation. I have said elsewhere that the great Negro leader during Reconstruction would have had the hardness of Nkrumah, the ascetic brilliance of Nehru, the Machiavellian adroitness of Franklin Delano Roosevelt, and the love-thy-neighbor vocabulary of Martin Luther King, Jr. He would have had a certain detachment from white values and supreme faith in himself and his mission.

The central weakness of Negro strategy in this period was its timidity and its subservience to Republican party policy. In one way or another, almost all Negro leaders looked to the Republican party, which talked a great deal about Lincoln and the war amendments but did little or nothing to remedy the situation in the South.

Despite this fact, Negro leaders continued to champion the party of liberation which, they said, was far better than any other organization. T. Thomas Fortune, editor of the *New York Age*, Peter Clark of Ohio, and George Downing of Rhode Island tried to organize an independent political movement; but the major Negro leaders and newspapers opposed the plan. Frederick Douglass said there was no way out of the Republican party that did not lead into the arms of the enemy.

Neither Douglass nor any other major leader invented a new structure. And extra-party action of some kind was an urgent necessity. Time and time again Douglass denounced the Republican party, but he never strayed outside the fold. It is difficult to avoid the conclusion that Douglass' leadership in this period was blunted by his identification with the Republican party. It is perhaps worth noting that Douglass was the last national protest leader with close ties to a regular party organization. Since Douglass, no Negro protest leader has been quite so hopeful of redress through political means alone.

To drain off threatened upswellings of indignation, the Republican party hierarchy invented "tokenism," a policy of doling out minor positions and perquisites to Negro leaders as a means of recognizing the race. This policy muzzled the protest of Negro leaders and maintained the fiction of Republican party interest. On the local level, some Negro leaders protested only the lack of adequate patronage and dissipated their energies in a futile pursuit of postmasterships.

It should be said in all fairness, however, that Negro leaders had few live options. The Democratic party was openly hostile; so was white labor. Negro leaders were also operating under a harsh imperative, the necessity of avoiding action that would unite whites in a war of extermination against all American Negroes.

Was Reconstruction then a failure? No, it did not fail where it was expected to fail; it was Athanasius *contra mundum*, as Du Bois said, but it was also Athanasius *pro mundum*. Back there, almost one hundred years ago, the American Negro struck a blow for the disadvantaged of all countries. Before the rise of the Afro-Asian states, before the emergence of the United Nations, the American Negro went forth to do battle for nonwhites. For the first time, nonwhites appropriated the symbols of Western political life. That attempt did not fail in the realm of the spirit; nor, for that matter, did it fail in the realm of the practical, for the Fourteenth and Fifteenth Amendments were permanent steps forward. If these Amendments had not been ratified in this area, they would never have been ratified. There has never been a period in America, before or since, when the climate of public opinion was favorable to the passage of national legislation of the breadth and scope of the Fourteenth and Fifteenth Amendments.

The war amendments burned the minds of men for a generation after the Bargain of 1877. In the 1880's and 1890's, there were periodic demands for enforcement of the war amendments; but after the failure to enact a bill for supervision of federal elections in 1890, the Negro dropped out as a national political issue. By 1913, the Republican party had dropped the ritual phrases in its platform that called for the enforcement of the Fourteenth and Fifteenth Amendments.

Throughout this period, Negroes held on to fragments of power in several states. They sat in Southern legislatures until the second decade of the twentieth century, and a Negro voice was heard in the council of Congress until 1901.

The last act of the Reconstruction drama unfolded in Virginia and North Carolina, where the first shots of the second Freedom movement were fired. In the 1880's, Negroes formed a majority of the city council of Danville, Virginia. Four of the nine policemen in the town were Negroes and all of the justices of the peace. On a Saturday before election in 1883, white conservatives staged a coup, killed four Negroes and systematically suppressed the Negro vote. A similar campaign in North Carolina in 1898 broke the back of Negro resistance in that state. Shortly before the election of that year, some fifty thousand rounds of ammunition and a carload of firearms were shipped to North Carolina by white supremacists in South Carolina and Virginia. Armed to the teeth, white Democrats, attired in red shirts, intimidated and harassed Negro voters and won the election. The blitzkrieg reached its height in Wilmington where a white mob, led by a former congressman, destroyed a Negro newspaper office, slaughtered eleven Negroes, wounded scores and chased hundreds into the woods. When the smoke cleared, the leader of the white mob was elected mayor of Wilmington.

The South secured its victory with a reign of white terror

which lasted for more than fifty years. No one knows how many Negroes were killed in this span. But Congressman Charles Williams of Wisconsin estimated in 1880 that 130,000 men had been murdered in the South for political activities.

During the white terror, the conscience of the American people went to sleep. The Negro's status in America rests on four very fragile props: the slumbrous American conscience, the Supreme Court, Northern public opinion, and world public opinion. In this age, the props collapsed, and the Negro stood alone before his ancient enemies: the terror, the fear, and the massive guilt of the American white man.

Northern liberalism, which had overextended itself in the abolitionist crusade, began a precipitate retreat from reality in the Reconstruction era. Frederick Douglass made a valiant effort to rally his old colleagues ("We need you now, almost as much as ever"), but they were busy, indifferent, or otherwise engaged. Some were hostile, saying with great stridence that Negro enfranchisement was a mistake.

There emerged in the 1880's a massive and intimidating mythology. A whole series of scientific and historical writings were launched to justify the Bargain of 1877. The Noble Slave now became The Wretched Freedman who was mercilessly lampooned on a thousand pages and a thousand platforms. A scene in *Huckleberry Finn*, published in 1884, reflected the spirit of the age. After a steamboat explosion, Aunt Sally said to Huck: "Good gracious! Anybody hurt?"

"No'm. Killed a nigger."

"Well, it's lucky because sometimes people do get hurt."

When freedmen looked abroad, they found the same hostility and indifference. Europe at that moment was embarking on the rape of Africa. Everywhere in this age men were taking the blessings of civilization to the natives and returning heavily laden with gold, manganese, and sugar. Everywhere—North, South, East, West—men were under a terrible compulsion to believe that nonwhites were innately inferior.

The Supreme Court, of all institutions, drove the last nail in the social coffin of the American Negro. In a series of decisions, the Court invalidated Reconstruction laws that protected Negro citizens. Then, going to the heart of the matter, the Court sucked the meaning out of the Fourteenth Amendment. In the slaughterhouse case of 1873, the Court said there were two kinds of citizenship, state and federal, and that the Fourteenth Amendment was designed to protect the rights of federal citizenship. And what were the rights of federal citizenship? The court was majestically vague. Most civil rights, it said, were derived from state citizenship and could not be protected against state action under the Fourteenth Amendment.

In the civil rights cases, decided in 1883, the Supreme Court of the land said that the Fourteenth Amendment forbade states, not individuals, from discriminating. Finally, in 1896, the Court formulated the doctrine of separate but equal, holding in *Plessy* v. *Ferguson* that laws requiring segregation were a reasonable use of the police power of the state. One Supreme Court justice protested. In two thunderous dissents, Justice John Marshall Harlan said, "the substance and spirit of the recent amendments of the Constitution have been sacrificed by a subtle and ingenious verbal criticism." The Plessy decision, the eloquent white Southerner said, "will, in time, prove to be quite as pernicious as the decision made by this tribunal in the Dred Scott case . . . [for] . . . in view of the Constitution, in the eye of the law, there is in this country no superior, dominant, ruling class of citizens. There is no caste here. Our Constitution is color-blind, and neither knows nor tolerates classes among citizens."

Not until 1954 would the Supreme Court catch up with John Marshall Harlan, the son of a Kentucky slaveowner. By that time, the damage Harlan predicted had been done. The Supreme Court decisions Harlan opposed denationalized civil rights, tied the hands of Negro militants and white liberals, and doomed millions of Negroes to a mood of futility.

Even more disastrous was the miring of the Negro's basic constitutional rights in legalism. No man is a citizen in fact whose basic constitutional rights depend on the good opinions of his neighbors or the skill of his lawyers. When the Supreme Court got through with the Fourteenth and Fifteenth Amendments, the Negro had no rights white men were bound to respect, unless the Negro in question had a large amount of money, a firm of superb lawyers and an infinite amount of time.

Bound and gagged by legalism and bad faith, the Negro walked down a road called freedom. As he walked, his enemies and his disabilities multiplied. The Supreme Court decisions, whatever their intent, were an open invitation to encroachment on the rights of Negroes; and Southerners did not wait long to pick up the option. Only Tennessee had a Jim Crow railroad law before 1881, but every Southern state enacted Jim Crow legislation after the civil rights decision of 1883. Only three states had required Jim Crow waiting rooms before 1899, but in the next three decades other Southern states fell into line.

Beginning with Mississippi in 1890, the South turned its attention to the Negro voter. Fraud and violence undergirded a legal framework of exclusion which consisted of poll taxes, "understanding," and property qualifications. "Pitchfork" Ben Tillman, the South Carolina demagogue, was frank. "We have done our level best," he said; "we have scratched our heads to find out how we could eliminate the last one of them [Negroes]; we stuffed ballot boxes. We shot them. We are not ashamed of it."

The Negro exclusion movement grew out of an acute class conflict between the poor whites and the old aristocrats. In the eighties and nineties, the long-subdued poor whites exploded in a burst of agrarian agitation. Particularly challenging to the old master class was the attempt on the part of poor whites to form a union with Negro farmers and laborers. In the first phase of the agitation, Populist leaders championed the rights of all poor Americans. Tom Watson, who later became a fire-eating racist, told Negroes and whites: "You are kept apart that you may be separately fleeced of your earnings."

On the local level, Negro and white Populists attended integrated picnics, meetings, and conventions in the South. State and local platforms of the party denounced lynch law and called for the defense of Negro political rights. Negroes were elected to state executive committees and attended national Populist conventions. By 1890, more than one million Negroes were members of a Colored Farmers Alliance which cooperated with the Populist movement. In 1894, Populists and Negro Republicans captured the political machinery of North Carolina.

Thoroughly alarmed by the entente between poor whites and Negroes, the Southern power structure ran up the flag of white supremacy and crushed the Populist movement. Reunited under a platform of white supremacy, demagogues and aristocrats decided to use prejudice as a political weapon to arrest the forces that were pulling Negroes and poor whites together. Their avowed aim was to create an unbridgeable gulf between Negroes and whites, to separate them completely and utterly in every aspect of life.

The name of this gulf was segregation, but segregation was only one arm of a huge octopus that spread tentacles into every area of black-white relations. A place was marked off for Negroes, and every instrument of control was used to drive them into that place. There had been ill will and hate before, but this was different. Now hate became a part of public policy and the instrumentalities of the state were nakedly and shamelessly used to deprive one part of the citizenry of participation in the public life of the community.

It was necessary in some places to prepare the proper climate. Hate is not natural to man, nor is segregation. Negroes and whites used common facilities in many localities in the South down to World War I, but demagogues steadily made inroads on their rights and prerogatives. This can be seen most clearly in South Carolina. In 1890, Governor Ben Tillman proposed the separation of Negroes and whites on streetcars. But the state senate refused to approve the measure. Francis Simkins, the Southern historian, wrote: "The growing sentiment for racial segregation had not as yet been sufficiently developed."

How was the sentiment developed?

It was developed by a massive assault on the minds of white people and the bodies of Negroes. Men stood on courthouse steps—a Tillman in South Carolina, a Vardaman in Mississippi, a Hoke Smith in Georgia—and held up to the startled vision of simple people the monstrous and fascinating image of the Black Male. Gazing on this image, brooding over their own inadequacies and remembering their own desire for black flesh, men grew fearful about their wives, their daughters, and their jobs. With a rush, sentiment changed, and laws permitting or encouraging separation in every area of life were passed. Negroes and whites were forcibly separated in public transportation, recreation, hospitals, orphanages, prisons, asylums, funeral homes, morgues, and cemeteries. The process was spread over a whole generation and reached a climax in the first decades of the twentieth century.

The laws and decrees were part of an overall system, a system designed to overawe, isolate, subordinate, degrade, push down—destroy. Tentacles of the system reached into the political, economic, and psychological realms. The thrust came from a variety of motives, the desire to avoid assimilation and to limit or eliminate competition for cherished values. But there was also a desire to discipline, control, punish, and humiliate. The legal system was buttressed by an etiquette of debasement which forbade whites to shake hands with Negroes or to call them by courtesy titles. Negroes, on the other hand, were expected, were required, in fact, to call all white people "Mr." or "Mrs." and to use the back doors of white homes and institutions. The etiquette of debasement was vigorously pushed by the power structure. For decades in the South, there was an unwritten rule that no Negro's picture could appear in the paper unless it was in connection with a crime.

This system was solidly grounded on economic exploitation. The great mass of Negroes were confined to Black Belt plantations by crop liens and vagrancy laws. Under the sharecropping system, Negroes worked the land of planters who supplied tools and advanced credit for clothing and food. In theory, the sharecropper and the planter split the proceeds from the crop. But the books were kept by planters who also marketed the crop. As a result, tenants usually remained in a state of perpetual debt. The longer the average sharecropper worked, the more he owed. Year by year, he slipped deeper and deeper into debt, the victim of some horribly tangible nightmare.

Conditions were equally bad in Southern towns where jobs had a name and a color. Negro jobs were dirty, hot, heavy, and unremunerative. White jobs, on the other hand, were clean, light, and well-paid. But the line between the two categories shifted with each business crisis. When white men were hungry, Negro jobs were reclassified. Step by step, Negroes were displaced as waiters, porters, draymen, cooks, caterers, and artisans. At the end of the Civil War, Negroes virtually controlled the building trades industry in the South. It has been estimated that only 20,000 of the 120,000 artisans in the South at that time were white. By 1900, the figures had been reversed.

The instruments of the state were freely used to minimize or eliminate Negro competition. A South Carolina law, for example, put stringent limits on the relations between Negro and white factory workers and had the general effect of barring Negroes from the new textile industry.

By state laws, by municipal decrees, by group pronouncements and vigilante action, Negroes were pushed out of the general community, and a biracial civilization was established. Every community became two communities—a city of Negroes and a city of whites. Although the two groups shared the same land, they dealt with each other like foreign countries, as enemies and strangers.

In the 1880-90 period, Negro businessmen—barbers, boot and shoe makers, butchers, restaurant owners, caterers—held their own in the open market, serving Negro and white customers in downtown locations. As Jim Crow grew, the Negro business world contracted. White property owners stopped leasing to Negro businessmen who began a one-way migration to the Negro Main Street—Beale Street in Memphis, Auburn Avenue in Atlanta, Church Street in Norfolk. Since white men controlled the power to license, it was relatively easy to push

Negroes out of coveted grades. In this way, the Negro lost his monopoly over barbering and catering.

Status fears played a large role in the severing of the community into two mutually hostile groups. For a long time in the South, white undertakers serviced Negro clients. But as the number of white undertakers increased, competition became more intense, and status entered the death business. When integrated cemeteries drew the veil over the grave, the cycle was complete—from birth to death.

The net effect of all this was to force Negroes to pay first-class fares for fourth-class accommodations. It was to force upon them inferior schools and to deprive them altogether of public facilities citizens usually take for granted. Until the late 1920's, there were no public high schools for Negroes in most areas of the South. As late as 1933, there was not a state-supported high school in Alabama or South Carolina offering a four-year course for Negroes.

Practically, then, as well as legally, Negroes were excluded from the mainstream community. From birth to death, they were enclosed in a system of maximum insecurity. They awoke to the world under a sentence which could be executed at any time by any white man. The ultimate sanction was lynching which reached staggering heights in the 1890's when a Negro was lynched somewhere every day or two. As the years wore on, lynching became more barbarous and lynchers became more sadistic. Negroes were burned at the stake, mutilated, hacked to pieces, and roasted over slow fires.

A large amount of energy went into the maintenance of the system. Whites watched carefully to see if Negroes knew their place and accepted it. It was not enough to accept sullenly—gleeful acceptance was demanded. Any infraction of the etiquette of debasement—a failure to say "sir," a smile in the wrong place or a forward word—was considered, correctly, as an attack on the whole system. In some communities, lynchings were carried out to awe Negroes. Clarence Cason, a Southern white man, said that the "conviction that the black man must now and then be intimidated, in order to keep him from forgetting the bounds which Southern traditions have set for him, is firmly rooted in the consciousness of many Southern people. So unquestioned is this philosophy that at times lynchings are planned and carried through—not under the fierce compulsion of mob hysteria—by men who have calmly resigned themselves to the performance of a painful duty, which, according to their lights, is necessary for the good of society."

Far more devastating than lynching was the impact of the

total system on the personality structure of Negroes who were penalized for expressing human impulses. The system penalized the Negro for resenting insult and defending his home; and it rewarded him for passivity, indolence, and ignorance. The system penalized the aggressive, independent Negro and rewarded the supplicatory, shiftless Negro. One could not become a high school principal in the old South, one could not hold a high position of any kind without going through the rituals of "good Negro-ness." And, of course, as Pascal pointed out, when one goes through the rituals long enough sooner or later the grace of faith is given.

Men who know better have spoken rhapsodically of the Golden Age of race relations in the South, of the time when Negroes and whites were friends, when "Mr. Southall," for example, knew "Sam" and "Mary" and "Jane" and "Sally." Speaking thus, of "Mr. Southall" and "Sam," men prove either their naïveté or their bad faith which, in the area of race relations, are pretty much the same thing. "Mr. Southall" did not know "Sam," though "Sam" probably knew "Mr. Southall." The tragedy of the South, and of America, is that the Sam Joneses and the Bill Southalls and all the rest could have been friends and never were. Oppression breeds hate and strife and struggle. The Sam Joneses and the Bill Southalls were at war in the old South and they are at war in the new. Nothing has changed—not even the name of the game. The game, to be plain, was "keep the Negro in his place"; and that game, as Paul Baker pointed out, was "a silent, dogged, sanguinary struggle" in which "the combatants never [rested] upon their arms."

Having consolidated their power in the South, demagogues and Bourbons moved to the offensive. Sure of themselves and rather contemptuous of Northern liberalism, which they perceived to be timid and ineffective, the South called for a repeal of the Fourteenth and Fifteenth Amendments. Congress became a sounding board for racist propaganda and in the whole land few white voices protested. In the 1890's, three Bourbon Senators demanded the immediate deportation of all Southern Negroes. Wilkinson Call of Florida suggested that America pay Spain fifty million dollars for Cuba as a dumping ground for rebellious Negroes.

There was also a great deal of talk in this era about a war of extermination. One cannot read the documents of this period without a gnawing feeling that white men were itching for a revolt by Negroes so they could shoot them down like the Indians, as a current phrase had it.

Against this system, against political, economic, and social strangulation, the Negro and his leaders went forth to do battle. They were a ragged host, standing exposed and alone on a broad plane with the high ground and the heavy weapons in the hands of men who feared and despised them. The Negro masses had displayed astonishing social sophistication in the Reconstruction period, but now they disappeared from the field of battle and were not heard from again for sixty years. Pushed back toward slavery, not knowing, having no way of knowing, really, what was happening to them and why, they grew sullen and silent and their will slept.

Thunderous messages were addressed to them and battle calls were sounded, but they did not hear; and if they heard, they did not respond. The Negro people were confined for the most part to enclaves in the Black Belt counties along the Gulf and the East Coast. No newspapers came to these oppressed enclaves. There was, in fact, little or no light from the outside and plantation bosses intended to keep it that way. And the local leadership? What local leadership there was—preachers, mostly, and fraternal leaders—was timid and afraid.

American Negroes have known many hours of despondency in America but never before or since have they seemed quite as lost and as helpless as they did in the post-Reconstruction period. Negro leaders organized equal rights organizations, issued resolutions, and vague threats. But nobody was listening, and nobody seemed to care. The only hope white men of goodwill offered Negroes was prayer—in "separate but equal" churches.

Millions prayed, but millions cast about for more worldly weapons. Frederick Douglass, now in the winter of life, went back into the trenches. He had made mistakes in his middle period, but now he thundered back, beginning a famous speech with the electric phrase: "Not a breeze comes to us from the late rebellious states that is not tainted and freighted with Negro blood." Douglass denounced the Negro's "so-called emancipation as a stupendous fraud—a fraud upon him, a fraud upon the world." America, he said, had abandoned the Negro, ignored his rights and left him "a deserted, a defrauded, a swindled, and an outcast man—in law free; in fact, a slave."

Douglass and other Negro leaders fought a defensive holding action, concentrating on retaining the war gains—the Fourteenth and Fifteenth Amendments—and throwing cold water on plans for the forcible deportation of American Negroes. In speech after speech, Douglass told America that it was courting social disaster. It was impossible, he said, to degrade Negroes without degrading the American social fabric. The continued perversion of the state legal processes would eventually force Negroes outside the community for "where justice is denied, where poverty is enforced, where ignorance prevails, and where any one class is made to feel that society is an organized conspiracy to oppress, rob, and degrade . . . neither persons nor property will be safe. . . . Hungry men will eat. Desperate men will commit crime. Outraged men will seek revenge."

Pointing to the summers of 1964 and 1965, Douglass said in 1894 and 1895 that America, if it did not alter its course, would create "an aggrieved class" of black rebels. And he added significantly: "We want no black Ireland in America."

All this was true and extremely enlightening. But what was to be done? Douglass said Negroes should refurbish their weapons, dig trenches, expose, warn, appeal, exhort—and contest every inch of ground. Negroes, he said, "should keep their grievances before the people and make every organized protest against the wrongs inflicted upon them within their power. They should scorn the counsels of cowards, and hang their banners on the outer wall." Time, he said, would fight the Negro's battles—time and the Negro birth rate. "Every year adds to the black man's numbers. Every year adds to his wealth and to his intelligence. These will speak for him."

The struggle, Douglass said, would go on. "Until the public schools shall cease to be caste schools in every part of the country, this discussion will go on. . . . In a word, until truth and humanity shall cease to be living ideas, and mankind shall sink back into moral darkness, and the world shall put evil for good, bitter for sweet, and darkness for light, this discussion will go on."

In 1895, the year of his death, a young Negro student approached Douglass and asked him what he should do with his life. The old warrior pushed himself up to his full height and his eyes blazed with the fury of his youth as he said:

"Agitate!"

"Agitate!"

"Agitate!"

Most literate Negroes followed Douglass to the end. They held mass meetings, wrote resolutions, and addressed messages to the nation. Equal rights organizations sprang up in every state, and attempts were made to mobilize white support. Provocative overtures were made to the burgeoning labor movement, but white workers were as hostile as white merchants. Between 1880 and 1890 there were more than fifty strikes in the North against the employment of Negro workers.

As in all ages of acute conflict, Negroes turned to black nationalism. Edwin P. McCabe, a former state auditor of Kansas, led a movement for the establishment of an all-Negro state in the Oklahoma Territory. The attempt failed, but all-Negro communities were organized in several cities in the South and North.

One of the most colorful of the Negro nationalists was Bishop Henry McNeal Turner, the last of what Du Bois called "the mighty men, physically and mentally, men who started at the bottom and hammered their way to the top by sheer brute strength . . . spiritual progeny of ancient African chieftains and the fruit of the African chief in America." A former member of the Georgia legislature and a former chaplain in the Union Army, Bishop Turner never forgave America for what he considered ungrateful treatment. The Negro, he concluded, had "no manhood future" in America. The AME bishop became so embittered that he refused to die on American soil. Feeling the approach of death, he dragged himself off to Canada and died there—defiant and discontented to the end.

There were some in this age who wanted to fight fire with fire. When Negroes in Clarksville, Tennessee, burned part of the town in retaliation for a lynching, the *Chicago Conservator* congratulated them. "We are loath," the paper said in 1880, "to advocate lawlessness. We deplore the necessity of resort to arson and rapine, but if such things come, let them come." Another fire-eating activist was John E. Bruce, a prominent journalist, who called for "a resort to force under wise and discreet leaders."

Increasingly, in this age, the voice of accommodation was heard. Uncle Toms came forward and put themselves at the disposal of the ruling class. More ominous still was the emergence of men who collaborated out of a mistaken sense of duty or fear. Such a man was Isaiah T. Montgomery, the only Negro member of the Mississippi Constitutional Convention of 1890. He not only voted for laws disfranchising Negroes, but he also made a strong speech in support of Negro disfranchisement.

Another factor having deep disintegrative effects was the fragmentation of Negro life and the emergence of a black elite based, in the main, on the house slave and the free Negro classes. The black elite was a contrast class, composed of opposite Negroes—Negroes, in other words, who defined themselves by acting just the opposite of the "crude masses." The Negro masses, according to the white stereotype, were loud, dirty, boisterous, carefree. The black elite, in reaction, became quiet, clean, polite, and rigorously dull. The Negro masses belonged to the evangelical Baptist and AME churches; the Negro elite joined the Episcopal and Congregational churches. In every aspect of life, the black elite made a desperate and, in the nature of things, futile effort to separate themselves socially and psychologically from the Negro masses.

The frailties and fears of the black elite took deep roots in Negro life during the years of reaction and terror. There emerged in this period the tendency of representing the masses instead of guiding them, of speaking for the masses instead of speaking to them, of attacking and defending the masses instead of organizing them.

No one had a better insight into the uses of Negro disunity than Henry Grady, the architect of the "New South." In the 1880's, Grady crisscrossed the North, preaching the gospel of conciliation and North-South trade. Before cheering audiences in Boston and New York, the eloquent Georgian made six points:

1) *White people in the North and South must unite on a common racial platform—white supremacy.* "Never before in this Republic has the white man divided on the rights of an alien race. The red man was cut down as a weed, because he hindered the way of the American citizen. The yellow man was shut out of this Republic because he is an alien and inferior. The red man was owner of the land—the yellow man was highly civilized and assimilable—but they hindered both sections and are gone!"

2) *There must be no agitation on the race question.* The problem, if there was a problem, must be left to the "conscience and common sense" of Southerners. "It must be left to those among whom [the Negro's lot] is cast, with whom he is indissolubly connected, and whose prosperity depends upon their possessing his intelligent sympathy and confidence." External pressure only irritated the Southern white man who loved Negroes with a love "you cannot measure nor comprehend."

3) *The Negro must remain in his "ordained place,"* for *"what God hath separated let no man join together."*

4) *The Negro must abandon politics and accept the "clear and unmistakable domination of the white man."* The whites "shall have clear and unmistakable control of public affairs They own the property. They have the intelligence. Theirs is

the responsibility. For these reasons they are entitled to control. Beyond these reasons is a racial one. They are the superior race. . . . This is the declaration of no new truth. It has abided forever in the marrow of our bones, and shall run forever with the blood that feeds Anglo-Saxon hearts." And yet, despite domination and separation, the two races could work together and "perpetual sunshine" would "pour down on the two races, walking together in peace and contentment" and "the race that threatened our ruin" will "work our salvation as it fills our fields with the best peasantry the world has ever seen."

5) *Negro leadership must accept, support, and sustain the racial policies of the white power structure.* To this end, it was necessary to keep a sharp eye on Negro education and Negro leadership. The Negro will "not vote except under persistent and systematic and inspiring organization, this organization cannot be effected or maintained against a powerful . . . social system that embraces the wealth and intelligence of the community." How was it possible to prevent "persistent and systematic and inspiring organization"? The white power structure planned to use the most talented Negroes to damp down the fires of discontent. "We have no fear of [Negro revolt]; already we are attaching to us the best elements of that race, and as we proceed our alliance will broaden." Of what use was the "best element" of the Negro race? The Negro, Grady said bluntly, "must be led to know and through sympathy to confess that his interests and the interests of the South are identical."

To know and to confess.

What a curious choice of words. More curious still is the fact that a black man came forward and confessed. Booker Taliaferro Washington was the flesh of Grady's vision. Like Grady, Washington indentified the Negro's interest with the interests of his oppressors. Washington, like Grady, spoke often and eloquently of "humble" Negroes, "the most patient, faithful, law-abiding, and unresentful people that the world has ever seen." The Southern Negro leader, like the Southern white leader, said the problem, if there was a problem, must be worked out by the Negro and his "best friend," the Southern white man.

Washington came onto the field in the middle of a great retreat. Like Douglass, like Langston, like practically all Negro leaders, he accepted the defeat. Unlike other Negro leaders, however, Washington applauded the peace terms and used his great influence to silence Negroes who said the terms were harsh and unjust.

There are situations no leader can change, situations that defy resolutions, speeches, pleas, even prayers. Faced with such a situation, the wise leader bides his time, marshals his resources, studies the terrain—prepares, in a word, for the next battle. He gives a little when necessary, but he gives grudgingly and continues to probe the line for weak spots. This was Frederick Douglass' reponse to the catastrophic defeat of 1877. And his response provides perspective to assess Booker T. Washington. Douglass made a strategic withdrawal; Washington capitulated. Douglass accepted fate, as all men must; Washington accepted fate and the enemy and the idea the enemy represented.

In his famous Atlanta Compromise address of 1895, the Tuskegee Institute president accepted the whole of Grady's program. He asked Negroes to forget politics, accept the domination of white people and concentrate on the essentials: Christian (i.e., humble) character, property, cleanliness, thrift, and Christian (i.e., industrial) education of the hand and the heart. Agitation, said Washington, echoing Grady, only irritated and impeded; there must be no outside pressure or national laws. Repeatedly, he urged Negroes "to manifest their gratefulness by showing a spirit of meekness and added usefulness."

Much of the confusion that surrounds Washington stems from an artificial dissociation of the man from his policies. Men say what they are, they propose what they are, they lead others down roads engraved on their own hearts.

And what was Booker T. Washington?

Washington was a meek, mild-mannered slave who became a meek, mild-mannered freedman. After graduating from Hampton Institute, he went to the Black Belt of Alabama and established Tuskegee Institute. To survive in Macon County, Alabama, he had to tickle the prejudices of white men. His tragedy was that he imposed his private and personal solutions on a whole race.

Like most young men of his time, Booker T. Washington was influenced by Frederick Douglass. Incredibly, inexplicably, he saw himself as a leader in the Douglass tradition. But the two men had little in common. Kelly Miller, the Howard University dean and essayist, made a penetrating analysis of Douglass and Washington that goes to the heart of two dominant tendencies in Negro leadership circles: accommodation and contention. This analysis, incidentally, was published while Washington was still alive.

"Douglass," Miller wrote, "was like a lion, bold and fearless; Washington is lamblike, meek and submissive. Douglass escaped from personal bondage, which his soul abhorred; but for Lincoln's proclamation, Washington would probably have arisen to esteem and favor in the eyes of his master as a good and faithful servant. Douglass insisted upon right; Washington insists upon duty. Douglass held up to public scorn the sins of the white men; Washington portrays the faults of his own race. Douglass spoke what he thought the world should hear; Washington speaks only what he feels it is disposed to listen to. Douglass' conduct was actuated by principle; Washington's by prudence."

The Tuskegee president was raised to power by white men who made him a virtual dictator of Negro America. He was the court of last resort on Negro political appointments. No Negro institutions, his critics said, with only slight exaggeration, could get a substantial amount of money without his approval. Supported by the Southern and Northern power structure, he made men and broke institutions with a word or a nod of his head.

During the years of his ascendancy, Washington set the mould for conservative, accommodating leadership. And his influence in attenuated form is still perceptible today. The avoidance of conflict, the search for "the right approach," the glorification of the better class of white folk: all this is straight out of the Washington vocabulary. Washington, like his modern counterpart, never went beyond an implication that the rights of Negroes were being invaded. And when he made a protest, it was in the interest of the power structure. "It is unreasonable," he said once in an oblique "condemnation" of lynching, "for any community to expect that it can permit Negroes to be lynched or burned in the winter, and then have reliable Negro labor to raise cotton in the summer."

Always careful not to offend Southern public opinion, Washington explained away or minimized segregation. He placed the blame for segregation on the shoulders of Negroes who were not ready for whatever they were demanding. "It is important and right," he said, "that all privileges of the law be ours, but it is vastly more important that we be prepared for the exercise of these privileges." In fact, Washington said, "we should, as a race, thank God that we have a problem. As an individual I would rather belong to a race that has a great and difficult task to perform, than be a part of a race whose pathway is strewn with flowers."

If Washington was not a Thomist (from "Uncle Tom"), he was the father of thousands. By his great prestige, he made collaboration fashionable. And for a generation afterward, the bowed head, the bared teeth, and the bended knee were accepted skills of Southern Negro leadership. Washington's leadership was no less disastrous in his years of power. By devaluing words and preventing Negroes and liberal whites from uniting on a common program, he shattered the feeble Negro protest movement. By suborning the Negro press and confusing the Negro masses, he destroyed the Negro's ability to protect himself at an hour when he needed protection most. And to all this must be added the obvious fact that the Washington policy of appeasement did not work. Cast down your buckets, Washington said in his Atlanta speech. Down went millions of buckets and up they came—filled with blood. The Great Accommodator accomplished some good. He championed Negro business and produced greater tolerance for Negroes at an hour when it was sorely needed—but the price was too high. The price, quite simply, was complicity in one's own degradation. And for this, leaders are responsible not only to themselves but to unborn generations.

Reading the accounts of his last years, one is convinced that Washington himself realized this. Raising the question, "Has the Negro had a Fair Chance?" he answered, author Francis L. Broderick said, with a "shuffling but nevertheless unmistakable No." Then, almost on his death bed, he completed an article, published posthumously, that condemned segregation.

Washington was opposed in his lifetime by a host of Negro militants and moderates. Five months after the Atlanta address, John Hope, a Morehouse College professor, denounced Washington and his strategy. Bishop Turner, Kelly Miller, and novelist Charles Chesnutt also condemned the accommodator. When Washington apologized for the disfranchisement of Negroes, Chesnutt exploded. "Washington," he said, "has declared himself in favor of a restricted suffrage, which at present means, for his own people, nothing less than complete loss of representation. . . . The time to philosophize about the good there is in evil, is not while its correction is still possible, but, if at all, after all hope of correction is past.

Until then it calls for nothing but rigorous condemnation. To try to read any good thing into these fraudulent Southern constitutions, or to accept them as an accomplished fact, is to condone a crime against one's race. Those who commit crime should bear the odium. It is not a pleasing spectacle to see the robbed applaud the robber. Silence were better."

Cast down by the great defeat of Reconstruction, the Negro masses suffered accommodating leadership in silence. But molecular processes were at work, healing the psychological wounds of defeat. A harbinger of coming change was the dramatic rise in the quality of Negro group life. By 1890, large numbers of Negroes in almost every city belonged to the Negro church, and fraternal orders were laying the foundations for the first Negro insurance companies.

Of even greater importance was the establishment of the pioneer Negro colleges which were legacies of white missionaries and philanthropists. As Myrdal has shown, missionary work in the South was, in part, a conscience salve for Northerners who were involved directly or indirectly in the abandonment of the Negro. Northerners, moreover, had to make a large concession in order to work in the South: they had to agree to forgo tampering with the fundamental relations between Negroes and whites. Despite certain limitations of vision and program, missionaries and philanthropists played an important role in moulding Negro leadership patterns. Each year the missionary colleges graduated little bands of potential rebels, and the new rebels were leaven in the lump of degradation and debasement. It has been said, with only slight exaggeration, that Negro colleges were primarily responsible for preventing the re-establishment of slavery. James K. Vardaman, the Negro-baiting Mississippi politician, recognized the importance of these institutions. "What the North is sending South," he said, "is not money but dynamite; this education is ruining our Negroes. They're demanding equality."

The first effective opposition to Washington's policy of submission came from men and women fired in the crucible of pioneer Negro colleges. Ida B. Wells, the great and neglected woman leader, was perhaps the most imaginative leader of the post-Reconstruction renaissance. The young Fisk graduate started a paper in Memphis and directed a withering fire at Southern bigots. Threatened with lynching, the elegant, striking-looking editor walked the streets of Memphis with two guns strapped to her waist. Driven from Memphis by mob action, she settled in Chicago. From this vantage point, she organized the first effective opposition to lynching, publishing a red book which was probably the first authentic record of lynching. The pioneer woman leader also conferred with presidents and went to England to rally world opinion against lynching and mob violence in America.

In the last five years of the nineteenth century, the isolated voices of opposition became a chorus. There was a flurry of organizational activity, an unfailing barometer of Negro unrest. In 1892, a doctor made a widely-publicized statement that there was not a Negro virgin in America over sixteen years of age. Outraged Negro women led by Mary Church Terrell and Josephine St. Pierre Ruffin organized in 1896 the National Association of Colored Women. Negro men organized the Afro-American Council which established local branches and pursued the battle with a strategy of litigation, and Negro intellectuals banded together in the American Negro Academy.

In the last year of the old century, the Negro conventions converged on Chicago. A contemporary news report said the conventions were the result of "a wave of intense feeling which has recently stirred American Negroes." Among the propulsive forces, the paper said, were "continued lynchings and disturbances, progressive disenfranchisement, the treatment of Negro soldiers and the hostile attitudes of trade unions." The report added: "The opposing forces [at the conventions] were easily distinguished; those who desired radical action in regard to lynch law, those who desired to defend the Republican Administration from attack, those who favor some schemes of migration, and those who desired above all to strengthen national organization."

Thus divided, looking both to the left and to the right, American Negroes crossed over into the twentieth century. The new century opened with the firing of cannons, the unfurling of flags, and the slaughtering of innocents. There were race riots in Harlem and several other Northern cities in 1900, and there were 107 lynchings in the South.

Back there, in the dawn years of the twentieth century, the white man bestrode the earth like a Colossus; and the future was bright with the promise of endless blue-eyed tomorrows. No one dreamed then that the Western world would soon come apart at the seams—no one, that is, except an obscure Negro scholar, W. E. B. Du Bois, who wrote, prophetically, that "the problem of the twentieth century is the problem of the color line."

II. RENAISSANCE

The Lions and the Foxes

THE Negro rebellion began not in Montgomery in 1955, not in Greensboro in 1960, not in Birmingham in 1963, but in Boston in 1905.

It began with an impertinent question, a batch of red pepper, and a riot in a church.

It began, as Emerson cogently noted, where all revolts begin: in the mind of one man.

William Monroe Trotter, who started it all, was the last abolitionist and the first modern rebel. Pudgy, black, and pugnacious, with quick, darting eyes and a whole-hearted commitment to integration and revolt, Trotter was the advance man of a new breed of black rebels who fleshed out the renaissance of the Negro soul.

An authentic radical, cast in the mould of the New England dissidents, Trotter was born in 1872 and raised in a Boston suburb saturated with abolitionist memories. After graduating from Harvard with honors and a Phi Beta Kappa key, the Boston rebel married into a socially prominent family and settled down to a promising career as a real estate broker. There stretched out before him then a bright vista of achievement and service in the echelons of the black elite. But this vision seemed somehow mean to Trotter who was haunted by the creeping misery of the Negro masses and the surging tide of accommodation. With scarcely a backward glance, Trotter repudiated the elite and became an activist. Aided by George Forbes, another well-educated member of the Boston elite, Trotter founded the Boston *Guardian* in 1901 and dedicated his life to the destruction of Booker T. Washington and the idea he represented.

Washington was quick to pick up the gage flung down by the young Boston activist. The Tuskegee president made a desperate and pathetic attempt to silence Trotter, subsidizing another Boston paper, and engineering costly and time-consuming suits against the rebellious editor. But nothing worked; the Boston Cato went his lonely way, thundering: Booker T. Washington must be destroyed. Worse, he followed Washington from city to city in an unsuccessful effort to question him about his equivocal words. This peripatetic campaign probably would have come to naught had not Washington made an uncharacteristic mistake. Overconfident, sure of himself and his power, he accepted an invitation to speak in Boston, the citadel of Negro radicalism. When the Great Accommodator rose to speak on July 30, 1905, at Boston's AME Zion Church, the Trotterites were ready. Ignoring the chairman, they leaped to their feet and shouted questions and insults from the floor. Trotter posed several loaded questions, asking: "In view of the fact that you are understood to be unwilling to insist upon the Negro having his every right (both civil and political) would it not be a calamity at this juncture to make you our leader? . . . Is the rope and the torch all the race is to get under your leadership?"

The restive audience exploded at this point, and policemen were called to restore order. When Washington resumed his speech, he unwisely told an equivocal anecdote about an old mule and the hall heaved in thunderous screams, shouts, and hisses. In the confusion someone threw a batch of red pepper and the crowd panicked, men and women trampling each other in a frantic attempt to reach the nearest exit.

Reports of the Boston "riot" and the "insult to the Negro's greatest leader" startled America—which was, I suppose, Trotter's aim. It had not been possible, up to that point, to get prime coverage of the seething ideological dispute in the Negro world. Having selected Washington as the Negro leader, the white power structure protected him from the enfilading fire of white and Negro malcontents; but it was impossible to suppress the Boston riot, and word went out that some Negroes were displeased with "their" leader.

The heavy-handed handling of the Boston riot (Trotter served a one-month jail sentence) was a catastrophic mistake. People who loathed Trotter began to sympathize with him. More ominously, for Booker T. Washington and the power structures, people on the perimeter began to move to the center of the arena.

The Boston riot, like the abolitionist demonstrations of the 1830's and the sit-in demonstrations of the 1960's, was more than a localized disturbance. Seen whole, within the context of forces contending for the public's ear, the riot was a plea, an appeal, and an argument. And the argument, clothed in the propaganda of a deed, was much more irresistible than mere words. Sixty-six years before, Wendell Phillips had been converted by an idea fleshed by risk and pain. Now, at another decisive hour in the history of the Negro protest, a hero came down off the fence. The convert was W. E. B. Du Bois, a thirty-five-year-old professor of economics and sociology at Atlanta University. Poet, scholar, mystic, seer, prophet, Du Bois had moved for years on the edge of the controversy, courted by both Washington and anti-Washington forces. Now he came down hard on the side of the radicals. "I did not always agree with Trotter then or later," Du Bois wrote. "But he was an honest, brilliant, unselfish man, and to treat as a crime that which was at worst mistaken judgement was an outrage."

Totally committed now, Du Bois moved out into the deeps as a fisher of men. This was a decisive moment in the history of the pioneer protest movement. Du Bois had gifts Trotter lacked. He was widely admired as an ideologue who could invoke a program in an epigram and rip an opponent to shreds in seven languages. Du Bois, moreover, was a man of genius whose academic distinction impressed both Negroes and whites.

Under Du Bois the protest movement moved to a new level of strategic and tactical effectiveness. More important, in the context of current realities, was Du Bois' role in the founding of the NAACP and the articulation of the attenuated abolitionist ideology which undergirds the modern protest movement.

Thirty-one years later, the NAACP said Du Bois' ideas had "transformed the Negro world as well as a large portion of the liberal white world, so that the whole problem of the relation of black and white races has ever since had a completely new orientation. He created, what never existed before, a Negro intelligentsia, and many who have never read a word of his writings are his spiritual disciples and descendants. Without him the [NAACP] could never have been what it was and is."

In typically immodest and yet truthful statement, Du Bois agreed. "I think I may say," he wrote, "without boasting that in the period from 1910 to 1930 I was a main factor in revolutionizing the attitude of the American Negro toward caste. My stinging hammer blows made Negroes aware of themselves, confident of their possibilities and determined self-assertion. So much so that today common slogans among the Negro people are taken bodily from the words of my mouth."

Who was this man who spoke with such frankness, such immodesty—and such truth?

William Edward Burghardt Du Bois was, almost despite himself, the Columbus of the Negro's New World. In his triumphs and in his failures, he personified the new Negro ethos which crystallized in the dawn years of the twentieth century.

Du Bois' life was a history in miniature of the death and rebirth of the Negro psyche. Born three years after Appomattox, one of a handful of black pebbles in the white sea of Great Barrington, Massachusetts, Du Bois was steeped from birth in the mute pains of violated black flesh. He was three when Grant was elected, eight when Queen Victoria became Empress of India, nine when Hayes betrayed the Negro, and ninety-one when the sit-in age began.

Like Trotter, like Walter White, like almost every protest leader, Du Bois was a child of the black elite; and his deficiencies, a certain snobbishness and disdain for the masses, were deficiencies of that structure. His family was among the oldest inhabitants of Great Barrington, and they tended, Du Bois remembered, to look down on Negro newcomers and Irish and German laborers. "A knowledge of family history," he said, "was counted as highly important."

Du Bois came early to indignation. As one of the few Negro students in the school system, he took great delight in besting his companions in letters and ideas. "The sky was bluest," he said, "when I could beat my mates at examination-time, or beat them at a foot-race, or even beat their stringy heads." At an early age, the future Negro leader decided that he was destined for greatness. How he learned this is a mystery. But we catch him at the age of fifteen in an extraordinary and, considering the circumstances, somewhat immodest act: collecting and annotating his papers for posterity.

With the help of scholarships, Du Bois graduated from Fisk and Harvard and went abroad to study at the University of Berlin. There, on his twenty-fifth birthday, the young mystic decided that he would become the Moses of the Negroes of America and Africa. Alone in his room, he made a "sacrifice to the Zeitgeist" of God and Work, performing a strange ceremony with Greek wine, oil, and candles. Then he made an entry in his diary.

> I am glad I am living, I rejoice as a strong man to run a race, and I am strong—is it egotism, is it assurance—or is it the silent call of the world spirit that makes me feel that I am royal and that beneath my

sceptre a world of kings shall bow. The hot dark blood
of that black forefather born king of men—is beating
at my heart, and I know that I am either a genius or
a fool . . . this I do know: be the Truth what it may
I will seek it on the pure assumption that it is worth
seeking—and Heaven nor Hell, God nor Devil shall
turn me from my purpose till I die. I will in this second quarter century of my life, enter the dark forest
of the unknown world for which I have so many years
served my apprenticeship—the chart and compass the
world furnishes me I have little faith in—yet, I have
none better—I will seek till I find—and die. . . .

These are my plans: to make a name in science, to
make a name in literature and thus to raise my race.
Or perhaps to raise a visible empire in Africa thro'
England, France, or Germany.

I wonder what will be the outcome? Who knows?

I will go unto the King, which is not according to
the scripture, and if I perish, I perish.

Returning to America in 1894 at the age of twenty-six, Du
Bois entered "the dark forest of the unknown world." He became a professor of economics and sociology and turned out a
series of monographs and books on the race problem. He believed then that truth, dispassionately presented, would set
men free. But he soon changed his mind. There were, he recalled later, seventeen hundred Negroes lynched between 1885
and 1894 and "each death [was] a scar on my soul." No less
distressing were the daily pinpricks he suffered as a resident
of Atlanta, Georgia. Proud and sensitive, Du Bois became a
virtual recluse, confining himself to the Atlanta University
campus, never entering a Jim Crow streetcar or a Jim Crow
theater. Those who knew him then could never forget the
looks of him: thin, aristocratic, aloof—a lonely man of terrible
pride who was never seen without gloves and a cane.

Somewhere in this dark age it came to Du Bois that truth
will only set men free if they have been actively seeking it.
And more: that truth, unsupported by organization and energy, is powerless among men running pell mell into darkness.
With Du Bois, analysis was always a prelude to action. Having
decided that knowledge was not enough, he began his slow
descent from the olympian heights of his ivory tower.

His first act was the publication in 1903 of a book of essays,
The Souls of Black Folk, which had an impact on its age not
unlike the publication of Baldwin's *The Fire Next Time* sixty
years later. With restrained passion that burned like ice, Du

Bois addressed himself to the issue of the day—freedom. To speak of Negro freedom in that day was to speak of Booker T. Washington; and Du Bois, who had tried to maintain a middle course, did not shrink from the task. In an essay, "On Mr. Booker T. Washington and Others," he aligned himself with Negro militants who opposed Washington, writing: "We have no right to sit silently by while the inevitable seeds are sown for a harvest of disaster to our children, black and white." Black men of America, he said, had a duty to perform, "a duty stern and delicate,—a forward movement to oppose a part of the work of their greatest leader."

And of what did this duty consist? "So far as Mr. Washington preaches thrift, patience, and industrial training for the masses, we must hold up his hands and strive with him, rejoicing in his honors and glorying in the strength of this Joshua called of God and of man to lead the headless host. But so far as Mr. Washington apologizes for injustices, North or South, does not rightly value the privileges and duty of voting, belittles the emasculating effects of caste distinctions, and opposes the higher training and ambition of our brighter minds, —so far as he, the South, or the nation, does this,—we must unceasingly and firmly oppose them."

So writing, Du Bois marked off the field of battles and divided the Negro community into "sheep" or "goats." According to James Weldon Johnson, Du Bois' little book had a sharper impact on the Negro community than any other book published since *Uncle Tom's Cabin.*

Two parties arose in the ghetto now, and every literate Negro had to take a stand on the respective programs of Du Bois and Washington. Between these two parties, Johnson wrote, "there were incessant attacks and counterattacks; the [accommodators] declaring that the [militants] were visionaries, doctrinaires, and incendiaries; the [militants] charging the [accommodators] with minifying political and civil rights, with encouraging opposition to higher training and higher opportunities for Negro youth, with giving sanction to certain prejudiced practices and attitudes toward the Negro, thus yielding up in fundamental principles more than could be balanced by any immediate gains. One not familiar with this phase of Negro life in the twelve- or fourteen-year period following 1903 . . . cannot imagine the bitterness of the antagonism between these two wings." The struggle continued until Washington's death.

The roots of this controversy lay deep. The surface disagreement over industrial vs. higher education obscured a fundamental disagreement over modes of being. The whole controversy turned on leadership, not trades; on power, not education. To Washington's program of submission, Du Bois opposed a strategy of "ceaseless agitation and insistent demand for equality [involving] the use of force of every sort: moral suasion, propaganda and where possible even physical resistance." Du Bois' primary interest was in the education of "the group leader, the man who sets the ideals of the community where he lives, directs its thoughts and heads its social movements." He therefore opposed Washington's stress on education of the hand and heart because without a "knowledge of modern culture" the Negro would have "to accept white leadership, and . . . such leadership could not always be trusted to guide the Negro group into self-realization and to its highest cultural possibilities."

To drive this point home, Du Bois created the myth of the Talented Tenth, the ideological substructure of the modern protest movement. "The Negro race," he said, "like all races, is going to be saved by its exceptional men. The problem of education, then, among Negroes must first of all deal with the Talented Tenth; it is the problem of developing the Best of this race that they may guide the Mass away from the contamination and death of the Worst, in their own and other races."

The important thing to note about this archetypal Negro myth is its neutrality. The myth forms the base of the leadership principle of organizations as diverse as the Roman Catholic church and the Communist party. Everything depends, in the final analysis, on the definition of the tasks of the Talented Tenth. In theory, members of the Talented Tenth were to awaken the masses, guide them, inspire them, and lead them. In fact, the early Talented Tenth consisted of talented men leading other talented men and issuing manifestoes, from afar, for the edification and instruction of masses who had never heard of Du Bois, Washington, or the Talented Tenth.

Sixty years later, the young rebels of the Student Nonviolent Coordinating Committee would convert this myth into an instrument of revolutionary ardor. But these rebels, some of whom were influenced by the early Du Bois, conceived of the Talented Tenth as a saving remnant who organized the masses and lifted them where they were. This seed was contained in Du Bois' original formulation but, curiously, neither Du Bois nor his disciples developed it. And it is difficult to avoid the conclusion that this was a conscious choice based on the strain of snobbery which is also a base element in elite myths—myths being defined here as imaginative interpretations of social reality which release energy for the reconstruction or the defense of the status quo. Du Bois later broke away from this constricting element in his thought, but by that time the minds he had helped to form were set in narrow moulds.

But none of this could be seen by either side in 1903. In the years between 1903 and 1915, when the Du Bois-Washington controversy was at its height, most Negroes lived in back-country enclaves and were not available as constituents for either Washington or Du Bois, both of whom appealed, by necessity, to educated elites. The issue was joined in 1905 with the organization of the Niagara movement, the first sustained instrument of indignation since the Reconstruction debacle. From Atlanta, in June, 1905, Du Bois issued a call "for organized determination and aggressive action on the part of men who believe in Negro freedom and growth." In July, twenty-nine business and professional men met secretly at Niagara Falls, Ontario, and organized the germinal Niagara movement. Du Bois and Trotter were the leading lights of the movement which demanded immediate and total integration. In 1906, the same year that Gandhi began his passive resistance campaign in South Africa, the Niagara militants abandoned caution and held an open meeting at Harpers Ferry, the scene of John Brown's martyrdom. This meeting, Du Bois said, was "in significance if not in numbers one of the greatest meetings that American Negroes have ever held . . . and we talked some of the plainest English that has been given voice to by black men in America." Raising demands that are still burning issues, the Niagara militants said:

> We will not be satisfied to take one jot or tittle less than our full manhood rights. We claim for ourselves every single right that belongs to a freeborn American, political, civil, and social; and until we get these rights we will never cease to protest and assail the ears of America. . . .
> In details, our demands are clear and unequivocal. First, we would vote; with the right to vote goes everything: freedom, manhood, the honor of our wives, the chastity of our daughters, the right to work, and the chance to rise. . . . We want full manhood suffrage, and we want it now, henceforth and forever.
> Second. We want discrimination in public accommodation to cease. Separation in railway and street-

cars, based simply on race and color, is un-American, un-Democratic, and silly.

Third. We claim the right of freemen to walk, talk, and be with them that wish to be with us. No man has a right to choose another man's friends, and to attempt to do so is an impudent interference with the most fundamental human privilege.

Fourth. We want the laws enforced against rich as well as poor; against capitalists as well as laborers; against white as well as black. We are not more lawless than the white race, we are more often arrested, convicted and mobbed. We want justice even for criminals and outlaws. We want the Constitution of the country enforced. We want Congress to take charge of the Congressional elections. We want the Fourteenth Amendment carried out to the letter and every state disfranchised in Congress which attempts to disfranchise its rightful voters. We want the Fifteenth Amendment enforced and no state allowed to base its franchise simply on color.

Fifth. We want our children educated. The school system in the country districts of the South is a disgrace and in few towns and cities are the Negro schools what they ought to be. . . .

These are some of the chief things we want. How shall we get them? By voting where we may vote; by persistent, unceasing agitation; by hammering at the truth; by sacrifice and work.

These were fine words if the Niagara militants could make them stick, but the odds were against them. Booker T. Washington controlled the power lines between the Negro and white communities and he counterattacked with devastating thoroughness, using his considerable resources to isolate the militants from white liberals and the Negro press. The movement was also hampered by internal problems. Du Bois and Trotter were not, by any means, organization men; the presence of both in one organization guaranteed strife and dissension. Between 1905 and 1907, the young movement was racked by a series of internal ideological explosions. Finally, in 1908, Trotter broke with his associates and founded his own organization, the National Equal Rights League.

Another factor in the eventual demise of the Niagara movement was its narrow base of membership. The membership consisted of a select group of ministers, educators, and professionals, a fact which pleased Du Bois who said he only wanted to attract "the very best class of Negroes." Full membership in the organization was confined to Negroes, but whites were eligible for associate membership. Among the white associate members was Mary White Ovington, a wealthy social worker who played a key role in the founding of the National Association for the Advancement of Colored People. By 1907, the organization had 236 members and 144 associate members.

The elite tone of this pioneer Talented Tenth organization disturbed some Negroes and whites. The editor of the (New) *Jersey City Appeal* told Du Bois that he "would do well to get closer to the people, I mean the masses as well as the classes." Mary White Ovington expressed a similar reservation. Pointing to the psychological and social chasm between the Niagara members and the Negro masses, she asked Du Bois to let her speak on the Negro and the labor problem at the 1908 convention. "I would like," she said, "to hammer that side of things into some of the aristocrats in the membership." Despite its narrow base, the Niagara movement fashioned a national organization and established local branches in Northern cities. In program and in structure, the organization was similar to the NAACP, with an action campaign based on lobbying, legal redress, and protest propaganda.

Buffeted by critics of the left (Trotter) and right (Washington) and hampered by defects of vision and structure, the movement limped along from crisis to crisis until 1910. Although the Niagara militants failed in their larger objectives, they succeeded brilliantly on another level. By hammering away at the national conscience, the militants created a climate of dissent. More significantly, the movement educated Negroes in a strategy of contention and laid the foundations for the National Association for the Advancement of Colored People.

Even as the influence of the Niagara group diffused itself through Negro society, a pivotal era in the social life of the Negro and of America was drawing to a close. New machines were changing the face of the world and the Negro was changing with it. Blacktop roads were poking inquiring fingers into the Black Belts of the South, and improvements in communications were bringing in rays of light. Of crucial importance in this connection was the Model T Ford which freed both Negroes and whites from the tyranny of the land.

Every throb of the engine, every turn of the wheel, loosened the Negro's chains. Men traveling in the South in this period noted a new phenomenon, Negro racial consciousness; and they began to warn the South that the Negro could not be held down forever. The new Negro racial consciousness sprang from conflict, segregation, and despair. But it had deep roots in dawning hope. The sharp rise in the number of Negro college graduates and the emergence of a new class of black Babbitts boosted Negro morale and stoked the fires of disaffection. Tangible proof of this new orientation was the growth of protest organizations. By 1908, the pioneer Niagara movement was sharing the national spotlight with Trotter's National Equal Rights League, Ida B. Wells's Antilynching League and the interracial Constitution League of John Milholland, a white industrialist.

Another factor in the growth of racial consciousness was the renaissance of the Negro press. As the Negro public increased in literacy, the number of Negro papers increased. As Negroes increased in militancy, the tone of the Negro press became more strident. William Monroe Trotter was, as we have seen, the father of modern protest journalism. But his contemporary, Robert Abbott, played an important role in refocusing the passion of the Negro press. Abbott was a Georgian who migrated to Chicago and started a paper in the kitchen of a friend's house. Sensing the new mood of urban Negroes, Abbott made an issue of every case of segregation and discrimination, hurling charges and recriminations in bold, red headlines which attracted the masses. In the process, he created a new tradition in the Negro press and made himself a wealthy man.

With the founding of the National Association for the Advancement of Colored People, the divergent strains of Negro militancy and white liberalism merged and the modern protest became organization. Sentiment for a national interracial organization was crystallized by a 1908 riot in Springfield, Illinois. A mob, which included, the press said, many of the town's "best citizens," took possession of Springfield for two days and surged through the streets, killing and wounding scores of Negroes and driving hundreds from the city. Shouting, "Lincoln freed you, we'll show you your place," bands of white ruffians lynched and flogged Negroes within sight of the emancipator's grave.

That this should happen in a city intimately associated with the early life of Lincoln horrified liberal America. William English Walling, a radical white Kentuckian, expressed the dawning sense of outrage in a newspaper article, "Race War in the North." It was time, Walling said, for national action. "Either the spirit of Lincoln and Lovejoy must be revived and we must come to treat the Negro on a plane of absolute political and social equality, or Vardaman and Tillman will soon have transferred the race war to the North. . . . Yet who realizes the seriousness of the situation, and what large and powerful body of citizens is ready to come to their aid."

No "large and powerful body of citizens" recognized the seriousness of the situation, but one woman did; and, in the end, that made all the difference in the world. Mary White Ovington, the young white social worker of the Niagara movement, read Walling's plea and sat down "within the hour" and penned an answer. Proposals and counterproposals were made and, finally, in the first week of January, 1909, a white Southerner (Walling), a Jewish social worker (Henry Moskevitz) and a white woman (Ovington) held a meeting in a Manhattan apartment, which changed the course of Negro history. It was decided at this meeting to enlist the aid of white liberals and Negro militants in a crusade for human decency. With the help of Bishop Alexander Walters of the AME church and Dr. W. H. Bulkley, a Negro principal of a white New York public school, the white liberals issued a call "for the discussion of present evils, the voicing of protests and the renewal of the struggle for civil and political liberty." Oswald Garrison Villard, then publisher of the *New York Post,* wrote the call which was issued on February 12, 1909, the centenary of Lincoln's birth. The Negro's legal status had been declining for more than sixty years. At that point it was not markedly different from the pre-Reconstruction period. With chilling eloquence, Villard, a grandson of William Lloyd Garrison, detailed the crisis of the hour.

> If Mr. Lincoln could revisit this country in the flesh, he would be disheartened and discouraged. He would learn that on January 1, 1909, Georgia had rounded out a new confederacy by disfranchising the Negro, after the manner of all the other Southern States. He would learn that the Supreme Court of the United States, supposedly a bulwark of American liberties, had refused every opportunity to pass squarely upon this disfranchisement of millions, by laws avowedly discriminatory and openly enforced in such manner that the white men may vote and black men be without a vote in their government; he would discover, therefore, that taxation without representation is the lot of millions of wealth-producing American citizens, in whose hands rests the economic progress and welfare of an entire section of the country.
>
> He would learn that the Supreme Court, according to the official statement of one of its own judges in the Berea College case, has laid down the principle

that if an individual state chooses, it may "make it a crime for white and colored persons to frequent the same market place at the same time, or appear in an assemblage of citizens convened to consider questions of a public or political nature in which all citizens, without regard to race, are equally interested."

In many states Lincoln would find justice enforced, if at all, by judges elected by one element in a community to pass upon the liberties and lives of another. He would see the black men and women, for whose freedom a hundred thousand of soldiers gave their lives, set apart in trains, in which they pay first-class fares for third-class service, and segregated in railway stations and in places of entertainment; he would observe that State after State declines to do its elementary duty in preparing the Negro through education for the best exercise of citizenship.

To right these wrongs, to call America back to the dream of the Founding Fathers, to remonstrate, to petition, to denounce —in order to do these things, hundreds of Negro and white Americans gathered in New York City in the last week of May, 1909. Some of the old abolitionists, notably Thomas Wentworth Higginson, and some of the sons of the abolitionists, notably William Lloyd Garrison, refused to attend because of the alleged "radical tone" of the conference. Among the prominent Negro participants were Niagara militants like Du Bois, Trotter, J. Max Barber and prominent women leaders like Ida B. Wells and Mary Church Terrell.

This decisive conference, on which so much depended, began with an astonishing exhibition. A Columbia University anthropologist and a Cornell University zoologist exhibited bottles containing the pickled brains of apes, Negroes, and whites. The two learned gentlemen then proved to the conferees and to the press that Negroes were human.

Having proved something, the conferees got down to the hard business of inventing a structure. It became clear almost immediately that the Negroes did not trust the white people and vice versa. Most of the white participants were moderates who did not want to offend Booker T. Washington. The Negro participants, on the other hand, were militants who doubted the good faith of white liberals.

The struggle over composition of the steering committee almost wrecked the meeting. When someone suggested Booker T. Washington's name, the meeting exploded. Villard was surprised that the "whole colored crowd" was "bitterly anti-Washington." The wrangle continued until past midnight when the nominations committee, taking "a middle course [which] suited nobody," announced its selections. Booker T. Washington was not nominated; nor were Negro radicals like Ida B. Wells and Monroe Trotter. Ida B. Wells went immediately to the chairman and insisted that her name be placed on the list; and the chairman, Mary Ovington noted, "illegally, but wisely" complied. Trotter maintained a nebulous relation with the NAACP for a few years and then dropped out, saying the organization was "too white."

One more hurdle, the resolutions, stood before the Negro and white conferees. A long and bitter debate ensued on almost every word and comma of the resolutions. The Negro militants turned on the white liberals with a cold fury, charging that "a traitorous clique" had captured the meeting; and a woman, probably Ida B. Wells, leaped to her feet and cried out, Du Bois wrote, "in passionate, almost tearful earnestness —an earnestness born of bitter experience—'They are betraying us again, these white friends of ours.'"

Suspicion and hostility reached such a pitch that Villard conferred with a white associate over the advisability of forming another organization with more restrained Negroes. Fortunately, for all Americans, the Negro militants and white liberals patched up their differences and worked out a compromise program. The program, in essence, was a watered-down version of the Niagara platform with stress on political and legal tactics. But there were some surprising omissions. Trotter could not persuade the liberals to support a federal antilynching bill. After an "acrimonious" debate, the conference endorsed a vague statement "opposing violence."

In compromise, then, and in caution, the NAACP embarked on an adventure of litigation, lobbying, and persuasion. At the second national conference in May, 1910, a permanent organization was effected. Moorfield Storey, a Boston lawyer, was elected president. The only Negro officer and the only Negro incorporator was Du Bois, who resigned from Atlanta University to accept the position of director of research and publicity. The new organization opened for business at 20 Vesey Street in lower Manhattan and hired a white woman, Frances Blascoer, as the first secretary. In the summer of 1910, the organization began its legal redress work by intervening in a murder case involving Pink Franklin, a South Carolina peon who had slain a constable who burst into his home at 3:00 A.M. The organization succeeded in getting Franklin's death sentence commuted to life imprisonment. Within three months, the first NAACP branch office opened in Chicago. In the next seven years, the organization grew slowly. By 1913, there were 1,100 members in a handful of Northern branches.

In the beginning, the NAACP was a typical American reform organization based on a middle-class membership and "respectable protest." The organization made no attempt to organize the masses; nor did it assume the proportion of a crusade. In essence, the NAACP was what Bunche called it: "an interracial petitioning and litigating body." This fact disturbed some of the Negro members. Archibald J. Grimké observed on one occasion that it required no special courage to sit in New York and issue manifestoes. He complained, according to Mary Ovington, because the NAACP was "not revolutionary."

The NAACP did not, as some contend, inherit the mantle of abolitionism. The abolitionists were radicals; the NAACP was militant. The abolitionists were "irresponsible" and nonrespectable; the NAACP was responsible and respectable. The abolitionists sent men and women out into the field to stir up people and disturb the peace; the NAACP cautiously assailed legal barriers.

The NAACP did not revive the abolitionist tradition, but it played an absolutely indispensable role in the renewal of the protest movement, opening the eyes of Negroes to a whole new vista of legal struggle. As editor of the *Crisis,* the NAACP's house organ, W. E. B. Du Bois played a major role in setting the tone of the organization. But it is essential to note that Du Bois never agreed with the main body of NAACP tradition. He was always one step ahead, or behind, the dominant trend. The association proceeded cautiously in the courts, but Du Bois scattered shots all over the landscape, attacking the church, the press, the white power structure, philanthropic foundations, and unions.

There was a tendency in the beginning for white liberals and moderates to patronize Negro militants. Mary White Ovington said that "few colored people were trained to take such executive positions as we had to offer" in the second decade of the twentieth century. Du Bois disagreed, saying that Negroes "must not only support but control this and similar organizations and hold them unswervingly to our objects, our aims, and our ideals."

It is at this point perhaps that we ought to pause for a moment and consider the ideals of Du Bois. The acerbic professor was the second stone in a line of leadership that started with

Frederick Douglass. Douglass, as we have seen, aspired to lead Negroes and questioned the right of white people to articulate the Negro's vision. Du Bois went further: he saw Negroes not only as leaders of themselves but as leaders of all the Negroes of the world. Visionary? Perhaps. But history records that Kwame Nkrumah, at least, and possibly Jomo Kenyatta and others caught the fire of his vision.

And what was Du Bois' vision? No man can say, really. Du Bois was complex, very complex. Almost anything you say about him would be true. He was a Negro nationalist, an ardent integrationist, a militant, a moderate, and an activist. There were two submerged but powerful strains in the thinking of the young Du Bois, "industrial democracy," and Negro nationalism. Du Bois loathed Anglo-Saxon civilization and came close to loathing Anglo-Saxons. Surely, he asked God, in a poem written after the Atlanta riot of 1906—"Surely Thou, too, are not white, O Lord, a pale, bloodless, heartless thing."

The corollary of Du Bois' myth of white decadence was the myth of the Negro's mission. Du Bois believed in the divine mission of Negroes and Africans and "their sweetness of soul." "In time," he said in a 1908 speech, "we [Negroes] are going to be the greatest people in the world, if only we do the work that is before us as it ought to be done."

Like Douglass, his sociological father, Du Bois championed struggle and eternal protest. Unlike Douglass, however, he placed severe limitations on his leadership. He despised, he said, "the essential demagoguery of personal leadership; of that hypnotic ascendancy over men which carries out objectives regardless of their value or validity, simply by personal loyalty and admiration." As a result, Du Bois became a leader of leaders, a leader who confined himself to "a leadership solely of ideas." Du Bois went out of his way to underscore his distaste for power. He could not be bothered by the rituals of leadership. "I could not," he said, "slap people on the back and make friends of strangers. I could not easily break down an inherited reserve; or at all times curb a biting, critical tongue."

The net result of all this was that Du Bois influenced people but never gained power. His influence, for all that, was important. As editor of the *Crisis,* Du Bois became a formidable force in the Negro world. By 1918, he was regarded as the most important Negro in the world. Many people, in fact, believed Du Bois *was* the NAACP, a belief Du Bois did nothing to contradict. Mary White Ovington said quite frankly that the *Crisis,* under Du Bois, was a "rival" of the parent organization.

This anomalous situation led to a series of internal explosions. Du Bois ran the *Crisis* as a personal fief and reserved the right to criticize the organization and other sacred cows in the organization's journal. Oswald Garrison Villard, the chairman of the board, claimed the right to "control" Du Bois and the *Crisis*. But Du Bois, who was also a board member, refused to consider himself a "subordinate" of the ruling white liberal elite. He demanded the right to articulate his own private vision, a vision that differed markedly from NAACP official policy. Things reached such a pass in the Manhattan office that Du Bois suggested, probably with tongue in cheek, the establishment of separate but equal divisions of the National Association for the Advancement of Colored People. When the board refused to curb Du Bois' acid pen, Villard resigned in protest.

After the 1913 resignation of Villard, the issue of white control simmered down. But the underlying issues were not resolved until the 1920's when Negroes achieved equality in the National Association for the Advancement of Colored People. The last white secretary was John Shillady who resigned in 1920 after he was thrashed on the streets of Dallas, Texas, by a mob which included a judge, several deputy sheriffs and other substantial citizens. Bruised in body and spirit, Shillady returned to New York City and submitted his resignation, saying: "I am less confident than heretofore of the speedy success of the Association's full program and of the probability of overcoming within a reasonable period, the forces opposed to Negro equality by the means and methods which are within the Association's power to employ." After resigning, Shillady drifted in and out of hospitals and died finally, "a victim," Walter White said, "of lynching as surely as any Negro who had been strung up to a tree or burned at the stake." Mary White Ovington added a mournful postscript: "He had believed in the way of order and law and he learned that this way did not exist when the rights of the Negro or of his friends were in question." Shillady was succeeded by James Weldon Johnson, the first Negro secretary of the organization.

The doubts that assailed Shillady were not entirely groundless. In the years between 1913 and 1920, the Negro's stock dropped to a new low. The wave of repression began, oddly enough, in 1913, the fiftieth anniversary of the Emancipation Proclamation, and grew in virulence. Laws requiring segregated residential districts were passed in Norfolk, Richmond, Roanoke, Greensboro, Atlanta, and Baltimore. North Carolinians were casting about in these years for effective ways to segregate farm land; and Chicago, Philadelphia, Columbus, and Atlantic City were considering the advisability of establishing segregated schools.

By singular circumstance, this white fury coincided with the inauguration of Woodrow Wilson, the first Southern-born President since Andrew Johnson. The Wilson Administration immediately eliminated Negroes from responsible government positions and instituted separate eating rooms and lavatories in federal buildings. In Congress, there was a similar assault on the rights of Negroes. Twenty bills proposing additional discrimination against Negroes were introduced in the first Congress of the Wilson Administration.

Until that moment, the federal government had been the repository of Negro hopes. Now the last fragile thread was broken and Negroes found themselves in a no man's land between a hostile state and a hostile white majority. "What happened in Washington in 1913," Henry Blumenthal wrote, "involved more than the growing toleration of petty prejudices. Worse than that, trust was violated, and hope was lost." Even Booker T. Washington spoke out. "I have never seen the colored people so discouraged and bitter as they are at the present time." Washington's rival, William Monroe Trotter, played a central role in a minor drama that was indicative of the spirit of the times. On November 12, 1914, Trotter stormed into the White House and had a jaw-to-jaw argument with Wilson. According to reports, he shook his finger at the Virginia-born President who dismissed him for "insulting language." The President, Trotter reported, said that segregation was in the best interest of Negroes.

Abandoned by their government and insulted by their President, Negroes transferred their allegiance and their hope to the NAACP, which organized a brilliant campaign of countermoves. On November 5, 1917, the NAACP won a Supreme Court decision which outlawed enforced residential segregation. The importance of this victory is seldom appreciated. If the residential segregation laws had not been struck down at that point, race relations in America probably would have settled down to the black-quarter bitterness of South Africa. The NAACP also won important legal decisions in the fields of suffrage and criminal court proceedings and initiated an antilynching campaign. By pitiless publicity and incessant agitation, the organization succeeded in reducing the number of lynchings. Although the NAACP failed in Congress, where Southerners filibustered antilynching bills to death, it played a large role at the bar of public opinion. When the NAACP campaign began, few men denounced lynchings; by the late thirties, almost no one defended the practice.

Fighting a defensive battle, with all the heavy artillery in the hands of the enemy, Negro leaders concentrated, as James Weldon Johnson graphically put it, "on saving the bodies of Negroes and the souls of white folk." Of the organizations sharing the field of battle with the NAACP, none was more important than the Urban League which was not, strictly speaking, a protest organization. Founded in 1910 by a group of whites and Negroes, the Urban League was a professional social work agency which concentrated on the socioeconomic woes of urban Negroes. Edwin R. A. Seligman was its first president and Eugene Kinckle Jones served for many years as executive director. Ruth Standish Baldwin, wife of W. H. Baldwin, an ardent Booker T. Washington supporter, was the dominant force in the formative periods of the organization which pursued a strategy of conciliation, using tactics of education, persuasion, and negotiation.

To avoid duplication of effort and jurisdictional disputes, the Urban League and the NAACP divided the battlefield. At a meeting of Negro and white men of power, it was decided that the Urban League would pursue a policy of conciliation and negotiation in the fields of social service and employment and that the NAACP would concentrate on protest and pressure in the courts and other theaters of power. The rationale behind this decision was explained by Mary White Ovington who said: "We could not have raised money for philanthropy as successfully as an organization with a less militant program, and securing employment is a business in itself."

The NAACP was founded in 1909, the Urban League was founded in 1910, and Booker T. Washington died in 1915. Between 1909 and 1915, the balance of power shifted in the Negro world from accommodators to militants and moderates; and the center of gravity shifted from Tuskegee and the South to New York City, the home base of the Urban League and the NAACP. During this same period, the Negro elite became a self-conscious structure of Negro decision making. At the policy-making Amenia Conference of 1916, Negro and white power-holders hewed out the boundaries, and the limitations, of the Negro protest. The conference, which was designed to unite the supporters of Booker T. Washington and Du Bois, was called by Joel E. Spingarn, then chairman of the NAACP board. About sixty Negroes and whites attended the deliberations at Spingarn's country home near Amenia, New York. For three days, the conferees debated the state of the race and the respective approaches of Booker T. Washington and W. E. B. Du Bois. They decided, predictably, on a *via media*, endorsing Du Bois' program of "political freedom" with a proviso that recognized "the peculiar difficulties" of neo-Washington leadership in the South. All this was put in a resolution and the power-holders went home, believing that "members [of the Amenia Conference] have arrived at a virtual unanimity of opinion in regard to certain principles and that a more or less definite result may be expected from its deliberation."

The first Negro summit conference was important and "a more or less definite" result followed, but it had no immediate effect on the lives of the vast majority of Negroes. The defense organizations were in New York; the masses were not. The defense organizations were middle class; the masses were not. Du Bois was brilliant, the NAACP was militant, the Urban League was moderate—and it made absolutely no difference at all, for Negroes in the Black Belt had never heard of Du Bois or the Amenia Conference or the NAACP. Far from the command posts, out of sight and sound of the manifestoes, the masses were engaged in the struggle of Sisyphus, pushing large stones up hills only to see them roll down again. And yet a feeling was growing, a clear sense: that things did not have to be that way, that somehow, somewhere life could be lived under more tolerable conditions. The feeling moved, became a mood and leaped from heart to heart, from plantation to plantation. Without preamble, without plan, without leadership, the people began to move, going from the plantations to Southern cities, going from there to the faraway concrete ghettos in the North. There they found jobs and wrote letters, saying to a cousin or a sister or an aunt: come. And they came, hundreds and hundreds of thousands in an elemental flood of people and hopes. The first great wave came between 1916 and 1919 and the second between 1920 and 1924. By 1930, more than two million Negroes had abandoned the plantations for the Harlems of the North.

The people moved for many reasons—because the sheriff was mean, because life was mean, because the white man was mean. They were pushed by drought, boll weevils, and tyranny; and they were pulled by the lure of employment in the burgeoning war industries. Labor agents of Northern industrialists stimulated the movement; so did Robert Abbott and other editors who printed great big headlines of welcome ("GOODBYE DIXIE"). New vistas, new jobs, new opportunities: all these were in the background of the most significant movement in the history of race relations. Seen thus, as an explosion of hopes and fears, the migration movement was a revolt, and that revolt continues today as a permanent element in the Negro protest. An idea—the idea of freedom—moved the people, sending them in ever-increasing numbers to Chicago, New York, Detroit, Pittsburgh, and Philadelphia.

In the great concrete wildernesses of the North, Negroes emancipated themselves, physically and spiritually, casting off the graveclothes of slavery and the feudal South. Under the impact of industrialization and urbanization, the Negro psyche changed, became more complex, more opaque. The Negro, in the city, became less religious, more skeptical, more knowing and more demanding. As Negroes entered new trades and new occupations, they developed new conceptions of themselves and acquired new personalities. Old patterns of behavior were shattered and new social types emerged, Babbitts and Biggers, Dawsons and Powells, Wrights and Baldwins. The Negro folk, in a word, became proletarians.

All this had a sharp impact on Negro leadership patterns. The Negro press took on the now-familiar militant tone, and Negro agitators came forward to challenge the *bona fides* of the black elite. As early as 1922, the white power structure of Chicago called upon "responsible" Negro leadership to curb the new Negro agitators.

As the Negro changed, the racial front broadened and assumed a national character. Confronted with the flesh and blood of Negro reality, the North began a retreat from racial reality. A Negro exclusion movement crystallized, a movement propelled by the real estate interests of the power structure, the status fears of the middle class, and the sex and bread fears of the lower class.

The entry of Negro workers into new industries terrified white workers who feared, above all else, the increasing ability of Negroes to compete for restricted values. Desperately insecure, soured by their own inability to live up to the great American Dream of Success, Happiness and Power, white ethic groups raised demands for exclusion and separatism. Even more persuasive in the crystallization of anti-Negro sentiment were emotionally-toned fears centering around the home.

At the very beginning, the race problem in the North became mired in the power structure's deepest obsession, real estate. Before the Great Migration, Negroes lived in practically every section of Northern cities. Back there, in the beginning, the appearance of a new Negro neighbor occasioned no particular outburst. When Negroes moved into one or two apartment buildings on 134th Street east of Lenox Avenue in Harlem shortly after the turn of the century, whites paid no attention. But as the Negro population continued to grow, a panic developed. Whites began fleeing, James Weldon Johnson said, ". . . as from a plague. The presence of one colored family in a block, no matter how well bred and orderly, was sufficient to precipitate a flight. House after house and block after block was actually deserted." The hysteria infected banks and lending institutions, and a quiet war of containment began.

Here, even in its embryonic form, it is possible to see the process whereby real estate became the principal dynamic in the ensemble of Northern race relations. The development of the pattern of exclusion can be traced in Chicago where a small Negro ghetto grew up on Dearborn Street near the red-light district of the First Ward. As the Negro residents in Chicago increased, the ghetto rolled south and east along State Street with whites fighting desperately to contain the black tide and Negroes fighting just as desperately to break out of the white noose. The first tactic used by white separatists was open violence. Between July, 1917, and March, 1921, fifty-eight bombs were hurled at Negro homes in Chicago.

Open violence gave way in the twenties to a campaign of coercion and intimidation led by property owners' associations and neighborhood improvement organizations. In January, 1920, the Chicago Real Estate Board congratulated the Grand Boulevard Branch of the Kenwood and Hyde Park Property Owners Association for its success in preventing Negro occupancy of fifty-seven houses south of Thirty-ninth Street. The next year, the board voted to expel any members who sold property to a Negro on a block occupied by whites.

The quest for a nonviolent instrument of exclusion continued throughout the twenties. Finally, on March 30, 1928, the *Hyde Park Herald,* a Chicago community newspaper, reported a speech proclaiming the end of the quest:

> . . . Judge _____ of the Chicago Real Estate Board, before the Kiwanis Club of Hyde Park at the Windermere East, in summarizing the earnest and conscientious work of the Board for the last twelve months . . . proceeded to explain the fine network of contracts [restrictive covenants] that like a marvel-

ous delicately woven chain of armor is being raised
from the northern gates of Hyde Park at 35th Street
and Drexel Boulevard to Woodlawn, Park Manor,
South Shore, Windsor Park, and all the far-flung white
communities of the South Side. And of what does this
armor consist? It consists of a contract which the owner
of the property signs not to exchange with, sell to, or
lease to any member of a race not Caucasian.

Within a short time, the "marvelous delicately woven chain
of armor" covered most of the "far-flung white communities"
of the North. The invention of this device gave the Negro exclusion movement a new twist. Coming as it did from the top
and not from the bottom, the restrictive covenant made bias
respectable. It became modish to live in an all-white neighborhood covered by a restrictive covenant, and poor whites hastened to adopt the prejudices of their betters. In a brilliant
analysis, Robert Weaver underlined the importance of the new
status symbol. Noting that "groups most recently Americanized
. . . have now become most vocal in their expressions of anti-
Negro and anti-Semitic attitudes," Weaver said that "it is common to explain this as an excess of the poorly educated or least
cultured persons in the community. Such deduction is superficial. Many of those who resort to violence against Negroes
entering new areas are giving a class expression to their
opposition; but the opposition represents an acceptance of the
standards of the higher-income groups and an attempt
to emulate the 'respectable people.' . . . A generation ago,
residents in the poorer sections of these cities thought little
about color. But soon after instruments to effect enforced residential segregation had become prestige-laden in the more
desirable areas, color consciousness and prejudice spread to
the more blighted areas."

Propelled now by man's desire to have someone to look
down on, the Negro exclusion movement raced across the
North. San Francisco and other municipalities sent experts
to the Midwest to study the techniques of Negro exclusion.
Even the federal government was drawn into the web of conspiracy. The Federal Housing Administration in its under-
writing manual (1938) listed "protection from adverse in-
fluences," including "inharmonious racial groups," as important factors in determining eligibility for a housing loan.

The very best people—bankers, realtors, editors, merchants,
and community leaders—led the Negro exclusion movement.
Although financial institutions made the largest contribution
to acceptance of the idea of Negro exclusion, churches, col-

leges, and universities did not lag behind. Among the signers of restrictive covenants were universities, churches, and "the better class of people" of all faiths.

Real estate interests and property owners' associations gave the campaign an inflammatory twist, inventing an ideology of Negro debasement, an ideology that struck deep roots in the political, social, and educational thinking of the North. The ideology was based on the myth of the Negro's innate inferiority and his alleged propensity for lowering community standards. In Detroit, Chicago, San Francisco, and other communities, property owners' associations became open and vociferous champions of segregation in schools and recreational outlets.

In the twenties and thirties, the flames of fear, guilt, and hate leaped higher and higher. As the struggle widened, even vacant land was assigned a color. Land was either black or white, and everyone—bankers, preachers, priests, rabbis, and policemen —knew the difference.

The struggle to preserve the racial integrity of the land assumed the proportions of a miniature war. Whites spoke in military terms of Negroes "invading" and "infiltrating" a neighborhood. It was necessary for whites to "hold the line" at "the perimeter" or the neighborhood would be "lost."

Thus, a quiet war emerged in the North. And in the North, as in the South, the combatants seldom, if ever, rested on their arms.

Organized white aggression evoked counterforces in the Negro community. Conflicts over segregated housing and segregated schools intensified Negro racial consciousness and welded all Negroes into a common group with a common sense of shared resentment. Negro Main Streets blossomed in every large Northern community. Gradually, almost imperceptibly, a new and different black world came into being in the heart of the American North.

One more moment in the history of the Negro and the white American had passed—never to be called back, never to be erased.

World War I, following close on the heels of the disenchanted black migrants, shattered America's unstable racial equilibrium. This war—the first war to make the world safe for democracy—was an axial event in the history of whites and nonwhites. Until the bloody carnage on the battlefields of Europe, it had seemed that white men would go from triumph to triumph, with nonwhites holding their hats and picking up the leavings. But 1914 and the years afterwards forced an agonizing reappraisal. It became clear in these years that things were far from simple. Machines had loosed a terrible force in the world—and the end was not by any means clear In the light of this knowledge, the whole moral and spiritual climate of the West changed. All over the world now, men grew anxious. They were not so sure—they would never again be sure —of the sanctity of their mission and of the sanctity of their white skin.

If all this was not clearly seen in the first years of the war, it was beginning to be clearly felt, even in the ghetto, where a new spirit of self-assertion rose. There was a new spring in the Negro's walk, a new gleam in his eye, a defiant tilt to his head. And this, of course, intensified the white man's anxiety and his determination to keep the Negro in his place. Simple people believed somehow that if they could keep the Negro in his place the terrors in the world would go away. Nothing else, I think, can explain the dreadful chapter in Negro-white relations of World War I Negroes tried hard to enter into the spirit of the occasion, but white men would not let them. At the beginning of the conflict, Du Bois wrote a famous editorial —"Close Ranks"—which urged Negroes to forget their special grievances for the remainder of the war. But the special grievances, like Banquo's ghost, refused to go away.

In this war, as in every other war, Negroes had to fight to fight. Then they were assigned to menial duties as orderlies and servants. Several Negro regiments were in the thick of the fighting, but most Negroes served in labor units. Worse than that was the open hostility of white officers, many of whom addressed Negro soldiers as "coons" and "niggers." The spirit of vindictiveness leaped the Atlantic. There was little Jim Crow in France, and Negroes ate in "white" French restaurants, lived in "white" French hotels and dated Frenchwomen, some of whom seemed to prefer black skin. White officers spent so much time trying to inoculate Frenchmen with their prejudices that militant Negro leaders said white Americans fought more valiantly against the Negroes than they did against the Germans Needlessly humiliated by rules and prohibitions that blatantly emphasized their subordinate status in the eyes of their government, Negro soldiers reacted with defiance and sullenness. One American soldier said his camp was a penal institution. "I am," he said bitterly. "beginning to wonder whether it will ever be possible for me to see an American white man without wishing he were in his

Satanic Majesty's private domain." Another Negro soldier, who later became a famous congressman, was so embittered by his treatment that he vowed never to fight again for America. William Dawson renounced this vow during World War II, but it is significant that so conservative a man was driven to so extreme a posture.

Conditions were equally bad on the home front, which was in a state of virtual siege. On July 2, 1917, several hundred Negroes were killed and almost six thousand were driven from their homes by a white mob in East St. Louis, Missouri. On August 23, 1917, members of the Twenty-fourth Infantry Battalion shot up Houston, killing several white persons, including five policemen. Although the evidence indicated that the soldiers were goaded into desperation by repeated acts of hosility, nineteen of the soldiers were hanged and several were given long-term prison sentences.

Embittered by open violence at home and insults abroad, Negro Americans became more militant and daring, and the NAACP emerged as the dominant Negro protest instrument. When America entered the war, the NAACP had only eight branches and some nine thousand members. By Armistice Day, the organization had more than three hundred chapters and more than ninety thousand members.

During the war, the NAACP branched out into mass action. On Saturday, July 28, 1917, two months after America's entry into the war, the NAACP sponsored a mass march in New York City. Some fifteen thousand Negroes and whites marched down Fifth Avenue in a silent protest against "segregation, discrimination, disenfranchisement, lying, and the hosts of evils" forced upon Negroes. Mass marches and other forms of mass pressure continued throughout the war. The white press countered with scare headlines ("Negro Trouble Caused by Hun Propaganda"), and the Wilson Administration considered and rejected a plan to arrest Negro editors and protest leaders. On one occasion, the FBI invaded the New York offices of the NAACP and asked tart-tongued Du Bois exactly what the organization was fighting for. Pulling himself to his full height, his eyes blazing with indignation, Du Bois replied: "We are seeking to have the Constitution of the United States thoroughly and completely enforced."

This was clear enough and, to racists, bad enough; and, as the war drew to a close, America braced itself for a racial explosion. It was felt by many that the Negro had learned bad habits in Europe where, according to the Ku Klux Klan, he had been killing white men and sleeping with white women. Many white men believed, therefore, that it would be necessary to take the Negro in hand. American fears were magnified by the May, 1919, issue of the *Crisis*, which sold an unprecedented one hundred thousand copies although it was held up for twenty-four hours by postal authorities. In a burning editorial in that issue, "Returning Soldiers," Du Bois hurled a defiant slogan: "We return! We return from fighting! We return fighting!"

This, as it happened, was perfectly true. The long-fermenting racial tensions exploded in twenty-six race riots in the Red Summer of 1919. For one whole day, the nation's capital was in the hands of a black mob. For thirteen days, Negroes and whites slashed, hacked, burned, and traded shots on the streets of Chicago. Troops were called out finally to put down these uprisings and similar disturbances in Omaha, Knoxville, Norfolk, and other cities. The most significant disturbance of this summer occurred in Elaine County, Arkansas, where Negro sharecroppers organized a defense organization, the Progressive and Household Union of America. While the sharecroppers were singing their theme song, "Organize, Oh, Organize," at a mass meeting, white men fired into the church. The sharecroppers returned the fire, and one white man was killed. White officials organized a posse, burned down the church and began a general massacre, killing fifty or so Negroes. Policemen then arrested eight hundred Negroes and charged *them* with insurrection. Twelve Negroes were sentenced to death and seventeen received jail sentences. The NAACP carried the case to the Supreme Court and established the important legal principle that a trial in an atmosphere of mob hysteria was a denial of due process of law.

The Red Summer of 1919 was the climax of a chain of events that changed the orientation of American Negroes. The indifference and hostility of the Woodrow Wilson Administration, the turbulence of the Great Migration, the riots, massacres, and humiliations of the World War I period: all these loosened the Negro's sentimental bonds to America and prepared the way for new frontiers of strife and controversy.

The mood of defiance reached a peak in the revolt of the twenties, a revolt based on a floodlike surge of racial consciousness. Negro nationalism, a new mass phenomenon grounded on the affirmation of Negro values and a mystical celebration of African ties, was the dominant theme of the cultural and spiritual explosions that rocked the ghetto in the postwar period.

The New Negro literary revolt, which ushered in the postwar period, dramatized the Negro's spiritual emancipation. In an extraordinary outburst of intellectual and artistic activity, Negro writers and artists dropped their masks and spoke with unparalleled frankness and bitterness. Taking a more objective stance toward their experience in America, poets like Langston Hughes, Claude McKay, and Countee Cullen blatantly projected Negroness and Negro values into the mainstream. Langston Hughes sounded the dominant note: "We younger Negro artists who create now intend to express our individual dark-skinned selves without fear or shame. If white people are pleased we are glad. If they are not, it doesn't matter. We know we are beautiful. And ugly, too. If colored people are pleased we are glad. If they are not, their displeasure doesn't matter either. We build our temple for tomorrow, strong as we know how, and we stand on top of the mountain, free within ourselves."

The works of Hughes and other Negro intellectuals reflected the inner migration of the Negro psyche. The New Negro artists spoke for a community that was outside the community; they spoke to America from another psychological country.

Listen, for example, to Claude McKay:

> *Your door is shut against my tightened face,*
> *And I am sharp as steel with discontent.*
> *But I possess the courage and the grace*
> *To bear my anger proudly and unbent.*

And to Fenton Johnson:

> *I am tired of work; I am tired of building up*
> *   somebody else's civilization.*
> *Let us take a rest, M'lissy Jane;*
> *I will go down to the Last Chance Saloon,*
> *   drink a gallon or two of gin,*
> *   shoot a game or two of dice*
> *   and sleep the rest of the night*
> *   on one of Mike's barrels.*
> *You will let the old shanty go to rot, the*
> *   white people's clothes turn to dust, and the*
> *   Calvary Baptist Church sink to the bottomless pit.*
> *You will spend your days forgetting you married me*
> *   and your nights hunting the warm gin Mike serves*

the ladies in the rear of the Last Chance Saloon.
Throw the children into the river; civilization has
given us too many. It is better to die than to
grow up and find that you are colored.
Pluck the stars out of the heavens. The stars mark
our destiny. The stars marked my destiny.
I am tired of civilization.

This was more than a literary pose. For Fenton Johnson and his colleagues, rebellion was a way of life, a quest for identity and meaning. There were three main threads in this quest: 1) a celebration of the nonmachine, non-Puritan, non-exploitative Negro folk tradition; 2) an identification with Africa; and 3) an affirmation of the validity and meaning of Negro experiences as revealed in the history of the Negro.

Reversing the scale of values, Negro intellectuals devised a conceptual defense, a network of counter-irritants, to the demeaning images encrusted in the dominant tradition. By manipulating symbols and images, the New Negro avant-garde tried to emancipate the Negro and to free him from white symbols and images.

Negro scholars played a key role in this germinal movement. Carter Woodson, the father of Negro history, produced a series of scholarly works that gave the movement an intellectual base. With the founding, in 1915, of the Association for the Study of Negro Life and History, Woodson created an ideological scaffolding for both Negro and white scholars.

In this same period, the Negro ethos reached out to the nonwhite peoples of the world. Du Bois, who envisioned an independent African state, held a pioneer Pan-African congress in 1919. By 1925, three Pan-African congresses had been held under the auspices of American Negroes.

The rolling waves of color consciousness reached full tide in the career of Marcus Garvey, one of the greatest mass leaders in the history of Negro protest. Pushing the nationalism theme to its extreme limits, Garvey fashioned a philosophy of black Zionism. A short black spellbinder with the emotional antennae of a psychologist and the reflexes of an actor, Garvey created the first Negro mass movement and stirred the ghetto as it had never been stirred before. And his success, as Myrdal noted, told of a dissatisfaction so deep and pervasive that it bordered on hopelessness of ever gaining a satisfying social life in America.

The founders of faiths and political systems are often maligned by history—thus we get a Torquemada from Jesus, a Booker T. Washington from Frederick Douglass, and a Marcus Garvey from Booker T. Washington. Incredible as it may seem, Marcus Garvey, the bombastic black nationalist, saw himself as a conservator of Washington values. Inspired by a reading of *Up From Slavery*, Garvey left his native Jamaica and migrated to America in 1916. Settling in Harlem, the gifted Jamaican organized a nationalist organization and used it as a springboard to world fame.

The hidden reasons for Garvey's triumph lay in the changing climate of the age. The postwar years were years of acute reaction. White men were anxious, and they lashed out at imaginary enemies—Jews, Roman Catholics, Negroes. Far-right organizations sprang up, the Klan was revived, and racial hate reached a fever pitch. There was, at the same time, a festering resentment in the ghetto, a resentment that found no outlets through established patterns of Negro leadership. A revelation of the depth of Negro discontent was a student strike at Fisk University which attracted national attention and spread to other Southern Negro colleges.

The indifference of white Americans, the impotence of "established" Negro organizations, and a black head of steam in the ghetto; these are the indispensable elements for a separatist or an activist movement. Shrewdly reading the signs of the time, Garvey placed himself at the head of a restless and discontented people. Renouncing all hope of understanding in white America, he called for a return to "Mother Africa." Compromise, contention, conciliation, litigation, direct action: none of these, he said, would change in any fundamental way the situation of a black minority in a land dominated by a white majority that feared and despised them. Pleas for justice in such a situation, he said, were words said to the wind. "Don't be deceived," he said, "there is no justice but strength. In other words, might is right; and if you must be heard and respected you have to accumulate nationally in Africa those resources that will compel unjust men to think twice before they act."

Like Herzl, the founder of Zionism, like Elijah Muhammad, the organizer of the Nation of Islam, Garvey sought allies in the enemy camp and used every instrument to increase minority discontent. Like Herzl, like every nationalist leader in the history of the world, he argued that minorities needed an independent country to achieve their destiny as a people. Using the slogan, "Africa for the Africans at Home and Abroad," he made African liberation a live issue in the minds of black Americans.

While waiting for the improbable transfer of Negroes to Africa, Garvey preached a gospel of race pride and united action. "If we must have justice," he said, "we must be strong; if we must be strong, we must come together; if we must come together we can only do so through a system of organization." Garvey's system of organization was spectacular. His United Improvement Association had local branches in cities across the country and several in foreign lands. An embryonic army, the African Legion, was set up with Garvey as commander in chief. Armed with swords and riding crops, members of the army policed Garvey meetings and made sure no one got in without proper credentials.

A master showman, the best one in the history of Negro America, Garvey used pageantry and processions to drive home his ideas. Millions of Negroes were thrilled by colorful Garvey parades led by the African Legion in blue and red uniforms and the Black Star Nurses in chaste white. The organization's flag was black (for the race), red (for the blood of the race) and green (for the hope of the race).

Always alert to the drama of his cause, Garvey established a chain of cooperative enterprises (grocery stores, laundries, restaurants, hotels, and factories). His biggest coup, however, was the establishment of the Black Star Line, a steamship company.

In 1921, Garvey, at the peak of his power, announced formation of an African republic. At his investiture as the provisional president of this phantom republic, Garvey was surrounded by a royal black court, consisting of Dukes of the Nile and Niger.

The provisional president was a brilliant propagandist, much more imaginative and profound than his latter-day imitators. He made a frontal attack on the myth of Negro inferiority, creating a countermyth of Negro superiority. Stealing the weapons of his enemies, the Negro intellectuals, he used Negro history to buttress his claim. "When Europe was inhabited by a race of cannibals," he said, "a race of savages, naked men, heathens and pagans, Africa was peopled with a race of cultured black men, who were masters in art, science and literature; men who were cultured and refined; men, who, it was said, were like gods. . . . Why, then, should we lose hope? Black men, you were once great; you shall be great again. Lose not courage, lose not faith, go forward. . . ." In order to instill race pride, Garvey exalted everything black. Black stood for strength, beauty, virtue. Even God was black; and, in Garvey's

African Orthodox Church, Jesus and the Virgin Mary were given suntans.

The counternationalism of the Garvey movement stirred every nerve fiber in the ghetto; and an unprecedented number of Negroes flocked to his banner. Garvey claimed six million followers in 1923, a claim most scholars discount. But even his severest critics conceded that he probably had a half-million or more dues-paying members. During his short reign, Garvey raised more money than any other Negro leader had ever dreamed of, collecting some ten million dollars in one two-year period.

This, of course, disturbed the Negro and white power structures. Negro leaders bombarded Garvey with verbal grenades; and Garvey, who loved a good fight, responded in kind. The black elite, he said, was composed of mulatto bastards, who were doing their best to prove to the world that they were not what they were, i.e., Negroes. Hammering away at the explosive internal color line, appealing to the dark-skinned masses in the big-city ghettos, Garvey said the black elite were ashamed of the Negro blood in their veins.

With a keen eye for the strong points, Garvey focused his fire on the NAACP and W. E. B. Du Bois. It was very difficult to tell, he said, whether Du Bois was running "a colored vaudeville" [at NAACP headquarters] or a white show." Du Bois, in turn, assailed Garvey "as the most dangerous enemy of the Negro race in America and in the world . . . a lunatic or a traitor." Garvey countered by "expelling" Du Bois from the Negro race. The virulence of the controversy can be gauged by the title of a Garvey pamphlet: *W. E. Burghardt Du Bois As A Hater of Dark People. Wholesale 10¢; retail 15¢.*

In his less polemical moments, Garvey admitted that educated Negroes were making just demands. "But the great white majority," he said, "will not grant them, and thus we march on to danger." Garvey urged Du Bois to join him in a fight against "the white beasts." A race war was coming, he said, and the black elite were doing nothing to prepare for it.

In vituperation, Garvey excelled; but he was something less than expert in the field of finance. Vain and autocratic, he blundered into a series of errors and was convicted of using the mail to defraud in a complicated scheme to finance his steamship company. After two years of imprisonment in the federal penitentiary in Atlanta, he was deported in 1927 to his native Jamaica. Before leaving America, the charismatic leader penned a swan song.

When I am dead wrap the mantle of the Red, Black, and Green around me, for in the new life I shall rise with God's grace and blessing to lead the millions up the heights of triumph with the colors that you well know. Look for me in the whirlwind or the storm, look for me all around you, for, with God's grace, I shall come and bring with me countless millions of black slaves who have died in America and the West Indies and the millions in Africa to aid you in the fight for Liberty, Freedom and Life.

Bombast? Perhaps. But the seed fell not on rock. Kwame Nkrumah, Jomo Kenyatta, and other African leaders have acknowledged their indebtedness to Garvey. Nkrumah named his ship company the Black Star Line. And the red, black, and green flag (with white stripes) of Kenya invokes the memory and dream of the eloquent black dandy who died in London in 1940, alone and forgotten.

Garvey's program, insofar as it related to removing Negroes from America, was escapist and wholly impractical; but his strategy was based on excellent psychology. He gave the Negro masses the first consciousness of their power and potentialities. And it is probable that the basic psychological orientation of Negroes was permanently modified by the Garvey crusade.

The gangrenous wounds Garvey uncovered were rubbed raw and filled with salt by the Great Depression. The era from October, 1929, to December, 1939, shook Negro America to its foundations and left permanent scabs of anxiety. Relief became a major Negro occupation in this era and alienation was chiseled forever into the private places of the Negro psyche.

The traumatic shock of the Depression can be traced with precision in the life of Dick Gregory, who later became a nationally-known comedian. During the thirties, Gregory was a poor black boy in St. Louis. His father, the victim of the continuing aggression against the Negro male, had abandoned the family; and his mother was fighting a heroic and, in the nature of things, losing battle against the Negro situation. Gregory grew up in a nightmare of anxiety, hating himself, hating his family, hating his situation. "The way they gave out relief," he recalled, "and the way they embarrassed Negroes, treating them like they were dirt, made me burn inside. They could have brought the food at night or they could have come down a dark alley—*they could have let a man have a little dignity.*

But, no—the big government trucks would pull up in broad open daylight and they would throw the food out in the streets and say, 'Come and get it.' "

Like millions of other Negro Americans, like the young James Baldwin, like the young Richard Wright, Gregory recoiled in horror from the Negro image he saw in America's eyes. One day, when he was in the second or third grade, he tried to buy some respect. "The teacher was calling on the children and asking them to stand up and tell how much their fathers had pledged for the Community Chest. I always sat in the back in the dumb seat. The teacher always had to comb my hair and arrange my clothes. I was something like the hunchback of Notre Dame—it almost makes me want to cry to think back on it. There were some pretty wealthy kids in that class and they got up, one after another, and said: 'My daddy said he would give three or four or five dollars.' I held up my hand —now everybody in that class knew I didn't have a daddy. But I said: 'My daddy is going to send fifteen dollars.' That bowled them over. The teacher, a Negro, said: 'You don't have no daddy. It's people like you and your kind we're taking this money up for.' From that day, I was a different person. I resented my mother, my brother, the relief, everything connected with our life. From that day, school meant nothing to me but a place where I could be hurt. So I got resentful. Going to school, I learned what I was—poor.''

Poor—poor and black: the Depression was a school in which many learned the meaning and the limitations of these two words.

It was a school, too, for Negro leaders. Before the Depression, race relations were relations between a handful of "responsible" Negroes and a handful of "Christian" whites. The Depression changed all that, sending thousands of angry black men into the streets and disrupting the delicate understanding between Negro and white men of power. New leaders came forward with new visions, and the range of strategies available to Negroes was enormously increased.

The white man's hold on the Negro's mind was jarred, as we have seen, in World War I; now, with a rush, all the mental bars came down, and black man and white man faced each other across a widening chasm. For a spell, men of God stemmed the whiplash of bitterness. Preachers said from many pulpits—some of them in the ghetto—that God was punishing the people for their sins. Some half-believed it with half of their minds—but not for long. Increasing misery begat increasingly bitter thoughts. And the people turned mean, saying the disaster came not from God but from the devil, a person defined variously, but usually as a white man. Thinking thus, black people, as always, sought new gods. Father Divine became modish; so did Daddy Grace; so also did Lenin. *The God That Failed* came, ironically enough, in the guise of white men and white women who talked equality and acted it—men and women who gave parties where dances and, for all we know, kisses were exchanged; men and women who said that God was all right perhaps in his place but that the central question of the hour was not the Hebrew children but bread.

Communists.

> *Good morning, Revolution.*
> *How do you do?*

This poem reflected a widespread mood of despair in the ghetto. Negroes were not committed to an alien ideology—"It's bad enough being black," they said, "why be red?"—but they were ready—it was said over and over at house-rent parties and in the bars—for a new roll of the dice.

Communists made a desperate attempt to convert the Negro masses, calling for a Negro republic composed of a swath of Black Belt counties across the bottom of the South. This was a disastrous reading of the Negro mind, and the campaign collapsed. Harold F. Gosnell estimated that only five hundred Negroes joined the party in Chicago during the fervid depression campaign.

Although Negroes shunned the party, they accepted the help of both socialists and communists. Left-wing agitators organized unemployment councils and led the Negro masses in direct assaults on structures of oppression. "Flying Squadrons," composed of adventuresome young men, dashed from apartment house to apartment house, preventing the eviction of Negro tenants. On occasion, radicals and family members sat on the furniture and sang the Negro spiritual, "I Will Not Be Moved." More ominous were pitched battles between Negroes and government officials. In Chicago, a group of unemployed Negroes attacked white laborers who were constructing streetcar lines on the South Side. They refused to leave until the mayor, the Negro congressman and several other officials assured them that Negroes would get a fair share of construction jobs on the South Side.

The Negro masses were moved, finally, not by reds but by whites. People in the mass learn not from books but from events; and events in this period welded Negroes into a community of conscious victims. A crucial factor in this development was the increasing effectiveness of mass communication. In the new era of the radio, a lynching or an isolated act of brutality had an impact that was immediate and overwhelming. As mass deprivation spread and as details of lynchings and other atrocities poured from radios, the Negro masses began to move to new positions. A member of a Negro protective association in Macon, Georgia, plumbed the depth of this migrating mood in a letter to the Attorney General. Said he: "It strikes us that the time is just about at hand when we must cast aside our Bible, stop offering so many solemn addresses to the Supreme Being, and fight for our rights. . . . We should defend ourselves by fighting like hell, for once. . . . We would prefer death in lieu of remaining here on earth and have our manhood trampled on."

An echo of this sentiment came from Alabama where Negroes were organizing sharecropper organizations. This was a touch-and-go guerilla operation, similar in tone to the SNCC campaigns of the sixties. Negro organizers lived in constant fear and changed their sleeping places nightly. But one old woman said the fight would continue. "We expect trouble but we don't care. I say stick together. . . . The only way to get anything in this country is to fight for it. We don't have anything to lose but our lives and they ain't worth much. They can't kill you but once."

So saying, the old woman sounded the dominant note in the imperative mood of the Negro masses: *the feeling that they had nothing to lose.* This feeling, faint and shapeless at first but waxing ever clearer, came out in the Harlem riot of 1935. In a spontaneous and incoherent protest, Negroes invaded the business district of Harlem and destroyed some two million dollars' worth of property.

Equally significant in the total scheme of things was a little-noted news item on William Monroe Trotter. The fiery Boston radical had continued his lonely crusade, denouncing both white liberals and black moderates and refusing to compromise. Faced with a choice between what he considered two evils, a Negro hospital, for example, or no hospital, Trotter chose neither and went his lonely way. Toward the end, it seems, he was a little downhearted and perhaps disoriented. But he brightened up appreciably on April 6, 1934, his birthday. That night, after dinner, he took a stroll, as was his wont, on the roof of his apartment house. Sometime before dawn, he took another stroll on the roof and toppled to his death. However he came to his end, whether by suicide or accident, his departure from the national stage was a bitter parable of a bitter time.

As despair deepened, Negro racial consciousness grew. One evidence of this was the national groping for some sense of identity with the nonwhites of the world. After the invasion of Ethiopia, Haile Selassie became a national hero and mass meetings were held all over the country for "the black brothers of Africa." During this same period, there was a dawning sense of identification with the nonwhites of Asia, particularly the Japanese, who were appropriating Western industrial techniques with astonishing rapidity.

Another result of the nationalist mood was the mushroom growth of separatist organizations. The 49th State movement led by Oscar C. Brown, a Chicago lawyer, asked the federal government to detach part of Texas and create an all-Negro state. Another separatist group, the Peace movement of Ethiopia, supported Senator Theodore Bilbo's Negro repatriation bill.

More important than either the 49th State movement or the Peace movement of Ethiopia was the Nation of Islam (Black Muslim) movement which was organized by a mystery man named W. D. Fard in Detroit. After Fard's mysterious disappearance, Elijah Poole, the son of a Georgia preacher, assumed control of the movement. Taking the name of Elijah Muhammad, Poole branched out over the North, establishing temples in Chicago and other cities. The Muslims called for total separation of Negro and white Americans and indicated their disdain for white civilization by dropping their "slave" names and substituting the letter "X."

There was despair in this period—stark, naked, black nationalist despair—and yet, incredibly, there was new hope. The emergence of the attenuated welfare state concept, the use of the state as an instrument of induced change, a series of liberal Supreme Court decisions, the New Deal: all these were cracks in the Chinese Wall of degradation. Even more significant for the future of the Negro was the repeal of the two-thirds rule, an act which stripped the South of veto power over the Democratic Presidential nominee.

As a result of these changes, Negroes gained a new confidence in their collective strength. For the first time since the Reconstruction era, they found themselves a part of a victorious national coalition, a coalition composed, to be sure, of an

unwieldy combination of Southerners, Negroes, and second-
and third-generation white ethnic groups.

It is impossible, really, to overestimate the importance of the
New Deal to Negro Americans. But it is significant that the
New Deal gave least to the Negro who needed it most. Equally
significant is the fact that Franklin Delano Roosevelt never
dared to confront the implications of the Negro's position in,
say, Birmingham or even Chicago. And yet, for all that, the
New Deal was a gain. Despite the fact that the New Deal financed discrimination and segregation in its grants to the
South, despite the fact that the New Deal made it easier for
Negroes to get relief than a job, despite the equivocation and
vacillation of the Roosevelt Administration—despite all that,
the New Deal marked a major turning point in Negro for-
tunes. There were new housing projects and relief checks and
token jobs for token Negroes. And, above all else, there was
the feeling that Negroes were once again a part of the country.

Negro morale was also boosted by the emergence of new
political leaders. Soon after the migration, Negroes got a foot
in the door of the corrupt, crime-ridden, issue-free political
machines of the North. Within a decade after the migration,
Chicago had elected two Negro aldermen, a state senator, four
state representatives, and a county judge. The election of a
Negro congressman, Oscar De Priest, in 1928 confirmed the
new bridgehead of power in the North. Another fillip to Negro
political expressiveness was the band of bright young Negroes
—Robert C. Weaver, William L. Hastie, Ralph J. Bunche,
William Trent, Jr.—who went to Washington as race relations
advisors to the Roosevelt Administration. This group and
Mary McLeod Bethune, a moderate Negro educator, formed
the core of the famous Black Cabinet.

By 1930, Negroes held the balance of power in several
Northern states. What this meant in terms of racial issues was
dramatized by a brilliant 1930 campaign organized by Walter
White, the new executive secretary of the NAACP. Mobilizing
his resources with superb skill, White forced the Senate to deny
confirmation to John J. Parker, a North Carolina judge who
had once opposed Negro suffrage. The *Christian Science Mon-
itor* noted that this was "the first national demonstration of
the Negro's power since reconstruction days."

But there was a basic difference between the new politics of
the thirties and the old politics of the Reconstruction era. The
new politics, despite occasional victories, was devoid of political content. Big-city political machines were composed of dis-

parate and mutually hostile groups pursuing a politics of stalemate. Within the boundaries of this situation, Negroes could veto openly hostile policies; but they could not translate voting power into positive political gains. As a result, Negroes were penetrated by feelings of political helplessness. Since politics had no relevance to their agony, since it was not an activity with which they could lift themselves, they began to look on it with indifference. Worse, they came to see politics as a marketable activity involving the trading of votes for petty political favors.

Passing from the Negro voter to the Negro politician we find a similar constriction of vision. The big-city machines, to repeat, were composed of whites, who hated Negroes, and Negroes, who feared whites. It was impossible, therefore, for the machine to articulate and carry through a sustained program that would change the Negro's position in any fundamental way. To do this, it would be necessary to raise the race issues; and to raise the race issues would lead, inevitably, to a fragmenting of the machines.

Hemmed in by these restrictions, Negro politicians became mere timeservers. Once in office, they made no attempt to change the lives of their constituents. They developed machines, yes; but these machines were organizations for perpetuating their power and not instruments for a sustained and coherent attack on the status quo.

To succeed in politics, in short, was to fail. For, paradoxically, the more successful a Negro politician became, the more harm he did to his own people who, unlike white voters, had nothing to give except votes.

The banalization of politics—the mortgaging of Negro interests to machines controlled by men hostile to Negro aspirations—can be traced in the career of Congressman William L. Dawson, the Chicago Democrat who began his career as a militant. As soon as his power was consolidated, Dawson became a neo-Washingtonian who frowned on militancy and the use of politics for political—in other words, group—ends.

In the thirties, and in every other period of Negro despair, Negro political impotence played a key role in fuelling the fires of revolt. Faced with the sheer irresponsibility of political instruments to Negro aspirations, the Negro masses turned receptive ears to men who pointed to the streets.

Another factor in the re-education of the Negro masses requires emphasis: the Scottsboro case. All the elements of Negro subordination—the manipulation of sex and status fears and the cynical use of political and judicial apparatuses—were dramatized by this case which became an international *cause célèbre*. The case began, innocently enough, with a handful of whites clambering on a freight train in Chattanooga, Tennessee, on a day late in March, 1931. The white hobos huddled in a gondola, a freight car with sides but no top, which was filled to two-thirds of capacity with crushed rock. At Stevenson, Alabama, twenty or thirty Negroes integrated the freight train, and one of the whites protested, shouting angrily: "You niggers get out of here." What happened next is shrouded in controversy. One of the white men said that he and six of his colleagues hastily abandoned the train. But his companions charged that the Negroes threw them out of the car. Be that as it may, it is established beyond doubt that the white men hurried to a telephone and called the sheriff. When the train stopped at Paint Rock, Alabama, the sheriff arrested nine Negroes and three white "men." Further examination turned up a disquieting fact: two of the white "men" were women in men's clothes. The two women, whose names would soon be emblazoned on the front pages of papers all over the world, were Victoria Price, a part-time prostitute and cottonmill worker, and Ruby Bates, another cottonmill worker of uncertain virtue.

The unmasking of the two white women gave the case a new face. With great relish, the Alabama officers seized on this new element, grilling the women for hours on details of the integrated train ride. Both women insisted that the trip was uneventful and that the Negroes had made no attempt to molest them. But the officers were not satisfied. They summoned two local doctors who found no evidence of criminal assault. But—and this was the heart of the case—the doctors found that both women had had sexual intercourse twelve or more hours previous to the time of the examination. Ruby Bates and Victoria Price admitted that they had had sexual intercourse with white men in the freight yard in Chattanooga. Still, the officers were not satisfied; nor, for that matter, were the good people of Paint Rock. They began to gather now in front of the jail and to discuss, as men will do, details of the crime. With each telling of the story, the white women's reputation for chastity and probity grew; so also did the nature and extent of the sexual atrocities allegedly committed on them.

Finding herself thus ennobled in the eyes of the public, Victoria Price changed her story, telling a harrowing tale of repeated sexual assaults. She said now that she and Ruby Bates had been sexually assaulted six times during the thirty-eight mile trip by Negroes who held long knives at their throats. Four years later, Ruby Bates said that neither she nor Victoria Price had been sexually molested; but now, as the fury of the crowd grew, she elected, for reasons of her own, to support Victoria Price's story.

The nine Scottsboro boys, one of whom was only fourteen years of age, were indicted on a charge of rape and tried in an atmosphere of mob hostility. Some ten thousand white men converged on the town to see that justice was done—and, of course, it was, according to the lights of Alabama white men. The Negro defendants were convicted, and all were sentenced to death, except the fourteen-year-old, who was given a life sentence.

At this point, a legal wrangle ensued between the NAACP and the International Labor Defense League, a Communist-dominated organization. The ILD won and began a series of appeals which kept the case in the public mind during the whole of the thirties. Left-wing agitators exploited the case, organizing mass meetings and mass appeals in cities all over the world. Negro leaders learned a great deal from what Arthur Schlesinger, Jr., called "the brilliant exploitation" of the Scottsboro case by left-wing agitators. The use of the case as a pivotal point to focus attention on all phases of bigotry was, in truth, impressive. But Negro leaders were repelled, and rightly, by the more disreputable aspects of the case, the raising of extraneous issues and the execution of incendiary acts that led many to believe that left-wingers were more interested in exploiting the case for party purposes than in saving the lives of the condemned. But beyond all that were the real and disturbing issues raised by the case. So compelling were these issues, so stark was the confrontation of white and Negro fears, that no Negro or interracial organization, however timid or cautious, could abandon the case without also forfeiting the allegiance of the Negro masses. Finally, after a great deal of wrangling, a politically neutral defense committee was organized and most of the defendants were freed.

The Scottsboro case heightened tensions between Negroes and whites; but it also accentuated schisms within the Negro group. From all sides, from the left and from the right, came demands for a shift in strategy and tactics. In the rhetoric of the Talented Tenth, it was considered a dangerous and provocative act to appeal directly to the masses. But the activists who came forward to exploit the mood of the thirties abandoned the Talented Tenth methods of polite protest and petition, calling the masses onto the stage of history and awakening them to open political struggle.

It is quite clear now, in retrospect, that the labor campaign of the thirties was decisive in the formation of new social types in the Negro community. In this decade, the CIO embarked on a scintillating campaign of conquest, breaking taboos (organizing Negro workers) and new ground (staging sit-down strikes). Negro and white workers debated issues together, circulated petitions and staged mass demonstrations. As a result, a large number of Negro workers were educated in the use of mass pressure techniques.

Equally decisive in the ascending curve of Negro protest was the Buying Power movement which started in Chicago on the lip of the Depression and leaped across the country in the thirties. Young Negro activists outside the regular organizations led the campaign which was designed to force white employers to hire Negro workers. Using direct action tactics (picketing, boycotting, demonstrations), the activists concentrated on lunch counters, dime stores, movies, newspapers, bakeries, milk companies, and public utilities. Emboldened by their success and the responsiveness of the masses, the leaders broadened the campaign which assumed the shape of a national movement. The leaders of the movement demonstrated unprecedented militancy, indicating a willingness to suffer and to serve long jail sentences. Although the movement itself was nonviolent, demonstrators were often attacked and manhandled by white bystanders and policemen.

By the mid-thirties, Negroes all over America, in Cleveland, in Los Angeles, in Richmond, were in the streets, marching, demonstrating, and demanding. The movement reached a peak in New York City where a young preacher, Adam Clayton Powell, Jr., made his entree to the public stage. Preaching the virtues of "nonviolent and direct social action," Powell moved to the forefront of the vigorous New York movement.

In a four-year campaign that touched all bases (the telephone company, the light company, the bus company, the beverage industry, the New York World's Fair, dime stores, and department stores), the New York group added some ten thousand jobs to the Harlem work force. The coordinating committee, led by Powell and William Lloyd Imes, could, it was said, pack the largest hall in Harlem in forty-eight hours. On one occasion, the New Yorkers brought Consolidated Edison to bay by threatening to call weekly "lightless Tuesdays." Another gambit, equally effective, was the threat to have three hundred thousand Negroes ask for the operator instead of dialing the telephone number.

The great restless ferment of the thirties led to a burst of organizational activity. On the national level, several groups were formed and at least one of them, the National Negro Congress, became a major competitor of the NAACP. The Congress was organized in Chicago on February 14-16, 1936, at a meeting attended by more than eight hundred delegates representing more than five hundred organizations. This meeting marked the first attempt of the Talented Tenth to organize a mass movement. What emerged from the meeting was a loosely structured federation of existing organizations, including the NAACP. Until 1940, when it foundered on the shoals of Communist penetration, the Congress made a large impress on the Negro protest. With Asa Philip Randolph, the founder-president of the Brotherhood of Sleeping Car Porters, as president, the organization established local councils in cities across the country and pursued a program based on mass pressure. In Washington and other cities, Congress councils launched bold direct-action campaigns and used mass appeals, freedom songs, and mass meetings.

Of all the groups organized in this germinal season of the Negro protest, none had more potential for good than the Southern Conference on Human Welfare. The conference was organized in Birmingham in September, 1938. Against the wishes of the sponsors, segregation was enforced at the founding meeting. But Eleanor Roosevelt, one of the main speakers, refused to observe the segregation edict, placing her chair in the center aisle between the Negro and white sections.

Dr. Frank P. Graham was the first president of the organization, which organized wide support for a bold program of economic, political, and civic democracy in the South. After 1938, the conference held unsegregated meetings in city and state auditoriums in Chattanooga and Nashville. This promising venture, the most radical ever formed by white Southerners, collapsed in the forties in the growing climate of hysteria and fear.

On the local level, too, the thirties unleashed dynamic new forces. Many of the local organizations were political in nature. Richmond's Democratic League, for example, held mass meetings and used freedom songs in a campaign of voter registration. The Third Ward Civic League of Houston was organized around the same theme: Seek Ye First the Political Kingdom.

Political salvation was also stressed by the Atlanta Civic and Political League which waged fights for equal salaries for Negro teachers and improved recreational facilities. By the mid-forties, there were scores of voters leagues in cities in the South.

Angry youth found a voice in the American Youth Congress, the American Student Union, and the Southern Negro Congress. In the latter part of the thirties, Negro and white students formed discussion groups, staged plays, interracial dinners, and interracial dances.

The Piedmont student complex, which would break out in open revolt thirty years later, was extraordinarily active in this season, and with many of the same tactics: boycotts and sit-ins. In 1936, the Student Interracial Commission of Greensboro boycotted a local theater which entered into an agreement to bar all movies portraying Negroes in other than menial roles. This period also yields perhaps the first modern sit-in. In Alexandria, Virginia, a group of young Negroes sat down in a municipal library and were arrested.

This burst of organizational activity was a direct challenge to "established" Negro leaders who had to adjust to the ground swell. The Chicago Urban League placed its facilities at the disposal of leaders of the Buying Power movement—but refused to take an active part in the campaign. A prominent official of the League told the national office in New York, "The time has come for a more aggressive attitude on the part of Negroes. We of the Chicago Urban League realize that fact, and our future programs will be far more aggressive than they have been in the past."

Face to face with a new mood in the Negro community, "established organizations" executed a tactical shift. A favorite tactic, one that recurs repeatedly in the history of the protest, was the preempting of an issue by forming an *ad hoc* organization of "respectable" leaders who entered the battle with the avowed purpose of restraining the more radical leaders. Another gambit, equally effective, was the Trojan horse technique of boring in from within and insisting on a better organized, i.e., more respectable, revolt. By a variety of tactics, some of them open and above board, some of them underhanded and devious, "established organizations" tried to prevent the revolt from overflowing channels and becoming a real revolt.

Does this sound cynical and calculating? It was not, really. Members of "established organizations" were, for the most part, honest and sincere. But they were prisoners of their own idea-system, an idea-system that placed severe limits on the tactical patterns of the Negro protest. The responses they made to the 1930 revolt were a function of caution, not cowardice. And yet, underneath all, there was a growing understanding of the seriousness of the situation and of the need to get in step with the temper of the times. More and more Negro middle-class members joined picket lines as the Depression wore on. By 1938, Drake and Cayton noted, it was respectable for the Negro elite to picket and demonstrate in the cause of civil rights.

But something more than a gesture was needed, and established organizations moved quickly to re-examine their basic premises. A second summit conference—the Amenia meeting of August 18-21, 1933—was held to plumb the thinking of the restive "New Negro" of the thirties. About thirty-five young college professors, librarians, social workers and assorted intellectuals met with the Elder Statesmen (Du Bois insisted on the capitals) of the race at Joel Spingarn's country estate. The dialogue was stimulating, to say the least. The NAACP and the Urban League were scathingly criticized by the young men who said that too much emphasis had been placed on the Talented Tenth and not enough on the Negro masses. Although the young rebels were unanimous in their condemnation of the black elite, they could not agree on a new program. The suggested approaches ranged from interracial cooperation to open revolution.

The crisis in Negro leadership reached a peak in *l'affaire* Du Bois. The acerbic professor had been thinking again—and that was always a dangerous sign. Watching the gathering clouds, musing and analyzing, Du Bois became convinced that the NAACP approach was totally ineffective. "One damned protest after another," he said, would never end Jim Crow. "By 1930," he wrote, "I had become convinced that the basic problems and ideals of the Association must be modified and changed: that . . . a mere appeal based on the old liberalism, a mere appeal to justice and further effort at legal decision, was missing the essential need."

Having decided that the NAACP was on the wrong track, Du Bois began to attack the NAACP, began, in fact, to attack himself, for he, more than anyone else, was responsible for the civil libertarian texture of the Niagara-NAACP idea. Du Bois tried first to change the political and racial coloration of the NAACP board, suggesting young radicals like E. Franklin Frazier and Abram Harris. Failing in this effort, he declared open war on the NAACP. What was worse he declared war in a series of 1934 articles in the *Crisis*, the NAACP's house organ.

The NAACP fight, Du Bois said, warming to the struggle, had proved futile. In fact, he said, there was more segregation in 1934 than there was in 1910 when the organization was founded. What then was to be done? Du Bois said that since segregation was inevitable Negroes ought to use it by organizing consumer and producer cooperatives and cultivating their political and social strength. This was, at bottom, a sophisticated form of black nationalism, a kind of Ivy League Garveyism.

The NAACP ruling elite were horrified. Joel Spingarn, Walter White and other NAACP leaders repudiated Du Bois' views in the *Crisis*, and Du Bois repudiated *them* in the *Crisis*. The whole argument became extremely bitter, and Du Bois resigned in a huff and returned to Atlanta University as a teacher. But the Pandora's box he had opened could not be so easily closed. Du Bois' attack was only one of a whole volley of anti-NAACP salvos. Segregation was, in fact, increasing; and the Negro's economic position was deteriorating. What kind of action did the NAACP intend to take?

The NAACP disarmed its critics by appointing a Committee on Future Plans and Program to prepare a revised program. The committee, under the chairmanship of Abram Harris, prepared a comprehensive statement which was approved in an amended form at the St. Louis convention of 1935. The new program called for vigorous economic action and unification of black and white workers. Among the secondary objectives were the organization of classes in workers' education, the creation of industrial and agricultural councils, and the setting up of workers' councils. Branch offices, under the new plan, were to become "centers of economic and political education."

Ralph J. Bunche, who analyzed the NAACP for the Myrdal study, said this program was never carried out. In the late thirties, Bunche said, the organization's main interests were antilynching legislation and equalization of teachers' salaries. Bunche added: "In an era in which the Negro finds himself hanging ever more precariously from the bottom rung of a national economic ladder that is itself in a condition of not too animated suspension, the association clings to its traditional faith, hope and politics." NAACP leaders, Bunche said, had "a narrow vision of leadership."

The NAACP did not move as far and as fast as its critics wanted it to—but it did move. Youth councils, as Bunche noted, were organized to curb the growing tendency of Negro youth to organize independent social action; and NAACP branches began to organize picket lines and demonstrations. Even more important was the organization of a sustained legal campaign. The association had won a series of brilliant legal victories in the fields of housing, suffrage and legal rights, but it had not scored a breakthrough. With diabolical ingeniousness, the South minimized each victory by token compliance or the enactment of additional laws which nullified court decisions.

A grant from the American Fund for Public Service enabled the association to map a long-range legal program whose importance did not become obvious until 1954. Nathan Margold, who later became United States solicitor, drew up a blueprint of sustained action. And the association, on October 26, 1934, hired Charles Houston, then vice-dean of the Howard University Law School, to direct the campaign. Houston's strategy was based on what he called "the soft underbelly" of Jim Crow—graduate schools. By filing a series of taxpayer suits attacking inequality in graduate school education, Houston planned to make Jim Crow prohibitively expensive. The campaign began in 1935 with a successful assault against the University of Maryland and picked up steam under Houston's successor, a Howard University Law School graduate named Thurgood Marshall.

In this same period, Negroes picked up powerful supporters in the white liberal establishment, which always bestirs itself when the Negro protest movement makes a dangerous turn. The history of interracial liberalism, in fact, can be traced by crises in the Negro world. The movement grew out of isolated efforts to reduce racial tensions during World War I and became a going concern during the racial crises of the twenties and thirties.

Most Negroes were openly contemptuous of the programs and policies of the interracial movement which was crisis-inspired and tended to disappear as soon as the temperature in the ghetto dropped to a "normal" level. Conflict-shy, conciliatory, and gradualistic, the movement tended to rely on the timid tactics of education, conciliation, and persuasion.

Despite serious limitations, the conciliators played a modest role in the struggle. The Southern Interracial Commission campaigned against lynching in the twenties and its effectiveness increased in the thirties with the organization of the commission-backed Association of Southern Women Against the Practice of Lynching. The commission and its affiliates brought new voices and new energy to the fight, but they were afflicted by the common liberal malady: timidity. The Association of Southern Women, for example, opposed lynching—but it also opposed laws forbidding lynching.

With the oncoming of World War II and the subsiding of the more extreme manifestations of Negro discontent, the interracial movement ebbed away. Liberals in the North and South became preoccupied with the defense posture of the United States; and Negroes, finding themselves neglected by both the government and their white friends, lurched forward with a new wave of demonstrations and boycotts.

By an odd coincidence, this campaign reached a peak in 1938, the seventy-fifth anniversary of the Emancipation Proclamation. Negro youth sponsored a series of mass marches that year in support of the Wagner–Van Nuys Anti-lynching Bill which was killed after a Southern filibuster. Chicago youth, with flaming torches, marched through the South Side, carrying signs of protest against the filibuster. In Harlem, more than one thousand youths, wearing black armbands as a sign of mourning, staged a mass rally.

By 1939, Negro discontent was straining toward new forms of expressiveness. In Chicago, in New York, in Los Angeles, Negroes were on the march. As the thirties and, as it happened, the old world, died, the wheel was turning, and men were thinking dark or, to turn the image, white thoughts. At the end of the decade, Ralph J. Bunche put down a prophetic line. "Never before," he said, "have Negroes had so much experience with picket lines, and it may be a lesson that will sink in."

III. REHEARSAL

Gandhi in Harlem

WHEN, in 1990 perhaps or the year 2000, men come to search for the truly decisive epoch in American race relations; when they try to set down, clearly and without bias, the point where the furies began to gather, where Negro and white Americans were enwebbed in a net of fate as impossible to evade, really, as death itself; when they seek the fork and the forces that sent black men and white men down different roads to a terrible confrontation, it seems likely that they will seize on the decade of the forties. For in that decade, men stopped playing. In the forties, the new departure of the thirties—direct mass action—was institutionalized and the rising tide of color forced a reopening of the national compromise of 1877. And once that door was open it could not be shut again until America had decided, once and for all, which god it served.

The grim alternatives—integration or violence, democracy or fascism—were stated starkly in a 1940 novel, *Native Son*, that was an extended metaphor of a decade of decision. By writing this important novel, by conjuring up out of the depths the menacing symbol of Bigger Thomas, Richard Wright performed an act of leadership that affected race relations as much as any act of any protest leader. For Wright's achievement lay, precisely, in this: he named the problem. And the problem, once named, was not and could not be experienced again in the same way.

What was the name of the problem?

Listen.

"Brrrrrriiiiiiiiiiiiiiiiiiinng!"

This aural image—of an alarm clock awakening Bigger Thomas and millions of his brothers—was a sign, a portent, an omen. Bigger Thomas rose from his bed of vengeance—for it was that precisely—and went out into the world and killed, quite by accident, a white woman. But he compounded the act by chopping up her body—Wright played savagely, diabolically, with the symbol of white illness, the white woman—and burning it in a furnace. Worse, Bigger took a strange pride in the deed, finding, so Wright put it, meaning and purpose in an absurd world by a total rejection of the moral and legal precepts of a society that had rejected him. Transformed by his bloody deed, feeling a terrible freedom he had never known, Bigger went on to bash in the head of his girl friend. After a mad dash across the roof tops of the South Side slums, he was cornered and brought to bay—in an incredibly prophetic touch—by barrages from water hoses.

Standing, now, within sight of the electric chair, Bigger faced up to the implications of his deed and accepted himself and what life had made him. Repelled by the religion of his mother ("That's for whipped folks") and the placebos of Negro protest leaders ("They almost like white people, when it comes to guys like me"), Bigger went to his death, rejoicing in the only thing that gave his life meaning—hate.

After all this had been set down in words, after men had become aware of the meaning of Bigger and of the pit of emotions swirling beneath the words "Negro" and "white," after the images and symbols that informed Bigger's life—fear, violence, hate, rape, blood—had become burning realities in the white and watchful streets, America was not, and never again could be, the same.

We are not concerned here with *Native Son* as literature. What holds our attention is Bigger the symbol and Wright the apostle of a new racial sensibility. Both Bigger and Wright were children of the plantation and the migration and the thirties. Wright was born in 1908 on a plantation near Natchez, Mississippi, and grew up in a nightmarish world of violence and deprivation. His father, driven to drink and ruin by the black man's burden, abandoned the family; and Wright and his mother wandered over the South, scrounging off friends and relatives. In an orphans' home, Wright learned how to curse. Begging pennies in saloons, he learned how to drink. At six, he was a foul-mouthed drunkard; at twelve, an accomplished thief. The future novelist was saved for posterity by an accidental introduction to the world of books—books that opened up a whole new world of ideas and images and sent him, at the age of seventeen, to Chicago and the dreams Chicago symbolized to the Negroes of the South. But Chicago was no Green Pastures and Wright, in despair, turned to communism, discovering, as he later related in *The God That Failed*, that the party was not heaven.

By this time, Wright was haunted by an image of revolt and revenge, an image of all the Biggers he had known—men who fought back with whatever they could lay hands on, men defined by the size of their pain and the size of their rebellion: men known, then and now, as "bad niggers." Wright saw the live models of Bigger in Mississippi and on the South Side of Chicago. "They were a wild and homeless lot," he said, "culturally lost, spiritually disinherited, candidates for the clinics, morgues, prisons, reformatories, and the electric chair. . . ."

By gathering up the fragments of the live Biggers and transmuting their lives with the alchemy of art, Wright held up a mirror to a world Negro leaders and white liberals were trying desperately to avoid. In this mirror, the white man—liberal, moderate, and racist—saw himself, and he was an oppressor. In this mirror, the Negro saw himself, and he was a victim mangled and eviscerated by complicity in his own degradation. These were unpalatable truths; and men, as usual, cursed the mirror that reflected their likeness. But it was too late for rituals of evasion. What Wright was saying—literary considerations apart—was that urbanization and industrialization had made the race problem so ominous, so personal, and so menacing that further evasion would lead to national catastrophe. To Bigger, Christian uplift and polite protest were not only futile and Philistine but dangerous.

Enter—at this precise moment—Asa Philip Randolph, a Negro activist who shared Wright's sense of urgency if not his apocalyptic imagery. Randolph, who was the third stone in the line of Negro leadership, saw the gathering storms of which Wright spoke and he tried, desperately, to change the patterns of Negro and white leadership. He failed, it is true, but through him new elements of meaning entered into the Negro-white dialogue.

Randolph was something new in the history of Negro leadership—a man with a sense of history, a broad understanding of pressure and power, and a total commitment to broad ends involving the Negro masses. A tall man, lean and bronze, with a deep vibrant voice and a fondness for Shakespeare, Randolph was, in the words of Roi Ottley, "all soul." What was also true, and more to the point, was that he was all commitment. And his sense of commitment stemmed from a total immersion in the sociography of Negro-white conflict. He was born in 1889 in Crescent City, Florida, the son of an AME minister. He was six when Booker T. Washington went to Atlanta to bless appeasement; and he was twelve when Trotter called for a remembrance of the abolitionist past. As a boy, Randolph drank deep draughts of black defiance. "Dad was a mighty Republican propagandist," Randolph recalled. "The Reconstruction era was over, but Dad talked forever of the great days when Negro Republicans had served in the Congress and the U.S. Senate. They were very much alive in his mind. At the same time he was close to being a black nationalist. Jesus Christ was not white, he would tell us. God is not white, angels have no color. God has none. We were steeped in the concept that race was no basic distinction. What mattered was merit, quality, worth."

What mattered, above all, was resistance. Randolph's boyhood idol was Henry McNeal Turner, the fiery AME bishop whom Du Bois called "one of the last of the mighty men." Turner believed that the Lord helped those who helped themselves, and two guns were a part of his ecclesiastical regalia. On one occasion, as a brown boy stood wide-eyed in amazement, the bishop parted his robes and checked the firing mechanism on his pistols, saying: "My life depends upon the will of God and these guns." It was an image, this, and Asa Philip Randolph never forgot it. Violence was not then and never would be his way—but defiance was.

Leaving the South, going with the other black migrants to the North, Randolph became a Harlem agitator. On soapboxes and street corners, he called for Negro and white unity and deprecated the program and policies of the Talented Tenth. With Chandler Owens, he founded the *Messenger*, "the only radical magazine in America." Randolph spoke out sharply against Negro involvement in the first war for freedom and spent several hours in a Cleveland jail. After the war, he founded and forced company recognition of the Brotherhood of Sleeping Car Porters. With the union as his base of power, he ranged out as an articulate advocate of a new departure. In the thirties, he was elected president of the National Negro Congress. He was at this juncture a socialist, but he loathed Communists; and he broke with the Congress in 1940, charging Communist infiltration.

As World War II neared and as Negro degradation increased, Randolph became convinced that new and different tactics were needed. Although defense industries were crying for labor, Negro unemployment was still at depression level. Defense industries, almost without exception, made it clear that Negro workers were not wanted. Some plants, in fact, welcomed all workers, "except Germans, Italians, and Negroes." Worse, infinitely worse, was the aura of bigotry surrounding preparations for an all-out war against racism. Although a Negro—Charles Drew—was primarily responsible for perfecting the blood bank technique, the Red Cross refused, at first, to accept Negro blood. And when Negro blood was finally accepted, it was segregated. Separatism also bloomed in the armed services. Negroes were barred from the Air Corps, the Marines and other branches of the service.

It was World War I all over again, but with a difference: neither the Negro nor the world was the same. Left to their own devices, deserted by white liberals, sensing another betrayal in the making, Negro Americans became bellicose and belligerent. "Established organizations" bestirred themselves, holding conferences and days of prayer and appeal. The NAACP organized a nationwide day of picketing of defense installations, and the National Urban League sponsored a national radio appeal. But something more substantial than appeals was needed. George S. Schuyler, the tart-tongued journalist said: "The masses of Negroes are getting fed up on these frauds." Schuyler called for an organization that "would have worked out some technique for fighting other than sending letters and telegrams of protest."

Asa Randolph's mind was running in the same groove. He had never placed great store in the traditional techniques of protest. The only thing that stayed power, he believed, was power. "Politicians only move when you move them."

More than any other leader in Negro history, more even than the leonine Douglass and the erudite Du Bois, Randolph focused on the aorta: power. He was interested in what power could do. He was interested, above all, in the only instrument of power available to a Negro leader, an instrument that, strangely enough, every major leader had avoided like a plague, the unpredictable instrument, the potentially explosive instrument: the Negro masses.

One day in 1940, Randolph left New York City and headed South on a speaking tour. As the train rolled across the Virginia countryside, where his forebears had served as slaves, Randolph brooded over the failure of the politics of talk. His mind went back to his father and to Henry McNeal Turner and to all the other men and women who had suffered and died while men talked. And, of a sudden, an idea—stunning and frightening in its simplicity—rose in his mind. Randolph turned to his traveling companion, Milton Webster, vice-president of the Brotherhood of Sleeping Car Porters, and made an incredible suggestion.

"I think," he said in his measured Oxford accent, "we ought to get 10,000 Negroes and march down Pennsylvania Avenue asking for jobs in defense plants and integration of the armed forces. It would shake up Washington."

Indeed, it would. "But where," Webster asked, "are you going to get 10,000 Negroes?"

Randolph could not be bothered by details. He was possessed now by the beauty of the idea and in his mind's eye he heard the sound of black feet tramping in front of the White House.

"I think," Webster recalled later, "the first place where Brother Randolph and I talked March on Washington was in Savannah, Georgia. The head colored man in town opened up the meeting, introduced me, and ran off the platform to the last seat in the row. It scared everybody to death."

And yet, underneath the fear, there was a strange fascination. Men turned away from the thing in dread; but they crept back, time and again, fascinated. No matter. Randolph went back to Harlem to the Brotherhood headquarters on the third floor of a building that housed beauty salons and dancing schools; and there, in the midst of the agony and the joy of Negro living, he started the wheels to rolling, conferring with "established Negro leaders" (Walter White, Mary McLeod Bethune, Lester Granger and others), winning either their silence or their consent. He then organized a national organization, using union outlets in various cities as a base. On May 1, 1941, he issued a dramatic call, urging ten thousand Negroes to prepare for a black invasion of Washington on July 1.

> Dear fellow Negro-Americans, be not dismayed in these terrible times. You possess power, great power. Our problem is to hitch it up for action on the broadest, daring and most gigantic scale.
>
> In this period of power politics, nothing counts but pressure, more pressure, and still more pressure through the tactic and strategy of broad, organized, aggressive mass action behind the vital and important issues of the Negro. To this end we propose that ten thousand Negroes MARCH ON WASHINGTON FOR JOBS IN NATIONAL DEFENSE AND EQUAL INTEGRATION IN THE FIGHTING FORCES OF THE UNITED STATES.
>
> An all-out thundering march on Washington, end-

ing in a monster and huge demonstration at Lincoln's Monument will shake up white America.

It will shake up official Washington. . . . It will gain respect for the Negro people. . . . It will create a new sense of self-respect among Negroes. . . . MASS POWER CAN CAUSE PRESIDENT ROOSEVELT TO ISSUE AN EXECUTIVE ORDER ABOLISHING DISCRIMINATION in all Government Departments, Army, Navy, Air Corps and National Defense jobs.

The Negro press, which had been cool to Randolph and his idea, warmed now to the struggle, printing big headlines of defiance. And the white press? The white press was wary, silent. But white men of power were watching, and Randolph knew it. Savagely, now, Randolph increased the pressure, calling a series of mammoth mass meetings across the country, coolly, shrewdly upping his estimate of the expected crowd with each new press release.

Now the white power structure began to move. But, and this is typical, no one said anything to Randolph. The moves were tangential, peripheral, seemingly unrelated to the pressure building up in the ghetto. On April 11, Sidney Hillman of the Office of Production Management urged defense plants to hire Negro workers. President Roosevelt followed this up with a personal letter to government agencies.

Randolph, smelling blood, so to speak, upped the ante, announcing almost total support from the Negro community. It was a naked war of nerves, but it was something else: Randolph was deadly serious. And when this became crystal clear, Randolph, along with Walter White, was summoned to a meeting in New York City Hall. At this meeting, Mayor Fiorello La Guardia, Mrs. Eleanor Roosevelt and other liberals urged Randolph to call off the March. It was unwise, they said, imprudent, and dangerous. Mrs. Roosevelt expressed deep concern over the plight of Negroes and promised to speak to the President about it. But a march, she said, was the wrong approach; it would do more harm than good. Randolph, measuring his old friends, said he was sure that the March would do some good. In fact, he said coolly, "it has already done some good; for if you were not concerned about it you wouldn't be here now. . . ." This was truth, stark, naked truth; and the liberals adopted another tack. Mrs. Roosevelt expressed concern over the personal inconveniences such a march would entail. The marchers, of course, would not be able to find

places to sleep and eat in the rigidly segregated capital. Ran
dolph answered—with steel in his voice now—that the demonstrators would march into hotels and restaurants and demand
service.

It does not take a great deal of time to get from Manhattan
to Harlem; but when Randolph returned to his Harlem office,
a telegram was awaiting him. High officials wanted him to
come to Washington "for a conference on your project."

On Wednesday, June 18, Randolph, Walter White, and T.
Arnold Hill of the National Urban League, were ushered into
the presence of Franklin Delano Roosevelt. The President sat
at his desk, flanked by the Secretary of War, the Secretary of
the Navy and other high officials.

"Hello, Phil," the President beamed, exuding his famous
charm. Putting his guests at ease, the President embarked on a
favorite stratagem, a long and amiable filibuster filled with
anecdotes and amusing stories. But Randolph was neither flat
tered nor amused.

"Mr. President," he said, cutting into an anecdote, "time is
running on. You are busy. We want specifically to talk to you
about the problem of jobs for Negroes in defense industries
Our people are being turned away at factory gates because
they are colored. They can't live with this thing. What are you
going to do about it?"

"Now you're quite right, Phil," the President replied. "And
I'm going to do something about it. Call off this march of yours
and we'll do something. Questions like this have sociological
implications. They can't be gotten at with hammers and tongs.
They can't be settled with marches."

Neither, Randolph said, in so many words, could they be settled with good intentions. The President looked at Randolph,
measuring him. How many people, he asked, will march? Randolph, without blinking an eye, said one hundred thousand
The President looked at Walter White and repeated the question. Walter White said one hundred thousand. Neither White
nor Randolph knew for sure; nobody would ever know It has
been suggested that Randolph was bluffing. If so, the bluff was
brilliantly successful.

The President was genuinely alarmed

"We cannot have a march on Washington," he said "We
must approach this problem in an analytical way "

"Then, Mr. President," Randolph replied, "something will
have to be done and done at once."

"Something will be done, but there must be no public pres
sure on the White House."

"Mr. President," Asa Philip Randolph said, his rich voice booming, *"something must be done now!"*

And something was done, almost immediately. Seven days later, President Roosevelt issued Executive Order No. 8802, establishing thereby a wartime Fair Employment Committee. And Randolph, carrying out his part of the bargain, went on the air and "postponed" the March, an act that did not please some of his followers. The young activists of the youth division —a young man named Bayard Rustin among them—condemned the postponement, and Randolph used the occasion to lecture his followers on the tactics of a mass pressure movement. Let us note five themes:

1) *Objectives must be concrete and specific.*

In the first place, the purpose of the march was specific, and not general. It was to secure an Executive Order from the President of the United States abolishing discriminations in national defense . . . [and] in the Federal departments of the Government.

2) *Objectives must be simple and vital.*

These were objectives that the people could understand, visualize, and feel. These objectives were developed in harmony with sound mass psychology; namely, that the people cannot struggle for an omnibus program with a multiplicity of aims, but must have one central and vital issue around which to rally. . . .

3) *Leaders must be flexible and tactically mobile.*

The strike vote is the positive, tangible expression of the will of the workers to strike if their demands are not complied with. However, the workers know, and so does the union, that all their demands will never be complied with. Therefore, when—as a result of negotiation and conference—the chief aims of the organization of the workers are realized, the proposed strike is called off.

This does not mean that another strike may not be proposed and scheduled.

4) *Mass movements must avoid romanticism.*

The Negro masses who want jobs now would have hurled curses upon the heads of the leaders of the Negro March-on-Washington Movement if they had sacrificed an immediate and practical opportunity to secure employment opportunities for Negro masses in defense industries in order to satisfy a handful of Negro youth who apparently were more interested in the drama and pyrotechnics of the march than in the basic and main issues of putting Negroes to work.

5) *Idealism is no program.*

It would seem to me that your first function as a serious group, devoted to the cause of the Negro masses, was to actually mobilize the youth of the country—at least of Harlem. This you never did. You were more articulate about what you hoped to do than what you actually did. It is a grave question in my mind whether the youth division would have actually mobilized 25 youths to go to Washington. There is no tangible evidence to the contrary.

In this letter, and in his vision of battle for the March, Randolph's fundamental traits as a leader emerged—boldness of conception, largeness of view, determination, and pragmatic shrewdness. It was said then that he lacked the administrative sensibility which is so dear to Negro militants and white liberals. But administration is one thing, and leadership is another. Administrative skills of the kind admired by Negro bureaucrats —attention to detail and paper work, the care and feeding of white liberal allies, etc.—would not have produced the great breakthrough of the first Presidential Executive Order on race relations since the Emancipation Proclamation.

Despite the opposition and/or silence of many Negro men of power, Randolph raised, almost singlehandedly, a new issue; and he focused the Negro's mind on a new technique and a new vision. Up to that moment, the dominant issues in Negro life were poll tax legislation, antilynching legislation, "separate-but-equal" school facilities and the white primary. Now, FEPC became the dominant myth, displacing other symbols and cares.

Although the wartime Fair Employment Committee did not accomplish a great deal, it was a point of focus which changed the climate of race relations and the vision of Negro leadership. Here now, for the first time since Reconstruction, was a decisive act by the federal government on behalf of Negro citizens. And hereafter Negro strategy would be based, implicitly or explicitly, on the necessity for decisive intervention by the federal government. It would be based, too, on the need for unrelenting pressure on the government. Roy Wilkins noted that the issuance of the Executive Order "was forced on the administration by the March-on-Washington crusaders, proving once more that we get more when we yell than we do when we plead."

So it seemed to many. When the shooting war began without any appreciable change in the situation of Negroes, yelling became a habit in the ghetto. Continued discrimination in defense plants, riots and revolts in army camps, and increased tension over housing and employment in Northern cities pushed Negro America to the edge of open revolt. Some Negroes like pacifist Bayard Rustin served prison sentences as conscientious objectors. Others like Lewis Jones refused to serve in a segregated army. Still others like Elijah Muhammad and his Muslim followers refused to fight for a segregated country.

Most Negroes backed the war effort, but they were clearly in a conditional mood. There was widespread apathy, cynicism, and demoralization in the rigidly segregated armed forces; and a Negro, in a letter to the *Raleigh News and Observer*, told America that time was running out. "This is very likely to be the last war," he wrote, "that the white man will be able to lead humanity to wage for plausible platitudes." More graphic was the epitaph a Negro soldier suggested for his tombstone: "Here lies a black man killed fighting a yellow man for the protection of a white man."

A measure of the wartime mood, and a thermometer of Negro despair, was the Sojourner Truth Housing Project riots in Detroit. When, in 1942, armed white men attempted to prevent Negro occupancy of a federal housing project bearing the name of the great Negro woman leader, Detroit was pushed to the edge of open war.

Negro leaders in Detroit and other cities said frankly that they no longer understood the Negro masses. Dr. J. S. Nathaniel Tress, a Charlotte, North Carolina, leader, said: "I am afraid for my people. They have grown restless. They are not happy. They no longer laugh. There is a new feeling among them—something strange, perhaps terrible."

It was obvious to millions of white Americans that something strange and terrible was moving behind the Negro mask. The implications of this thing that nobody dared to name were shrewdly weighed in an editorial in a New York newspaper, *PM*. "At no time in American history has the Negro enjoyed so much liberty as he does today. At no time has the Negro been so conscious and so resentful of the injustices and indignities still imposed upon him. Unless Americans understand this paradox and *act upon it quickly* the all-out war drive may be gravely handicapped."

Propelled by the imperative mood of the Negro community and the charismatic challenge of Asa Philip Randolph, "established organizations" shifted tactically. The NAACP sponsored direct-action thrusts (mass marches for integrated army divisions, picketing of defense plants) and adopted a tougher, more polemical posture. As a result, NAACP membership rose sharply. By 1945, the organization had some five hundred thousand members, as compared with the 1940 membership of sixty-five thousand.

Walter White, the blond, blue-eyed executive secretary of the association, emerged in this period as a talented advocate and a superb lobbyist. He succeeded, at least during the war period, in transcending the narrow limits of the protest tradition.

White was an interesting figure—colorful, dramatic, energetic. The fair-skinned son of a fair-skinned postman, he was born in 1891 in Atlanta and raised in comfortable circumstances. After a brief career as an insurance man, he joined the NAACP in 1918. The young NAACP worker attracted national attention with a series of articles on lynching. Bold and courageous, he "passed" as a white man and uncovered facts which were unavailable to Negro investigators. On at least one occasion, this stratagem backfired. A white mob, forewarned, awaited his arrival with some interest. When White arrived, a local Negro flashed him a warning. White retreated immediately, catching the train just as it was pulling out. A conductor said it was a shame that he had to leave so soon, "There's a damned yellow nigger down here passing for white and the boys are going to get him." White said that he hated to miss "the fun," but business had to come before pleasure.

A cool customer, White—cool, confident, and ambitious, never at a loss for a ready retort or a revealing fact. These qualities helped White survive white mobs and a series of internal NAACP wars with W. E. B. Du Bois who did not, to put it mildly, like White. When James Weldon Johnson resigned in 1930, White became acting secretary and assumed full control the next year. But the NAACP secretaryship does not, as White soon learned, make one a leader. It carries with it the possibilities of leadership. But the office itself, like the office of executive director of the Urban League, is a clerkship—and clerkship, as Richard Neustadt pointed out in quite another connection, is not leadership. But clerkship, for all that, is important, at least negatively. By carrying out the duties of his clerkship, an NAACP executive plays a modest, but nonetheless important, role in racial affairs. If he has no talent for making things happen, he can, at the very least, stop things from happening. But something more is required—as Garvey reminded White's predecessor, James Weldon Johnson, and as King reminded White's successor, Roy Wilkins, and as Randolph reminded White himself—for creative leadership. White succeeded by great dexterity in surviving his temporary eclipse by Randolph. By the late forties, he was one of the most important Negroes alive. It is true that he did not alter in any fundamental way the tactics and strategy of the NAACP; it is true that he, like his predecessors and his successor, had no answer, outside lobbying and litigation, to the question: what can the average Negro do now? But he did expand NAACP influence, creating a Washington office and youth and church divisions. He also carried out his clerkship with unprecedented flair, distinguishing himself in the process as probably the best lobbyist Negro America has produced. It can also be said, I think, that White demonstrated great agility in the forties by moving the NAACP structure in the direction of the dominant, direct-action trend. But this, as it turned out, was a temporary stratagem and not a long-term shift in strategy.

White has been criticized severely for alleged shallowness and dilettantism. In a brilliant essay, "Negroes in Gray Flannel Suits," Lillian Smith argued that White's approach, and the NAACP's approach, was shallow and socially naïve. There was truth in this, but it was not the whole truth. White was an uncomplicated, middle-class American type. He was a gregarious man who loved good food, old wine, and the company of important white people. If, as his critics contend, White occasionally confused the state of social justice with the number of important white people he could call by their first names, he did see clearly the perils of gradualism. He also played an important role in popularizing the basic NAACP legal shift from an attack on "separate-but-equal" facilities to an attack on segregation per se.

In this season, the Negro press was also very active, making the slogan, "Victory at Home and Abroad," a part of the mental equipment of almost every Negro. So insistent were Negro newspapers that the government considered and rejected pleas for the arrest and incarceration of Negro editors.

As a result of the unrelenting pressure of Negroes of every creed and class, America began a slow retreat from the bastion of white supremacy. Negroes were accepted into the Air Force, Marines, and WAACS. Segregated officer candidate schools were abolished; and, as a direct result of the brilliance of a Nazi General, Negroes fought with white men in combat units to roll back the bulge.

If Negroes were growing more set in their determination, the wrath of white racists was also rising. There was virtual panic in some areas of the South, and some white journalists and businessmen said that if winning the war meant Negro equality then they preferred to lose the war.

The world was changing—brown men and black men were pushing their heads up above the water—and white men, feeling themselves watched, observed, and judged, were afraid. That feeling came out in a resolution of the South Carolina House of Representatives:

"We reaffirm our belief in and our allegiance to established white supremacy as now prevailing in the South and we solemnly pledge our lives and our sacred honor to maintaining it. Insofar as racial relations are concerned, we firmly and unequivocally demand that henceforth the damned agitators of the North leave the South alone."

It came out in the anguished plea of a Mississippi Democrat who asked Northern Democrats to kill FEPC. "I come to you as an American asking you as another American, for God's sake to help us."

There was an hysterical note in this, and this hysteria doomed white liberalism. Walter White noted presciently in 1942 that "the highest casualty of the war to date" was white liberalism in the South. Before Pearl Harbor, interracial dinners, interracial meetings, and interracial dances were not uncommon in the South. Men, at that point, did not take their lives into their hands when they spoke out in favor of racial equality. As late as 1944, it was possible for Senator Lister Hill of Alabama to vote for an FEPC appropriation. And as late as 1946, the North Carolina Baptist Convention endorsed (and quickly reconsidered) FEPC.

Now all this changed markedly. The South became a closed society which did not tolerate dissent. Ralph McGill, who later broke away from the Southern tradition, fulminated in this age against the NAACP and federal intervention. The Atlanta editor opposed the poll tax, but cheered a Southern filibuster against the poll tax because, as he put it, "the motives behind the bill are probably the most sordid and hypocritical ever introduced into the Senate chamber."

With hysteria mounting in the South and fear spreading in the North, America faced a national crisis. "Nearer and Nearer the Precipice," was the summation of a "liberal" Southern writer in the *Atlantic Monthly*.

How does America meet a racial crisis?

By insisting, first of all, that a crisis does not exist; by insisting, secondly, that Negro leaders join in this petty deceit. Failing in both these two tactics, America falls back to a strategy of talk—of promises, of reports, of conferences, of surveys—

and a strategy of mirages, of token appointments of token Negroes. If these stratagems fail to take the force out of the approaching hurricane, America makes a concession in form, taking care to emasculate even the form in application.

These archetypal responses were tried in the forties and, inexplicably, all of them failed. Men who took the trouble to inquire discovered a disquieting fact: Pearl Harbor had killed or, at least, had seriously wounded Uncle Tom. It had been possible, before Pearl Harbor, to get Negro leaders to denounce malcontents. Now they not only refused to denounce "agitators"; they said, with disturbing unanimity, that the "agitators" were telling the truth. When Negro leaders were summoned to the Office of Facts and Figures, they astounded official Washington by declaring, to a man, that Negro morale could not be improved unless the Negro condition were improved. There was a similar failure of the old tactic of co-optation—appointing a Negro to a symbolic but powerless position. William Henry Hastie was named civilian assistant to the Secretary of War, but he resigned, in an unprecedented act, and denounced discrimination in the armed forces.

It was the same old ball game on the same diamond with the same two teams—but the men in dark skins were playing by a new set of rules. To make things even more vexing, Randolph chose this moment to introduce a foreign variation—Gandhism. Sensing the mood of the people, he called for a national campaign based on "nonviolent goodwill direct action." "The American Gandhi," as newspapers called him, proposed school, streetcar and bus boycotts, mass marches on city halls and the White House, and the maintenance of a picket line around the White House "until the country and the world recognizes the Negro has become of age and will sacrifice his all to be counted as men, free men."

Gandhism was not an entirely new development in the ghetto. In the early twenties, when Gandhi began his nonviolent resistance campaign in India, hearts picked up and men said, why not here? E. Franklin Frazier, an angry young man of the day, examined the matter at some length in the *Crisis* and counselled against Gandhism. There would be a "blood bath," he said, if a Gandhi arose to lead Negroes. As for loving one's enemies, Frazier said he was "primarily interested in saving the Negro's self-respect," adding: "If the masses of Negroes can save their self-respect and remain free of hate, so much the better for their moral development. . . . I believe it would be better for the Negro's soul to be seared with hate than dwarfed by self-abasement." All in all, Frazier concluded, nonviolence was neither practical nor expedient. He did not believe in "wholesale violence," but he was convinced that "violent defense in local and specific instances has made white men hesitate to make wanton attacks upon Negroes."

This did not end the speculation which continued throughout the thirties. During this decade, bands of black men made pilgrimages to the brown man of India. Howard Thurman, then dean of the Howard University chapel, was the leader of a group of American Negroes who were told by Gandhi that perhaps it would be through the American Negro that the principle of nonviolence would enter the world. It was at least a possibility, and Adam Clayton Powell, Jr. and other activists kept the option open during the thirties. More persuasive perhaps than either Gandhi or the Sermon on the Mount was the success of John L. Lewis with his blitzkrieg series of sitdown strikes in 1937.

Randolph, watching and weighing the mood of the people, fused the indigenous tactics of the labor movement and the ideology of Gandhi. In 1942 and 1943, he succeeded in creating the first American nonviolent movement and the first Negro mass movement that was not based on black nationalism. His March on Washington movement had fire in it; it moved, pulling people along on a surging tide of discontent and defiance. Local branches, based on his union outlets, were organized in Northern and Southern cities. In the summer of 1942, Randolph staged a series of mass meetings of a size and intensity unparalleled in the history of the Negro resistance movement.

"The power of the new movement is mysterious," Edwin Embree wrote. "It has almost no organization, no big machine for promotion and publicity. Yet it grips the people's imagination and holds their loyalty. Masses of the darker common people are looking to Randolph as the Modern Messiah."

All this was of vast importance in the political education of Negroes. For the first time, the Negro masses participated in a social crusade. Hundreds of thousands of lower-income Negroes came to social maturity in the feverish days of Randolph's crusade.

By 1942, Randolph was at the zenith of his power, and men were hailing him as "the mightiest man since Frederick Douglass." But there were doubters and scoffers. "Established Negro organizations" were horrified, privately, by Randolph's reliance on combat tactics—picket lines and mass demonstrations. And some noted—and this was the heart of the matter

—that the March on Washington movement did very little marching.

White liberals, as usual, agreed with Randolph's goals but not his methods. Liberals, moreover, were mortally offended, or so they said, by the exclusion of whites, as a matter of policy, from the March on Washington movement.

Randolph united his detractors by a bold 1943 call for a national civil disobedience movement. The *Pittsburgh Courier* said:

> A. Philip Randolph is guilty of the most dangerous demagoguery on record.
>
> The "March on Washington" plan was bad enough, but alongside a call to civil disobedience, it seems quite sane.
>
> For a stated period Mr. Randolph is suggesting that colored citizens disobey all Jim Crow laws as a demonstration of their dissatisfaction with them (and presumably he is prepared to lead the way) but there is to be no violence!

The *Courier* went on to say that such a campaign would "offer irresponsible and vicious elements an excuse for slaughtering thousands of colored citizens." The *Courier* did not doubt that Negroes would remain nonviolent, but pointed out that whites would certainly use violence.

Randolph struck back, calling his detractors "petty black bourgeoisie" who wanted "results without risks, achievement without action." The MOWM planned, he said, to hold nonviolent institutes to train Negroes in the techniques of Gandhian nonviolence.

As for mass action, he said: "The immediate, positive and direct value of mass action pressure consists of two things: one, it places human beings in physical motion which can be felt, seen and heard. Nothing stirs and shapes public sentiment like physical action. Organized labor and organized capital have long since recognized this. This is why the major weapon of labor is the STRIKE. It is why the major weapon of business is the Lock-out and the Shut-down. All people feel, think and talk about a physical formation of people, whoever they may be. This is why wars grip the imagination of man. Mass demonstrations against Jim Crow are worth a million editorials and orations in anybody's paper and on any platform. Editorials and orations are only worthwhile and effective when they are built around some actual human struggle for specific social and racial rights and against definitive wrongs.

"Mass social pressure in the form of marches and picketing will not only touch and arrest the attention of the powerful public officials but also the little man in the street. And, before this problem of Jim Crow can be successfully attacked, all of America must be shocked and awakened. This has never been done, except by race riots that are dangerous socio-racial explosions. Moreover, mass efforts are a form of struggle for Negro rights in which all Negroes can participate, including the educated and the so-called uneducated, the rich and the poor. It is a technique and strategy which the 'little Negro' in the tavern, pool-room, on the streets, jitterbugs, store-front preacher, and sharecropper, can use to help free the race."

As for white participation, Randolph said: "Now, the March on Washington Movement is an all Negro movement, but it is not anti-white, anti-American, anti-labor, anti-Catholic or anti-Semitic. It's simply pro-Negro. It does not rest so much upon race as upon the social problem of Jim Crow. It does not oppose interracial organizations. It cooperates with such mixed organizations as the National Association for the Advancement of Colored People and the National Urban League, and churches, and trade unions. Its validity lies in the fact that no one will fight as hard to remove and relieve pain as he who suffers from it."

Speaking thus, of pain and petitions and physical action, Randolph gave notice that a civil disobedience campaign was imminent. No one knows what would have happened had Randolph continued with his plans. For at that juncture the pain bubbled to the surface and America was face to face with that which informs all race relations discussions: miniature civil wars. There were riots in the summer of 1943 in Harlem, Mobile, Los Angeles, and Beaumont (Texas). The most tragic event of that summer, and in some ways the most tragic event of the decade, was Detroit's "Black Pearl Harbor" of June 20. Thirty-four persons were killed and more than one thousand were injured in rioting which raged until federal troops were called out.

The riotous summer of 1943 was a basic turning point in the Negro-white dialogue. The riots of that year illuminated the outstanding debts and the outstanding hatreds. Fearful of similar explosions, cities all over America "discovered" the race problem. By 1945, more than four hundred committees, official and unofficial, had been established by American communities. Most of these committees accomplished nothing; many, in fact, closed shop after the danger of widespread rioting passed.

After the riot season of 1943, the great tide of revolt
subsided and Negro leaders, finding themselves on exposed
beaches in ridiculous poses, retreated to islands of petition.
Hopes of changing the world by direct assault dwindled, and
men looked to God—or Thurgood Marshall—for surcease.
The 1943 March on Washington Convention "deferred" action
on the proposed civil disobedience movement and "postponed"
the March on Washington.

The great crusade was over.

The crusade failed for many reasons—the failure to develop
a stable following, the hostility of Negro and white men of
power, bad timing, bad luck. All these played a part. So also
did Randolph. By failing to produce ("Success," the cynical
French say, "hides many errors"), by failing to stage a march
or, failing in that, to get arrested, Randolph probably dimmed
the ardor of his following. Moreover, as some of his followers
later admitted, it was a mistake to call for a national civil disobedience movement without adequate local preparation.
Randolph, unlike King, started at the top with a call for a national movement. But it is significant that King has not yet
reached the point where Randolph started.

Although the crusade failed, it was not without a certain
significance. "No daring," Rene Crevel said once, "is fatal."
What is also true is that no daring goes unnoticed by the
young. Seeds were sown in this season—a Bayard Rustin
in New York City, an Ed Nixon in Montgomery—that would
bear fruit before the game had run its course. And a structure
—the Congress of Racial Equality—was organized to sustain
the spirit of the forties.

CORE, as the Congress is called, grew out of a memorandum, "Provisional Plans for Brotherhood Mobilization,"
prepared by James Farmer, a young graduate of Wiley College and Howard University, on February 19, 1942. The
Farmer memorandum envisioned a national movement based
on the Gandhian tactics of direct, nonviolent action. But
Farmer warned against "an uncritical duplication of the Gandhian steps in organization and execution." He suggested a
five-year or ten-year plan, "after which, it is to be hoped, re-
lentless noncooperation, economic boycott, civil disobedience,
et cetera, will be thrown into swing wherever and whenever
necessary."

Farmer miscalculated by ten years. National CORE, an
interracial organization using sit-ins and picket-line tactics,

was organized in 1943. By 1953, the end of Farmer's first ten-year plan, CORE was a paper tiger with a token staff. But ten years later, CORE and Gandhi and "et cetera" were a part of the American language and the Negro mind.

Nobody could foresee that development in 1943. The "riot season" served to consolidate the position of militants and moderates. "Established organization" emerged from the shadow of the crusade and resumed control of events with Randolph as an ally. At this juncture, the civil rights movement entered an interesting phase, which continues today, of *ad hoc* coalition building. Instead of expanding vertically by sending roots down into the Negro masses, Negro leadership decided to expand horizontally by allying with labor, religious, and civil libertarian groups whose roots, on the race issue anyway, were shallow indeed. The first fruit of this development was the National Council for a Permanent FEPC, co-chaired by Randolph and Allen Knight Chalmers, a Congregational minister and professor. The committee did not succeed in attempts to push an FEPC bill through Congress, but local units, some of them autonomous, were successful in drives for state and municipal bills.

One of the important byproducts of this movement was the engagement of the energies of the Negro church. Until the middle forties, the Negro church was a major accommodating and accommodative instrument in the Negro community. Run by cautious, conservative men who looked for salvation "up yonder," the church held itself aloof from the social struggle. In an exhaustive study, B. E. Mays and J. W. Nicholson noted in 1932 that "the church's program, except in rare instances, is static, non-progressive, and fails to challenge the loyalty of many of the most critically-minded Negroes. . . ."

The FEPC struggle gave the Negro church an opportunity to redeem the pledges of Richard Allen and the pioneer Negro preachers; and sensitive men seized the opportunity, traveling to Washington to buttonhole congressmen and senators, and sponsoring rallies and mass meetings in their sanctuaries. In 1944, the Fraternal Council of Negro Churches gathered in Washington in response to a "mandate issued by the Negro people calling upon the church to present their cause to our Government and its lawmakers." It was noted that "this was the first time in Negro Church History that such a legislative project was initiated by the Church and it represented a distinct departure from traditional ecclesiastical procedure."

The reverend lobbyists were no more successful than their secular brothers. Although they learned something about life and politics in the FEPC movement, they were not yet, as Louis C. Kesselman noted, "politically emancipated." They were not fully committed; they were "unwilling to take steps to advance the FEPC movement if it meant the assumption of risks or interference with their own church activities." And it was becoming clear, hour by hour, that risks and total engagement were necessary for a meaningful assault on the barriers of Jim Crow.

The postwar world ushered in a new period of reaction and fear. Congress was dominated by a loose coalition of Southern Democrats and Northern conservatives, most of them Republicans, who chipped away steadily at New Deal social and economic gains. Worse, a climate of fear was moving over the Western world in the wake of communist gains in Europe and Asia.

This was a time of disillusionment and defeat for Negro Americans, of riots in Columbia, Tennessee, Athens, Alabama, and Chicago, Illinois, of isolated attacks on Negro veterans in the Black Belt areas of the South. They were singing, in these years, "When the Lights Go On Again All Over the World"—and only the Negro seemed to remember that the lights had not shone now in Mississippi for more than one hundred years.

Richard Wright packed his bags and went to Paris, saying goodbye forever to America. W. E. B. Du Bois, back at the NAACP with a vague title, began his migration to the left; and Paul Robeson, huge, black, and eloquent, moved, voice and baggage, into the left-wing camp. Asa Philip Randolph, sensing what he called a tide of reaction, called for the establishment of a third party.

A chilling barometer of Negro despair was an absolutely astounding act by the conciliatory NAACP. On October 23, 1947, the NAACP filed "An Appeal to the World" with the United Nations and asked that august body to intervene in America's domestic affairs on behalf of a suffering and oppressed minority.

What this all meant—the NAACP petition, Wright, Randolph, Robeson, and Du Bois—was that the pain was becoming unendurable, and that some men were willing to bet their careers, their honor, their very lives on human grandeur. And once that point was reached, as Myrdal pointed out obliquely in 1944, somebody had to do something.

There were men in America who knew this. They knew the

war had internationalized the color problem and that the coming struggle for power between Russia and America made some concession to Negroes and Equality absolutely necessary. There were, to repeat, some men who knew this. But what they did was entirely disproportionate to the amount of cramp and pain Negroes felt. President Harry Truman appointed a Civil Rights Commission which brought in a long and admirable report. The report was glowingly eulogized in the press, filed, and forgotten.

But men were waiting and watching; among them, Asa Philip Randolph. For the second time now, Randolph raised a new issue, thereby illustrating the duty of a leader to educate the masses, both Negro and white, by forcing them to confront new elements in a changing situation. In the latter part of 1947, Randolph began to agitate for an integrated armed forces. When President Truman called for a peacetime draft, Randolph acted. To the consternation of millions of Americans—Negroes and whites—Randolph announced that he would lead a civil disobedience movement against the draft. With Bayard Rustin and other young activists, Randolph established the League for Nonviolent Civil Disobedience Against Military Segregation. The league's objective was a Presidential executive order against segregation in the armed forces.

President Truman called Randolph and other Negro leaders to the White House. But Randolph was bargaining from a position of strength and he and Truman knew it. The conference was amiable until Randolph said that his travels across the country had convinced him that "Negroes are sick and tired of being asked to shoulder guns in defense of democracy abroad until they get some at home. They are prepared to resort to civil disobedience and refusal to register for the draft if it means serving in a Jim Crow Army."

Truman flushed and said heatedly, "I wish you hadn't said that. I don't like it. I'm doing the best I can. You know what I have asked Congress to do."

Randolph refused to back down, pointing out that he was not questioning the President's integrity but his sense of history.

"I don't like it at all," the President cut in. "I wish you hadn't said that."

Randolph said he was sorry he had to say it, but truth was truth.

Called before the Senate Armed Services Committee with

Grant Reynolds, co-chairman of his committee, Randolph repeated his threat.

"I personally pledge myself," he said, "to openly counsel, aid and abet youth, both white and Negro, in an organized refusal to register and be drafted."

"It may lead to indictments for treason and very serious repercussions," Senator Wayne Morse warned.

"We are willing to pay that price," Randolph shot back, noting pointedly that "Senator Morse has never felt the sting of Jim Crow. . . . I believe any of you men would raise hell in America if you felt the indignities and injustices that are suffered [by Negroes] in America."

Hell was precisely what Randolph intended to raise. He went immediately to a soapbox and urged draft-age youth in his audience not to register with their draft boards. "I am prepared," he announced, "to oppose a Jim Crow Army until I rot in jail."

The power structure moved now to its basic tactic: divide and segregate. Established Negro leaders were summoned to a conference with Secretary of Defense James Forrestal and other functionaries. Forrestal suggested the appointment of an advisory committee of prominent Negroes; but the prominent Negroes balked, demanding a token of good faith. Not only did the group refuse to repudiate Randolph, but they, in effect, supported him by flatly refusing to form the advisory committee. Lester B. Granger, executive director of the National Urban League, announced after the conference that "the group agreed that no one wanted to continue in an advisory capacity on the basis of continued segregation in the armed services."

Meanwhile, a great debate raged in the Negro community over Randolph's strategy. Most Negro leaders avoided open repudiation of Randolph, hoping that the threat would win basic concessions. *Newsweek* noted that Walter White, "the careful and cautious" NAACP secretary, "did not share Mr. Randolph's faith in the efficacy of a civil disobedience campaign," but that the only alternative was "the immediate and total abolition of segregation." The magazine concluded that Randolph expressed what a vast number of Negroes, particularly young Negroes, felt and thought about segregation.

Faced again by a determined Randolph and a Negro community teetering on the edge of revolt, white men of power retreated. On July 26, 1948, President Truman issued two executive orders, creating an FEPC board to eliminate racial discrimination in federal employment and a President's Committee on Equal Treatment and Opportunity in the armed services. This was not, by any means, what Randolph had demanded. But he accepted the olive branch and called off the civil disobedience movement, noting that the campaign had forced issuance of two pivotal executive orders and had "jarred Negro spokesmen out of tolerating compulsory racial segregation, in war or peace."

Though Randolph was appeased, other activists were not; and the new Progressive party provided an instrument for venting despair. Calling for a basic change in the Negro situation, eschewing the token approach of the Democrats and Republicans, the Progressive party raised racial tensions to a new high. Prominent Negroes—Paul Robeson and several "respectable" doctors and lawyers—were given positions of real power within the party; and more than thirty Negroes ran for state and federal offices on the party ticket. Henry Wallace, the Progressive party's Presidential candidate in 1948, campaigned in the South with an integrated staff.

In several states, notably North Carolina, mobs attempted to break up integrated Progressive party meetings. When Glenn Taylor, a United States senator and the party's vice-presidential candidate, attempted to enter a Negro church in Birmingham through a door marked "Negro," he was arrested on a charge of resisting a police officer.

The Progressive crusade was a basic and bare-knuckled challenge to the power structure which reacted with basic and bare-knuckled tactics. Pointing to the Communists, who were an undoubted part of the crusade, the power structure ruthlessly counterattacked. White men of power were particularly apprehensive about the Negro community. After all, there were real grievances in the Negro community; and Wallace, a former U.S. vice-president, was promising to redress these grievances. Would Negro leaders abandon their basic strategy of maneuvering between the two major parties? Would Negroes release the emaciated Democratic bird and reach for the elusive but temptingly fat Progressive bird in the bush? Discreet calls were made in almost every community. In *Community Power Structure,* a study of decision-making in Atlanta, Georgia, Floyd Hunter traced the lineaments of deliberation.

> Many of us [Negro leaders], a Negro leader reported, were in sympathy with the aims of the Progressive party, but we felt that more could be gained ultimately by sticking to the older parties. We discussed

the matter of alignment very carefully among ourselves [the top leadership group], and decided to play a waiting game. We knew that the Progressive party was scaring the leaders uptown and we thought the fright was good for them. If the party gained strength we could always threaten to go along with it, but we would wait and see.

All of the leaders have one or two white men they can go to and discuss various matters that concern us. Whenever there is a threat of trouble or when the police get too brutal, we can get help from some of the men we know personally. *At the time of the Progressive party activity the white men got in touch with us.* They wanted to know how our people were reacting to the propaganda being put out by this party. They said they were very much against the party and hoped we were. They said they had helped us in the past and they wanted our help now.

We discussed this among ourselves and we agreed to let the uptown boys dangle a little. We finally told them, however, that we were not for the Progressive party ourselves and we would do what we could to discourage it in the community here. We said we could not act openly, but we would do what we could. We figured that we would really gain more by such a move on our part. As things turned out the Progressive party was a flop. I definitely think we gained something by not going too radical. *Our strategy is to get places for ourselves in the older parties.* [Emphasis supplied.]

Because of the total opposition of Negro and white men of power and the flagrant machinations of Communists, Negro voters elected to keep the bird in hand. But they profited, so to speak, from the fall-out of the movement. The Progressive threat probably forced the Democrats to take the "strong" 1948 stand on civil rights. And it convinced many of the necessity of making at least a token move toward Negro equality.

Equally persuasive was the specter of Paul Robeson who went to Paris and said it was unthinkable *to him* that American Negroes would fight against Russia. After returning to America, Robeson was the focal point of a series of riots and disturbances in Peekskill, New York, and other communities. Aided by Du Bois, who resigned from the NAACP and aligned himself with the left, Robeson attempted to create a People's movement. The attempt failed; Negroes, then and now, disavowed the ideology of the elder Du Bois and the embattled

Robeson. Still—and this should be noted well—Robeson and Du Bois remained—and remain—persuasive symbols of revolt for hundreds of thousands of Negroes.

The Robeson drama, the Progressive Crusade, and the Cold War fear were pivotal elements in the collapse of the revolt of the forties. A great retreat began after the Progressive crusade. The NAACP, the Urban League and the liberal establishment began to clean house, barring Communists and silencing radicals. Picketing and mass demonstrations became dangerous forms of dissent. The word masses assumed an ugly meaning; and polite protest was enshrined as the only means of struggle.

By 1949, the great rehearsal was over and men crept back, sheepishly, to the dressing room to exchange masks of rebellion for masks of acceptance under protest. It was all over; but nothing was forgotten. Seeds were stirring under the great white snow; and, in season, the flowers of rebellion would grow.

IV. LULL

Bigger in Wonderland

BIGGER THOMAS stood on a Southside street corner. Around him swirled the sound of the slums and, high above, an airplane dipped in and out of the clean white fluffs of clouds. Bigger watched the plane for a moment and, of a sudden, all the horror of his life bubbled to the surface.

"Goddamit!" he said, focusing his anxieties on the faraway symbol of white power and white control—"Goddamit! They won't let us do nothing."

These words, spoken in the 1940 novel *Native Son,* seemed, to some anyway, oddly unrealistic in the early fifties. By that time, "they" were "letting" Negroes do a great many things no one dreamed of in the forties. Negroes were flying airplanes and making them. There was a black general in the Air Force, a black star with the Brooklyn Dodgers, and a black administrative assistant in the White House. The Myth of Negro Progress, which is the only thing that stands between the Negro and revolt, seemed real enough in those days. The myth was tangible, the myth was palpable. You could see it, you could touch it—the brass ring was gold.

As the midcentury mark passed, Negro Americans thought they could see the beginning of the end. The great burst of reform projects of the thirties and forties lost their savor, and the ghetto surrendered to what C. Wright Mills called the optative mood. In this mood, men speak of things hoped for as though they existed, and the substance of things dreamed of becomes the evidence of things not seen. Racial strife in America is punctuated by such periods of relative calm during which the greater fury of the next phase silently gathers itself. Coming, as it always does, between two periods of acute tension, the optative mood bridges past and future, giving men time to count their winnings, leading them on to absurd exaggerations of their gains, preparing them, unwittingly, for the next period of excruciating disappointment. When the optative mood seizes the ghetto, when dreams become things, and mirages, realities, protest organizations lapse into somnolence, activists become clerks, and paper work replaces demonstrations.

The period between 1950 and 1954 was a classic example of optative evasion. Some men announced, with incredible optimism, the imminent disappearance of Negroes. The *Detroit News* spoke of "the eventual disappearance" of all-white neighborhoods in that city. The Colored Methodist Church and several other organizations met and solemnly removed the word "colored" from their titles. In keeping with the spirit of racial ecumenicity, some Negro writers announced that they would henceforth write about people—and not Negroes. At least one prominent novelist said publicly that he was through with the race struggle, and several of his colleagues resigned, insofar as that was possible, from the race. Charles S. Johnson, an eminent Negro sociologist who was then president of Fisk University, sounded the dominant note of the period in a 1953 speech. "We are changing," he said, "from a racial society in many respects to a human relations society."

So it went everywhere, men dreaming dreams and seeing them.

How explain this?

First of all, by the spirit of the age. This was a time of fierce affirmation, of frenetic and sometimes ludicrous attempts on the part of all Americans to accentuate the positive. This mood was linked to disturbing changes in the world, to the contraction of the European ego abroad, the explosion of the atom bomb, the rise of Afro-Asia, and the red clouds over Europe.

Another factor in the damping down of discontent was fatigue. Men cannot live forever at fever heat. The ghetto had been in almost constant turmoil now for some twenty years. Negroes were tired; they stopped now on the ledge of the mountain to catch their breath and consolidate their gains. Finally, and most significantly, there was the simple and unalterable fact of progress. *The brass ring was gold or, at least, gold-plated.*

Negro gains were more apparent than real, but they were real enough for all that. Negro workers were making four times as much as they made in 1940. By 1953, Negroes owned almost a third of the dwellings they occupied, a two-thirds rise over 1940. Negro college enrollment was up 2,500 per cent over

1930. Negroes, moreover, were receiving unprecedented recognition. There was a new sensitivity to Negro demands at the national level. The "great experiment" of integration in the armed forces was initiated and ripples from this great wave spread, beneficently. The Eisenhower Administration continued the postwar policy of appointing Negroes to highly visible posts, naming J. Ernest Wilkins assistant secretary of labor and E. Frederic Morrow administrative assistant in the White House. There was, additionally, a bumper crop of new Negro judges on the federal, state, and local level.

The North just then was beginning the open-city leap the South would make ten years later. As a result of direct-action probes (sit-ins and stand-ins) by CORE and other organizations, and litigation or the threat of litigation by local NAACP chapters, public facilities (lunch counters, restaurants, hotels, recreational facilities) in downtown sections in Chicago and other Northern cities opened their doors to Negro citizens. The most dramatic change was the integration of Washington, D.C., as a result of court orders and prodding by the Eisenhower Administration. Some public facilities were also desegregated in Baltimore, St. Louis and other Border State areas.

Tangible gains were also evident in the old states of the Confederacy. By 1953, almost one million Negroes were voting in the South. Negroes had been elected or appointed to boards, commissions, and public offices in Atlanta, Richmond, Nashville, Winston-Salem and other urban areas in the South. After a trip through Dixie, Roi Ottley, the Negro author, reported an air of expansiveness in the Negro sections of urban areas. Some Negro matrons, Ottley reported, believed cities like Nashville and Atlanta were making more progress than Chicago and New York. According to these informants, department store clerks were addressing Negro customers as "Mr." and "Mrs." and were permitting them to try on clothes and other articles before purchasing them. Ottley also reported a big building boom. With one eye on the Supreme Court and the other on Thurgood Marshall and the NAACP legal staff, mayors were feverishly building schools and hospitals for "our Negro citizens."

In both the South and North, Negroes were holding on to their war gains and breaking new ground. Department stores and public utilities (telephone companies, bus companies) were hiring a small number of Negroes. The Korean War added to the climate of general prosperity by keeping the labor market tight. As a result, money flowed freely and credit was easy to get. Negro-owned businesses, especially savings and loan associations, reported record earnings. By the early fifties, there were some fifty thousand Negro-owned businesses, including about fifty insurance companies and fourteen banks.

The net result of all this was an enormous expansion of the Negro middle class. The proliferation of clerks, technicians, secretaries, and professional people changed the tone of life in the ghetto and paved the way for the confrontation of the sixties. Middle-class groups are generally useless in a social revolution, but, paradoxically, a middle-class core seems to be a prerequisite, in the West anyway, for a social revolution. The children of the new Negro middle class and some of the more sensitive adults found the fruit rotten on the vine; and their despair, and the despair of the deprived underclass, would be decisive in the upheaval of the sixties. But none of this could be foreseen in the halcyon days of the fifties. The new middle class, pitilessly described in E. Franklin Frazier's *Black Bourgeoisie,* inherited the hand-me-down brownstones and Georgians of whites who were fleeing the city. Gilded ghettos sprang up in Chicago, Atlanta, Detroit, New Orleans and other urban areas. With new grass to mow, with shiny new gadgets to explore (hi-fi sets and washing machines and power mowers), the Black Bourgeoisie became desperately serious Babbitts. *Time* magazine reported in 1953 that the number of Negro golfers in Chicago "had gone up from 25, a few years ago, to more than 2,000." On Lenox Avenue in Harlem, the magazine reported, "Cadillacs are so commonplace that nobody turns around to look at them anymore." Some of the "Cadillac prosperity," *Time* concluded, "is obviously false or forced." Still, the magazine said, coming dangerously close to a provocative quote of Marie-Antoinette, "for most Negroes, the problem is no longer jobs, but better jobs; for many, it is no longer bread, but cake."

A great deal of this progress stemmed from impersonal changes in the world: the increasing industrialization of the South, the artificial expansion of the Cold War economy, and the changing tone and texture of power relations in the world beyond the Atlantic. Even more persuasive was negative democratization, the wooing of Negroes by white men of power who needed their voices or, at least, their silence in the ideological struggle against Russia. Nor does the chain of causation end there. The Negro revolts of the thirties and forties were major causative factors; so, to be sure, were Negro radicals like Paul Robeson who frightened America into a course of action that would have come with better grace from an internal consciousness of the acute need for change.

For all these reasons, and for others, America began to cash the blue chips of Negro citizens. The Supreme Court—signaling the beginning of the era of integration as it signaled in the Reconstruction era the beginning of the era of segregation —began in the late forties to define with greater precision the equal part of the "separate-but-equal" myth. What was more important were several hints from the Court that it was ready to go beyond "separate-but-equal" and rule on segregation per se. The Court's drift toward truth was, in part, a result of the changing climate of the age; but it was also a tribute to the patient, plodding, persistent efforts of Thurgood Marshall and the staff of the NAACP Legal and Educational Fund. The grand outcome was a series of decisions that doomed the white primary, restrictive covenants, and segregation in colleges, graduate schools, and interstate travel.

All of this—the increasing sensitivity of the federal government, the series of Supreme Court decisions—reflected a new level of concern in white America. In this period, there was a rash of books and movies (*Home of the Brave, Pinky, Lost Boundaries*) and a paroxysm of organizational activity. It was estimated that there were some one hundred official and some four hundred unofficial race relations committees in the North by 1950. By that time, according to press reports, white people were expending voluntarily nearly one hundred million hours a year in organized efforts to improve the climate of race relations.

Most of this activity was busy work which merely scratched the surface. It seems, in retrospect, that most Americans were engaged in a huge conspiracy to deny the reality of their eyes. The "gains" most people praised were confined almost entirely to the Negro middle and upper classes. Some of the "progress," moreover, masked dangerous setbacks. Negro "gains" in the housing markets, for instance, solidified housing and school segregation. As whites fled to the new bedroom dormitories in the suburbs, the ghetto expanded enormously. More ominous yet was the crystallization, in the wake of the suburban boom, of the new idea of one-color, one-class, one-kind neighborhoods. Robert Weaver, almost alone among the social commentators, noted that this idea, in and of itself, was a clear and present danger to American democracy. But it would take time to see this—time and the polarization of the American community. In the fifties, Negroes did not look gift horses in the mouth. As whites moved out, they moved in. House by house, block by block, the ghetto marched toward the city limits of scores of municipalities. This was not, all things considered, an unmixed blessing but it was not a clear-cut gain.

Beyond the horizon were other dark clouds. White fear, as expressed in the resurgence of the Ku Klux Klan in the South and the growth of property owners associations in the North, was growing. This fear bubbled to the surface periodically in violent episodes like the bomb-murder of Harry Sims, the Florida NAACP official, in 1951, and the Cicero (1951) and Trumbull Park (1953-56) housing riots in Chicago. Although 1952 was the first year without a single reported lynching, terrorism and intimidation, often under the color of law, was common in the South. And to all this must be added the obvious fact that almost everyone was dealing with symptoms not causes. Segregation was not decreasing; it was growing. The South was still spending five, six and seven dollars for white education for every one dollar spent on the education of Negro children. There were more books in the Oklahoma state penitentiary than in the state's Negro university. In progressive Atlanta, there was not a single kindergarten for Negroes in the early fifties, not one community center and only one Negro park. In Chicago and other Northern cities, schools were segregated, dilapidated and transparently unequal.

Deep in the heart of the ghetto, unnoticed by most commentators, things were going from bad to worse. Nearly a third of all Negro homes were dilapidated, as compared with less than 10 per cent for the nation as a whole. Worse, more than 20 per cent of all Negro homes were overcrowded. Although the citizens of *this* America shared to an extent in the general prosperity of the period (via easy credit plans), they were, on the whole, sitting ducks for the series of recessions which began in 1952 and became progressively worse as the years wore on. The full impact of all this, and of the hidden threat of automation, would not be felt until years later, but the signs of impending disaster were clear to some men.

The rippling tensions beneath the placid surface of Negro life can be studied with profit in the lives of two men who would soon be better known. James Baldwin and Malcolm Little, like millions of other Negroes, were looking, in this period, for a place to call home. Baldwin and Little found no meaning in the two values that informed Negro life: *appropriation* (the assimilation of the white man's technique and sensibility through repression and education) and *protest* (continuous knocking on doors with the implicit understanding that it would be a long time before the doors opened).

It seemed to Baldwin and Little, as it seemed to many later, that the changing face of the world (the rise of Afro-Asia, the urbanization and creeping degradation of the masses) had rendered obsolete the premises that guided Negro policy. This was not, it should be noted, an intellectual pose. For Baldwin and Little, the change was a felt, an experienced reality that impelled them to run real risks and articulate real solutions. The truth of the matter is that Baldwin and Little had no intention of meeting, in any way, the white man's idea of what a Negro ought to be. Both men, in fact, had rejected not only the *white* man but the society the *white* man had made and the place he had prepared in it for Negroes. In a sense, Baldwin and Little were throwbacks to the archetypal Negro figure, "the bad nigger." They had chosen to put themselves on trial, turning away from the categories of American life and digging deep within themselves for meaning and identity. Baldwin had fled America in horror and was living in Paris. Malcolm Little, fleeing the same reality, had performed radical surgery on himself, excising his name and his identity, becoming an apostle of Elijah Muhammad, the Black Muslim leader. How came these two men to such extreme postures in an age of bonhomie and racial good cheer? By a radically different analysis of Negro reality. They did not see what their contemporaries saw or, to put it another way, they saw what their contemporaries did not want to see. Most commentators focused on surface events; Baldwin and Little dug down to the subsurface. (In a sense, they *were* the subsurface.) Most commentators celebrated the real material advances of the Negro middle class; Baldwin and Little deplored the deepening misery of the masses and what they believed was a failure of the middle class to confront the reality and meanness of their lives. Most of all, Baldwin and Little deplored the inarticulate major premise of American life (Negro inferiority), a premise that made every Negro's life a series of guerilla actions on a Kafkaian battlefield. Baldwin and Little will repay some study: they were mirrors reflecting the swirling forces in the subcellar of the Negro mind.

Baldwin was, in his own words, "a very tight, tense, lean, abnormally ambitious, abnormally intelligent, and hungry black cat." Like Little, he was a product of the concepts that inform this study—abortive emancipation, continuous migration, urbanization, increasing self-consciousness, and alienation. He was born on August 2, 1924, in New York City or, rather, Harlem; for, as he later said, the Negro's New York and the white man's New York are not, by any means, the same place. Baldwin was marked, for good or ill, by a strong-willed father who hated white folk; and his recorded reminiscences of life with father are among the most painful and most moving in American letters. A strong father figure is rare in Negro life; it is perhaps significant that not only Baldwin and Little but also Martin Luther King, Jr., were moulded forever by the fire and fury of men who, whatever their failures and successes, were real presences in their homes.

Baldwin's father, David, was a page out of the Negro past. The son of a slave, he was of the first generation of free men. Born in New Orleans in the germinal days of jazz, which he loathed, Baldwin the elder moved North after 1919 with the other black migrants. Settling in Harlem with his wife, a native of Maryland, he managed somehow to keep together his brood of nine children. It has never been easy for a Negro to be a man and a father in America; it was close to impossible for the men of the generation of the migration and Depression. The Baldwins were often on relief; and it was necessary, from time to time, for the children to scrounge in the streets for sustenance. No good is done to men by exposing them thus to the contempt of their children. Baldwin's father had been reasonably happy it seems; he was a preacher-laborer who was given to bouncing his children on his knee. But the happy days did not last long. Something happened to the old man, and all the joy went out of him. The eyes turned mean and desperate; the voice became harsh and rasping; the man became petty and vindictive, a paternal tyrant who vented his spite and his fears and his phobias on his family. "I do not remember," Baldwin has written, forgetting somehow the happy years, "in all those years that a single one of his children was ever glad to see him come home." How and why did the old man change? Baldwin does not know or, at least, he gives no hints in his obsessive return to this strange and compelling figure who was filled with so much impotent rage and so much— Baldwin uses the word time and time again—power.

Drake and Cayton (*Black Metropolis*) divide the Negro lower-income group into "shadies" and "respectables." The Baldwins were of the "respectables." Old man Baldwin tried desperately to shield his children from the pimps, prostitutes, and "shadies" of Lenox Avenue. He succeeded in a way, but he also failed. For as the dangers without grew greater, he became more desperate, driving everyone and everything from him. Betrayed by life, betrayed even, or so Baldwin says, by his children, who could not and would not communicate with him, the old man locked himself in a world of fantasy and rage. The whole history of frustrated Negro masculinity is conveyed in Baldwin's terrible image of the old man sitting by a window in the living room of his Harlem flat, shouting, singing, praying—alone. The old man's retreat from reality created an archetypal vacuum which Baldwin's mother, the matriarchal image of millions of self-sacrificing Negro mothers, filled.

Out of this matrix came James Arthur Baldwin who grew up hating himself and the world his father had made. He was a talented young man who began writing early and became a full-fledged preacher at fourteen. Under different circumstances, he would have become a talented lawyer or professional person and would never have been heard from again. There was no money, however, to finance a college education and Baldwin, moreover, had, so he says, nothing but contempt for the typical Negro products of the American educational mill. After graduating from high school, Baldwin entered "the world of commerce and industry," working as a waiter, copy boy, and laborer. As a factory worker in New Jersey in the early days of the war, Baldwin came face to face with the terrifying power of the white world. Refusing to bend to Jim Crow, he was embroiled in a series of adventures. Going one night with a white friend to a restaurant, he was refused service. He said later that something snapped in the back of his head when the white waitress said the ritual phrase: "We don't serve Negroes here." Eyes blazing, lips trembling, Baldwin tried to get the waitress to come closer. He wanted her within reach of his hands; he wanted to get his hands around her throat—he wanted to strangle her to death. Fortunately for American letters, the waitress backed away in fear; and Baldwin, frustrated, flung a glass of water at her, missing, and shattering a mirror. The shattering glass awoke Baldwin from his murderous rage, and he beheld in horror what he had done and what he had wanted to do to an American white woman. Spinning on his heels, he dashed for the door, fighting off white men as he ran. With the help of his white friend, he eluded pursuers and made his way to his rooms. By such narrow margins are Negro geniuses separated from Negro criminals.

Baldwin returned, almost immediately, to Harlem, where his father lay dying. The old man, his body consumed by tuberculosis and his mind feverish with desperate fears, refused to eat, convinced that his family was trying to poison him. After his death, as David Baldwin lay in a funeral home, Harlem exploded in an apocalypse of violence, the Harlem riots of 1943. Baldwin rode with his father for the last time through streets littered with glass and debris from the riots. "He had lived and died," Baldwin has written, "in an intolerable bitterness of spirit and it frightened me, as we drove him to the graveyard through those unquiet, ruined streets, to see how powerful and overflowing this bitterness could be and to realize that this bitterness was now mine."

After his father's death, Baldwin fled Harlem and went to Greenwich Village to live. There he managed to finish several pages of a novel which he showed to Richard Wright, his idol. Wright, who was then at the height of his fame, helped Baldwin get a fellowship. In 1948, Baldwin followed Wright to Paris. He left America, he said, because he was afraid America would destroy him, that he would kill someone or be killed. In Paris, Baldwin "vomited up most of [his] hatred" and placed America "in perspective." His career began, oddly enough, with a revolt against Wright and a passionate attack on "protest" literature. When Baldwin, with incredible self-assurance, attacked "protest" literature, blandly citing *Native Son* as a prime example of the limitations of the genre, Wright hit the ceiling. Baldwin, with not a little naïveté, professed astonishment over his erstwhile mentor's chagrin. He tried to explain what he *really* meant, but the controversy became quite heated and the two men drifted apart. The controversy hinged not only on "protest" literature, but also on the Negro identity. Wright was saying, in these years, that there was more freedom in one block of Paris than in the whole of America. Though Baldwin loathed the American façade, he disagreed with Wright's assessment, partially, one suspects, because it was Wright's assessment, which is only another way of saying that Baldwin was of that breed of men who have a need to find and articulate their own vision. Rejecting Wright's vision, Baldwin embarked on a perilous personal journey, a journey, ironically enough, that ended in the sixties in a place not unlike the place invented by Richard Wright.

What Baldwin wanted to know, above all, was: Who am I? Where do I belong? These are dangerous questions for any American. A Negro American who asks them in all seriousness finds the ground opening beneath his feet. By daring to ask the unaskable, by plunging into the deeps of his soul, disregarding friends who urged him to take a life jacket, Baldwin came at last to the end of himself which was, in a manner of speaking, the beginning of himself. Ruthlessly honest, Baldwin asked himself, in the beginning, what was the meaning of Negroness. What relation, if any, did he have to the Western tradition and to the congealed products of that tradition, Rembrandt, for example, Chartres, the Empire State Building? In the end, he recognized or "was forced to recognize" that he was "a kind of bastard of the West."

What did this mean?

It meant, Baldwin said—and his argument here is not wholly convincing, culture being a construct of the mind and not of the genes—it meant that he stood somehow in a different relation to the cultural products of the West. He was, in short, "an interloper'" who "had no other heritage [he] could possibly hope to use." It was necessary, therefore, for him to "appropriate these white centuries . . . to make them mine." Baldwin admitted that he hated and feared white people, but he did not, on that account, love Negroes; on the contrary, he despised them—and any Negro who has not emancipated himself, as Baldwin was doing, could make the same confession—"possibly because they had not produced Rembrandt."

The net result of this soul-searching was a series of elegant essays which attracted a great deal of attention but did not solve Baldwin's personal problems. A true outsider, Baldwin lived in Paris in the crevices between cultures and communities. "When Jimmy was in his 20's in Paris," one of his friends explained, "he thought seriously of never being a Negro again—certainly never a Negro in America." When a dark-skinned Negro decides in all seriousness that he will never be a Negro again, he is not far from the discovery that he can be nothing else. Oscillating between Negroness and X and between Paris and America, Baldwin suffered what he calls "a species of breakdown" and was sent by friends to a village high in the Swiss Alps. There, in the Swiss village, with the mountainous Alps towering over him like a great white whale, the black boy from Harlem listened to two Bessie Smith recordings and learned, he says, what it means to be black in a white world. He learned something else, too: that life is full of sharp edges and blind alleys and that a man accepts his fate—which includes his color and his place of birth—with equanimity and poise. In 1953, with the publication of his first novel, *Go Tell It on the Mountain,* Baldwin began his meteoric climb to fame, effecting a truce with reality—and a truce, he said, was the best a Negro could hope for. As he said later in *Nobody Knows My Name:* "My revenge, I decided early, would be to achieve a power which outlasts kingdoms."

Malcolm Little's kingdom was of this world. He asked himself the same questions Baldwin posed, but he reached strikingly different solutions; and his solutions, like Baldwin's, grew out of and were reinforced by an intensely personal relation with an extraordinary family and an extraordinary father. Little, like Baldwin, was moulded by the Negro religious tradition. Like Baldwin, like King, like Asa Philip Randolph and many other Negro leaders, he was the son of a preacher. His father, a Baptist minister, was a black nationalist disciple of Marcus Garvey, the spellbinder of the twenties. A man of considerable power and energy, Little the elder loathed white people and envisioned an all-Negro state controlled and run by black men. The father lived for several years in Omaha, Nebraska. Here, in 1925, during the dying days of the Garvey Movement and the heyday of the modern Ku Klux Klan, Malcolm Little was born. At an early age, he moved with his family—there were, all told, eleven children—to Lansing, Michigan, where the father opened a store. The family prospered, but not without a certain dissension. Malcolm's father was a bumptious man who did not bite his tongue, and he was soon in trouble with local white folk. The whole thing came to a head on the day the Little store burned down. "The firemen came," Malcolm remembered, "and just sat there without making any effort to put one drop of water on the fire. The same fire that burned my father's home still burns in my soul." Not long after the fire, the mangled body of the father was found beneath a streetcar. Malcolm believed until the day of his assassination in Harlem that his father was murdered by evil white people.

After the death of the father, the Little family disintegrated. Malcolm landed in an institution for boys where he attracted the attention of the white matron. "She was good to me," he recalls. "I followed her around like a little puppy. I was a kind of mascot." It is a point of immense and ironic significance that the youth who became Malcolm X had, in a manner of speaking, a "white mammy." At that juncture, young Malcolm believed apparently in the traditional Negro values of litigation and appropriation. The most popular image of the age was Thurgood Marshall who had succeeded in dramatizing the legal approach. Under the influence presumably of the Marshall image, Malcolm decided that he wanted to be a lawyer. Given the circumstances, it would have been difficult, though not impossible, for Malcolm to have achieved this ambition which seems to have awed the directors of the institution who suggested that perhaps carpentry or some other trade would be more appropriate for a boy in Malcolm's position.

This advice enraged Malcolm who perceived in it a subtle condescension and an *a priori* judgment on the Negro's place. At that precise moment, Malcolm Little began his drift away from American society. Since he could not become a lawyer, he would become a lawbreaker. The process, as it worked itself out in his life, was more complicated than that. But there can be little doubt that Malcolm moved by successive stages to that position. Leaving the institution, he drifted east and immersed himself in the shadowy underworld of Harlem. Within a short time, according to him, he was making up to two thousand dollars a month and was wearing two-hundred-dollar suits. He dealt in dope, bootleg whiskey, women—you name it and "Big Red," as he was called in those days, could supply it. "Big Red" was arrested finally and sent to prison on a charge of burglary. In 1947, in the maximum security prison at Concord, Massachusetts, "Big Red" became a follower of Elijah Muhammad, the Black Muslim leader. The words and images of "the prophet of Allah" opened Malcolm's eyes, taking him back to the vision of his father and of his father's mentor, Marcus Garvey. Listening to the words of "the honorable Elijah Muhammad," Malcolm learned, he said, who he was and where he came from. And who was he? He was a black man, one of "the chosen few" who would inherit the earth after "all the white devils" had been destroyed. One day in a cell of the Massachusetts prison, Malcolm Little died; in his body rose a new man, undefined, unpredictable, unnamed—Malcolm X. The new convert immediately gave up alcohol, nicotine, and pork. Returning to the ghetto, after completing his prison sentence, he threw himself into the organizational work of the Black Muslims. With his great charisma and his razor-sharp mind, he was soon among the leaders of the community. As Negro leadership slumbered in an easy placidity, Malcolm and his brothers struck deep roots in the subsoil of Negro discontent.

In their different ways, Malcolm X and James Baldwin fleshed out the accumulating tensions in the ghetto. But few people took them seriously. Not many people, in fact, knew of their existence, and almost no one was prepared to deal seriously with the problems they symbolized. Negro leadership was preoccupied with the legal campaign, which was going well. There was little or no leadership outside the areas of litigation and lobbying. Perhaps the best indication of the state of militancy was a precipitous decline in NAACP membership which plummeted to about two hundred thousand, as compared with the wartime high of some five hundred thousand.

The biggest decline, the NAACP said, was in the larger cities, in Detroit, New York, Chicago, Los Angeles, Cleveland, and Washington. Despite the drop in membership, the NAACP virtually monopolized protest leadership. This was, it should be noted, an unusual situation. NAACP leadership, as we have seen, was strongly challenged in the twenties, thirties, and forties. By the early fifties, however, activists of the left and right were scattered and disorganized, and the NAACP held undisputed sway in the middle of the field. The organization shared leadership with a small number of moderate educators and foundation executives. The "Big Ten" of Negro leadership, Roi Ottley reported, consisted of three educators, two labor leaders, two race relations professionals, a politician, a scholar and a foundation executive, namely: Mary McLeod Bethune, Charles S. Johnson, F. D. Patterson, A. Philip Randolph, Willard S. Townsend, Walter White, Lester A. Granger, William L. Dawson, W. E. B. Du Bois, and Channing Tobias. As a group, Ottley noted, the Big Ten was the epitome of what Du Bois envisioned "40 years ago—a 'Talented Tenth' who form the negotiators and architects of the Negro's future." With the exception of Randolph and Du Bois, the dominant characteristics of the group were moderation and conservatism. There was not, Ottley concluded, "a spellbinder in the group."

This was a period of confusion and fragmentation in Negro leadership circles. "There are fewer outstanding leaders on the national scene today than ever before," *Time* magazine said. "Negro leaders have found that, as their people's status improves, the business of leadership gets tougher. . . . Today's Negro leader concentrates on getting things done on specific issues. Emancipated to a large extent from the white professional liberals and their pet slogan, 'education,' he tries, for instance, to get a court ruling on segregation in Pullmans instead of trying to 'educate' millions of individual Pullman passengers. Today's Negro leader does not want to be known as a firebrand; the compliment he prizes most is to be called a good tactician. One symptom of the change is the fact that Booker T. Washington, a superb tactician whom most Negro leaders in the '20s and '30s denounced as an 'Uncle Tom,' is being rediscovered by Negroes as a great man."

What was true of Negro leadership was true also, perhaps to a lesser degree, of the articulate layers of the followership. There was, if one can credit the oracles, a remarkable lack of bitterness in the ghetto. One reporter noted that Negroes no longer used the disparaging term "ofays"; nor did Negroes, in the presence of white reporters anyway, call white people "Mr.

Charlie." All in all, or so the media said, Negroes were happy with their lot. To be sure, there was some bitterness. It was noted in the South that there were too many "whole hog or nothing" Negroes. But, the press said, what little bitterness there was, was modified by hope, patience, and humor. One white reporter, with extraordinary ingenuity, managed to find a Negro who had almost forgotten that he was a Negro. A lieutenant colonel, a G-I officer from Washington, D. C., told the press: "I think about the color problem about once a day; when I shave in the morning."

To support this desperate optimism, there did appear from time to time encouraging flickers of light. It is important to note however that Negro optimism was based not on the flickers of light but on an apocalyptic belief that the full prize, complete and equal citizenship, was within grasp. The NAACP Legal Defense and Educational Fund and its director, Thurgood Marshall, were making real progress in the courts and the ghetto watched, fascinated, as the walls of color-caste came tumblin' down. As 1954 neared and as Thurgood Marshall and company leaped from plateau to plateau, hopes in the ghetto reached a feverish pitch.

The very extravagance of Negro hopes contained the seeds of a very real danger. It can be said, in fact, that this was the seed period of the great revulsion of the sixties. From the great peak of hope, Negroes were pitched down, by successive disappointments, to a depth that revealed to them the full horror of their situation, a depth, to be more accurate, that made it impossible for them to evade the implications of their situation. All this—the great fall, the dashing of the great hope—was perhaps a necessary part of the disillusionment and re-education of the Negro masses.

From the age of Washington to the age of the great hope, Negro strategy was based on some very questionable assumptions about the rules of the game. Of all the assumptions, none was more questionable than the premise that the game was being played by rules. As a matter of hard cold fact, Negroes were engaged in a life-and-death struggle with an antagonist who improvised rules as the game progressed and changed them whenever it was to his advantage. The whole point of the game, in fact—and every Negro and white man knew this in the deeps of his viscera—was that no Negro could win because he was a Negro. Since this fact, total capriciousness and an absolute lack of order, was too horrible to bear, Negroes and whites imposed an order on their lives, telling themselves that the game was being played by rules. The first rule of this fictional framework was a denial that the game had no rules. An understanding of this surrealistic sleight-of-hand—which seems mad, which was mad, which is mad—as absolutely indispensable for an understanding of the inner migration of Negroes which has consisted of the ripping away of successive veils of illusion. It was believed for many years that Negro claims would be honored when Negroes proved themselves by appropriating the white man's techniques and values. This comforting belief, comforting to both Negro and white leaders, was a casualty of the Depression and Pearl Harbor. By the end of the war, no one believed, really, that the game was being played by *that* rule, though some men found it useful or profitable to pretend that they still believed in the racial Santa Claus. The increasing harshness of Negro-white confrontations and the increasing desperation of men like Wright, Du Bois, Baldwin, and Malcolm X were reflections of an interior spasm resulting from an intuitive perception of the void at the center of Negro-white relations. But the collapse of the veil of appropriation did not destroy at one fell blow the racial equilibrium. Most Negroes were shielded from the great void by yet another illusion—litigation. Despite the evidence of their eyes, despite the whole history of race relations, most Negroes succeeded in the fifties in convincing themselves that the game was being played by the rules of law. To believe this, men had to shut their eyes to a great many things. Law is not an independent variable in the social system; it is, on the contrary, an essential prop of the social system, a prop that sustains and reflects the dominant myths. Moreover, law, as Thurmond Arnold and others have pointed out, is, in part, a social ritual designed not to solve problems but to evade them. A social movement which ignored these realities was, of necessity, riding for a fall. It was necessary, to be sure, to bulldoze, via court suits, the structural framework of color-caste, but the bulldozing alone would not create a new structure. Law, in short, was a necessary but not a sufficient tool. This was, in a manner of speaking, the fine print in the contract, and fine print carried no weight with the dreamers of the fifties. With reckless enthusiasm, Negroes of all ranks and creeds pooled their emotional resources and placed a reckless collective bet on the slow grey horse of Law. The horse won, but the house refused to honor the winners' claims, enraging them and sending them in ever-increasing numbers into the streets. But no one could foresee this development in the fifties. As the slow grey horse of Law rounded the turn and started down the back stretch, with Thurgood Marshall firmly in the seat, a panic of hope convulsed the ghetto.

Thurgood Marshall, the man in the saddle, was the great symbol of this age of hope. He was also the bulldozer of the Negro revolution of the sixties. By rewriting almost single-handedly crucial parts of the constitutional law of the land, Marshall cleared away the legal rubble and placed Negroes within striking distance of their goals. The limitations of the legal campaign were not necessarily Marshall's limitations. It was not his fault, really, that men were not playing the game they said they were playing. Marshall's greatest contribution perhaps was the ripping away of the last veil of illusion that enabled men to pretend. By succeeding brilliantly in the courts, he demonstrated the limitations of the courts. By becoming the indispensable hope of the ghetto, he proved, in the end, that no one man could do it alone. Yet, for all that, Marshall came close. Although he was a lawyer, his leadership ranged far beyond the confines of the courts. He dramatized litigation, made it understandable, and gave Negroes a new vision of battle. Because of him, the Fourteenth Amendment became as real and meaningful to Lenox Avenue as the cop on the beat.

The man who made the Supreme Court comprehensible to Lenox Avenue, and Lenox Avenue comprehensible to the Supreme Court, was of the second generation of protest leaders. Born in Baltimore in 1908, the son of a country club steward and a teacher, Marshall was graduated from Lincoln University (Pa.) in 1930 and went on to Howard University Law School where he became a protégé of Charles Hamilton Houston, a steel-willed, grey-eyed lawyer who was trying to create a West Point of Negro leadership. Marshall said later that Houston, who was born in 1895 and died in 1950, was primarily responsible for the Supreme Court decision of 1954. The son of a well-to-do Washington lawyer and a graduate of the Harvard University Law School, Houston was a rarity in legal circles, a scholar with social sensitivity and great breadth of vision. Houston excelled not only in details of the law but also in long-range planning. In order to fight, he said, Negroes must have a caste of warriors. As vice-dean of the law school, Charles Houston set himself the task of creating such a caste of legal warriors. He insisted that Negroes were losing Supreme Court cases because of shoddy preparation. This was, at best, a half-

186   *Confrontation: Black and White*

truth. The other part of the truth was that the Supreme Court had, as a matter of policy, shut its eyes to racial reality, refusing, in the twenties and thirties, even to take judicial notice of segregation. The best that Negro lawyers could get in those years was a ruling on whether separate facilities were "substantially" equal. Houston was aware of this, but he insisted that judicial hostility was no excuse for poor preparation. Under him, the Howard Law School became a tool of precision and purpose. He was given, Marshall recalled, to telling students on opening day: "Look at the man on your right and the man on your left. By the end of the year, two of you will not be here."

Among the few who survived was Thurgood Marshall who graduated *magna cum laude* and opened a small office in Baltimore where he was soon in the thick of the civil rights struggle. In 1935, only two years after his graduation from law school, Marshall scored the first substantial victory against *de jure* segregation, forcing the University of Maryland to admit a Negro student, Donald Murray, to its law school. Houston, who was then special counsel of the NAACP, asked his star student to give up his Baltimore practice and join him at the NAACP. Marshall became assistant counsel in 1936 and special counsel on the resignation of Houston in 1938. In 1939, the NAACP legal staff became a separate organization and Marshall was elected director. The new organization, the NAACP Legal Defense and Educational Fund, was a child of the American way of giving. Unlike the parent organization, which engaged in lobbying, the legal organization was eligible for tax-free gifts. By 1955, the legal defense fund was a separate organization in name and fact.

As director of the new organization, Marshall played a key role in the most important shift in Negro policy since Reconstruction. NAACP strategy in the 1930-45 period was based on the premise that suits seeking absolute and complete equalization of curricula, faculty, and physical equipment of Negro schools would make bias so prohibitively expensive that the South would voluntarily abandon segregation. It did not take long to discover that this approach would not produce the desired results. So, beginning in the early forties, the NAACP began to re-examine its premises and strategy. One day in 1945, a handful of Negro decision-makers (Marshall, Walter White, W. H. Hastie and others) met in Manhattan and decided that the time had come for a frontal attack on segregation. This decision, one of the most important in the history of race relations, was later confirmed by a larger group of lawyers and race relations professionals. Powerful men in local power structures in the North and South objected strenuously, but Marshall and Walter White carried the day. This was a fundamental turning point in the Negro protest, for the shift from attacks on the inequality of separate facilities to open demands for integrated facilities involved a shift not only in strategy but in orientation.

This shift was based, in part, on several decisions of the Supreme Court which was drifting away from the "separate-but-equal" fiction. Practical considerations also dictated a change. The South was growing accustomed to NAACP strategy. A suit attacking unequal facilities produced yawns, if not sneers, in the South. But a suit attacking segregation, Marshall noticed, produced immediate results. Legislatures hurriedly met and appropriated additional money for Negro schools. Mayors and city councils called special meetings. The ink was hardly dry on some petitions before bulldozers appeared to prepare the way for bright new Negro school buildings. But all this was too little, too late, too grudgingly given. Beginning with the pivotal *Sweatt* v. *Painter*, an attack on the segregated law schools of the University of Texas, Marshall succeeded in getting the Supreme Court to rule on the validity of segregation. Using expert testimony from anthropologists, psychologists, and sociologists, Marshall and other NAACP lawyers convinced the Court that equality involved more than physical facilities. In 1951, NAACP attorneys, and attorneys representing local organizations in Washington, D. C., began to attack segregation on the elementary and secondary school levels. As expected, the five cases from South Carolina, Kansas, Virginia, Delaware, and Washington, D. C., were lost in lower courts. Twice, in 1952 and 1953, they were argued before the Supreme Court. John W. Davis, an eminent constitutional lawyer, headed a battery of lawyers representing the segregationist view. Thurgood Marshall was anchor man for the opposing side which was represented by a disproportionately large number of graduates of Charles Hamilton Houston's West Point of Negro leadership, Howard University. Significantly, the federal government intervened on the side of the Negro petitioners. Secretary of State Dean Acheson stressed, as did others, the international implications of the case. On December 2, 1952, Acheson submitted a statement to the Court. "The continuation of racial discrimination in the United States remains a source of constant embarrassment to this government in the day-to-day conduct of its foreign relations; and it jeopardizes the effective maintenance of our moral leadership of the free and democratic nations of the world."

Legalism apart, the Court was being asked by both segregationist and integrationist to decide a question that was never stated.

What was America?

This question, stark and brutal, was coiled in the dry words of the disputatious briefs and no one could avoid it any longer.

In neither their questions nor their manner did the justices indicate the drift of their minds. After the arguments ended, they filed out quietly, their faces masked, their manner grave. Days passed, weeks, months. But the Court was silent. Once a week, on Mondays, the justices filed into the chamber, transacted business and filed out again, giving no hint in anything they said or did of the day or the hour of the decision that was on everyone's mind. As the Mondays passed, a panic of hope and fear seized America. Herman Talmadge and others announced that "riots, strikes, bloodshed and even lynchings" would occur if the *Plessy* v. *Ferguson* doctrine of separate but equal were overturned. Of words, of threats, of prayers, there was no dearth in the early days of 1954. Only the Court remained silent. March passed, and April, and May came.

Monday, May 17, 1954, was a Monday like all the other Mondays. There was a shower in Washington in the morning, but it brightened appreciably toward noon. As usual, there was a large gathering at the Supreme Court building. Among the dozen or so Negroes present were Thurgood Marshall and Attorneys George E. C. Hayes and James Nabrit. Marshall and his associates leaned forward, trying to pry from the faces of the justices a hint as to the meaning of the day. But the nine justices sat impassive before the maroon velour drapery. And everyone waited, tight with tension. The Court disposed of routine business. Then, leaning forward, Chief Justice Earl B. Warren began to read from a sheet of paper. It was 12:40. Warren held the Crowd in suspense by reviewing the history of the cases. Then, abruptly, he came to the core of the matter.

"Does segregation of children in public schools solely on the basis of race, even though the physical facilities and other 'tangible' factors may be equal, deprive the children of the minority group of equal educational opportunities?" Warren paused and said: "We believe that it does." He added: "We cannot turn the clock back to 1868 when the [Fourteenth] Amendment was adopted, or even to 1896, when Plessy versus Ferguson was written. . . . We conclude that in the field of public education the doctrine of 'separate but equal' has no place." The decision was unanimous.

This decision dealt with the narrow issue of segregation in public schools, but it had the general effect of re-defining the Negro's role in American life. Men greeted the change in different places according to their different lights. A man called Walter White, executive secretary of the NAACP, and shouted: "The NAACP is going out of business." Down in South Carolina, James Hinton, who sparked the NAACP drive in the key Clarendon County case, closed his life insurance office and hurried home to get the [colored] people ready." In Virginia, Barbara Trent, a sixteen-year-old Negro girl, broke down in tears when her teacher announced the decision. "We went on studying history," she said, "but things weren't the same, and will never be the same again."

There was a party that night at NAACP headquarters in Manhattan. Ecstatic workers hailed the approach of the bright new dawn with cheers, toasts, and impromptu dances. A great hulk of a man wandered, morosely, through the party, frowning. "You fools go ahead and have your fun," Thurgood Marshall said, "but we ain't begun to work yet." This, as it happened, was perfectly true. The Supreme Court, moving gingerly, had set no date for compliance. It asked, in fact, for additional arguments on this point. A year later, the Court ordered public school desegregation "with all deliberate speed." It seems clear, in retrospect, that this was a disastrous error. The cause of the Commonwealth would have been better served at that moment by a remembrance not of Blackstone but of Shakespeare: "If it were done when 'tis done, then 'twere well it were done quickly."

Since it was not done quickly, the initiative passed into the hands of reactionaries. During the year of delay, a strong resistance movement crystallized in the South around the White Citizens Councils and other racist groups. Encouraged by the timidity of the forces of law, the councils and other groups became increasingly bold, pursuing their goals by tactics of economic intimidation and terror. Public officials, who had greeted the initial decision with restraint and caution, changed now, announcing a massive campaign of litigation and official harassment. These currents mingled, the defiance of public officials reinforcing the terror and intimidation of the underground forces. By 1955, the Southern climate was hot with hate. Public schools were bombed, and mobs pelted Negro students with rotten fruits and stones. National Guard troops were called out in Kentucky, Tennessee, and other states to put down the white revolt.

The first of several climaxes in the second Reconstruction of the South came in 1957 in Little Rock, Arkansas, where howling mobs attacked Negro students and reporters. Defying the federal court, Governor Orval Faubus used national guard troops not to protect the Negro students but to bar them from the school. Faubus' stand stemmed, in part, from the ambivalence of President Eisenhower who indicated privately that he thought the Supreme Court decision was imprudent and who said publicly that he could conceive of no situation in which he would use federal troops to back up orders of the federal court. Faubus' revolt was a direct challenge not only to Eisenhower but to the authority of the federal courts and the supremacy of federal law. Eisenhower, whatever his personal reservations, met this challenge head-on, federalizing the Arkansas national guard and dispatching federal troops to Little Rock. At 9:45 on Wednesday morning, September 25, 1957, soldiers with drawn bayonets escorted six girls and three boys into Central High School, and America's confrontation with itself, and with the Negro, began. This confrontation was forced not so much by Southern defiance as by a new Negro mood as expressed most vividly by the nine Negro children of Little Rock who refused to withdraw from the struggle, thereby indicating their willingness to face the very real possibilities of maiming or even death in the cause of an ideal that had become central in their orientation toward life.

Massive defiance of the Supreme Court ended with Little Rock, but guerilla action continued. Because of the failure of nerve of the federal government, because its actions were sporadic, disjointed and unfocused, guerilla action largely nullified the spirit and letter of the Supreme Court decision. Of greater immediate consequence was the revelation to Negroes of the tissue of relationships in which they were enmeshed.

Were Negroes citizens?

Were they entitled to the full and equal protection of the laws?

What, in fact, was law?

Was there one law for white people and another law for Negroes?

What, precisely, was the Negro's *real* relation to America?

The era of bad faith, of troops and tanks and skirmishes in schoolyards, gave rise to basic questions and changed the tone of race relations in America. Bigger awoke to find himself bilked. A new tone, a tone of anguish and exile and alienation, rose on the ruins of hope. Daisy Bates, the heroine of the Little Rock struggle, sounded the dominant chord. "We've got to decide," she said, "whether it's going to be this generation or never."

V. CATALYST

Martin Luther King, Jr.

THE Cleveland Avenue bus rolled through Court Square, where Negroes were auctioned in the days of the Confederacy, and braked to a halt in front of the Empire Theater. This was a moment the South would never forget, but no one remarked it then. Neither the driver nor his passengers knew that a revolution was about to begin that would end with thousands of Negroes shouting and screaming and praying in the streets. It was a quiet, orderly day in Montgomery, Alabama, the Cradle of the Confederacy; but it was unseasonably hot for December 1.

Six white people boarded the bus at the Empire Theater, and the driver stormed to the rear and ordered the foremost Negroes to get up and give their seats to the white citizens. This was an ancient custom, sanctioned by the peculiar mores of the South, and it excited no undue comment. Three Negroes got up immediately, but Rosa Parks, a mild-mannered seamstress in rimless glasses, kept her seat. For this act of defiance, Rosa Parks was arrested. Local leaders called a one-day bus boycott on December 5, 1955, to protest the arrest. The one-day boycott stretched out to 385 days; the 385 days changed the face and heart of Negro America, creating a new idea and a new movement that raced across the South.

Out of Montgomery came a remarkable fisher of men, Martin Luther King, Jr., and a new ideology, nonviolence. It is not profitable really to ask whether the event of Montgomery "made" King or whether King "made" the event. What is more important is that King made the Myth of Montgomery which cannot be understood without reference to this exceptional young man who is, beyond doubt, the most brilliant Negro leader since Frederick Douglass and one of the most brilliant moral leaders in the history of the Commonwealth.

As a catalytic agent, King created a revolutionary point of departure, a new tissue of relations and hopes. As a magnet and exemplar myth, as an invitation to a new way of life and struggle, King attracted and released the energies of men and women of varying viewpoints. Among the men and women who found a new sense of purpose and passion after Montgomery were Bayard Rustin, the brilliant veteran of the crusade of the forties; and Ella Baker, a former NAACP staffer who found traditional Negro leadership techniques stultifying and cramping.

Beyond all that, King must be seen as a man who solved a technical problem that had stumped Negro leaders for generations. As a powerless group living in the middle of a powerful majority that hated and feared them, Negroes could not stage an open revolt. To go into the streets under those conditions with open demands for change was suicidal. As I have indicated elsewhere, King and the sit-in students solved the technical problems by clothing a national resistance movement in the comforting garb of love, forgiveness, and nonviolence, a transformation that enabled Negroes to stage an open revolt without calling it an open revolt.

The net result was a return on a higher level to Asa Philip Randolph's war without violence of the forties. Randolph's revolt failed, but King's succeeded, largely because of the changing climate of the age and the fact that King, unlike Randolph, had a base, the Negro church, deep in the psyche of the Negro people.

Though King worked primarily in the South, he had deep popular roots in the North. The acclamation he received at the Prayer Pilgrimage of 1957 confirmed beyond doubt that King had popular backing of a depth and passion unprecedented in America since the days of Booker T. Washington and Frederick Douglass. Significantly, King's support, like Douglass' and Washington's, transcended racial lines.

Behind King's sensitivity lay a long and relevant experience. The son of a Baptist minister, he was born and raised in the Negro religious tradition. Sociologically speaking, he was a child of the class E. Franklin Frazier called "Black Puritans." But through his father and his paternal grandfather, he was marked by the plantation and the agony and passion of the Negro folk.

King's story begins, in a manner of speaking, with Frederick Douglass' end. In 1894, the year before Douglass' death, the year before Booker T. Washington blessed appeasement, King's maternal grandfather, A. D. Williams, took over a dilapidated church in Atlanta. Within a short time, the strong-willed patriarch had made Ebenezer Baptist Church one of the strongest institutions of its kind.

During this same period, another man, a man born under a different star, was sharecropping on a plantation in Stockbridge, about twenty miles from Atlanta. Part Negro and part Irish, James Albert King was a hard-working man who dreamed of buying a small farm for his wife and children. But the dream never did come true. As King sunk deeper and deeper into debt, he gave up hope. Retreating within himself, he spent his weekends trying to drink himself into forgetfulness.

To this sharecropper, in this situation, were born ten children. The child who holds our attention, the male child Martin who became Martin Luther King's father, was born in 1899. Repelled by the enforced degradation of plantation life, he left Stockbridge and went to the big city of Atlanta. Ambitious and energetic, he worked hard, saved his money and put himself through Morehouse College. While still a student, he met, wooed, and married A. D. Williams' oldest daughter, Alberta. The young man later succeeded his father-in-law as the pastor of Ebenezer Baptist Church.

King's father and his grandfather were among the pioneers of the Negro protest movement. The grandfather, who was one of the early leaders of the NAACP, played a key role in the boycott of a racist Atlanta paper and helped to pressure into existence Atlanta's first public high school which was named, ironically, after the man who loathed pressure tactics, Booker T. Washington. King's father was also a staunch leader in the NAACP tradition.

Out of this soil came Martin Luther King, Jr., who was born on January 15, 1929, in a big rambling two-story house on "Sweet Auburn Avenue." King and his brother and sister were raised in comfortable middle-class circumstances. As a child, King had the usual brushes with Jim Crow (incidents on buses and in stores), and he suffered the usual trauma of discovering that there was a name—Negro—in the world and that that name applied to him and set him off somehow from other children. None of this apparently left deep scars. King's early racial experiences, compared, say, with the experiences of Baldwin, were almost peripheral. His childhood, unlike Baldwin's childhood, was marked by order, balance, restraint.

It is not necessary really to seek in King's childhood for the origins of his ideas on nonviolence. What we must seek in King's past is not the provenance of his theory of nonviolence but the pattern that gave him the insight to recognize a good idea when he saw it and the inner mechanism that inclined him toward a radical rejection of the dominant myths of his environment. The record, which is contradictory, seems to indicate that King was not a youth who went out of his way to find a fight; but the record, particularly the reminiscences of his childhood friends, indicates clearly that "Tweed," as he was called, did not run away from many scuffles.

Beneath the surface of King's life other currents moved. The young boy dissented apparently from crucial parts of the Black Puritan world view. Black Puritans, then and now, worshipped success and held themselves aloof from the Negro masses. But King had, and has, deep sympathies for the Negro masses, and a barely concealed contempt for the standards of success of his class. Even more striking is the fact that King was repelled by the Negro religious tradition. It may be that King was exercising the normal male prerogative of rebelling against a strong-willed father. The father, a man of considerable parts, wanted King to be a minister, but King decided quite early that he was not going to be a minister. It seemed to him then that religion, as he put it, could not be intellectually respectable and socially relevant. He thought, at first, that he would like to become a doctor; but he changed his mind later and decided to study law.

As a student, King was exceptionally bright, skipping the twelfth grade at Booker T. Washington High School and entering Morehouse College in 1944 at the age of fifteen. This was the first of several turning points in his life. Morehouse College was an all-men's school famous for turning out leading members of the Negro leadership group. It was served at this juncture by a number of outstanding men, including Dr. George W. Kelsey, head of the department of religion, and Dr. Benjamin E. Mays, the president. Both Mays and Kelsey were seminary-trained ministers and their sermons, socially relevant and intellectually stimulating, changed King's mind about the ministry. In 1947, King was ordained in his father's church and named assistant minister. The next year, after graduating from Morehouse, he became one of the few Negro students at Crozer Theological Seminary near Philadelphia. Competing for the first time with white students, King blossomed into an aggressive student leader. He led his class and became the first Negro to serve as president of the student body.

At Crozer, King developed an interest in the ideas of Walter Rauschenbusch, the articulate exponent of the "social gospel." The main thrust of the "social gospel"—the idea that the church should take a more active role in the struggle for social justice—became a central element in King's philosophy.

Leaving Crozer in 1951, King entered Boston University, where he earned a Ph.D. degree in systematic theology. In Boston also, he met Coretta Scott, an Alabama beauty who was studying voice at the New England Conservatory of Music. They were married in June, 1953, in her hometown of Marion, Alabama. In 1954, a bare fourteen months before the beginning of the boycott, King and his wife returned to Alabama, where he began his pastorate at Montgomery's fashionable Dexter Avenue Church.

Although King had a passion for social justice, his approach to the racial problem at that juncture was rigidly conventional. He leaned apparently toward the NAACP approach, but he also championed the gradualistic tactics of organizations like the Alabama Commission on Human Relations.

Into this quiet and conventional life came the bombshell of Rosa Parks. Ed Nixon, a Pullman porter who had participated in Randolph's crusade of the forties, seems to have taken the lead in the first phase of the protest. It was he who bailed out Rosa Parks; it was he apparently who suggested that something should be done. After a great deal of telephoning, it was decided to hold a one-day boycott, and King, a relatively new member of the leadership community, was elected president of the boycott directorate, the Montgomery Improvement Association.

Under King's leadership, the nature of the Montgomery struggle changed. What began as a "peaceful" struggle for more equitable treatment within the system became a "nonviolent" struggle to smash the system. With consummate skill, King and his aides, particularly the No. 2 man, Ralph D. Abernathy, organized a car pool and outmaneuvered the city officials who were frankly bewildered by the unorthodox behavior of the once-docile Negro community. Of even greater significance was King's role in the adoption of the nonviolent ideology. Contrary to common impressions, King did not enter the struggle with a program of action. As an educated man, he had a certain familiarity with the main outlines of the Gandhian struggle. He had heard lectures on the subject by Mordecai Johnson, then president of Howard University, and others. But it would be a mistake to conclude from all this that the King of 1955 was a Gandhian. The truth is at once more prosaic and more striking. *King convinced himself, and, in convincing himself, he convinced others.*

In the beginning, nothing apparently was further from the

minds of Montgomery resistants than Mahatma Gandhi. King and other leaders urged Negro boycotters to remain calm and peaceful, but they relied primarily on the words of Jesus and the traditional Negro leadership rhetoric that Negroes could never win with violence. Although the leaders stressed peaceful protest (they had no choice, really), they also believed in the Western tradition of self-defense. Nothing indicates this more clearly than King's application, shortly after the boycott began, for a permit to carry a gun. The application was denied. By that time, however, King was convinced that self-defense was wrong.

King came to this extraordinary view by a roundabout way. The original impetus seems to have come from a Southern white woman. Soon after the boycott began, Juliette Morgan, a white Montgomery librarian, remarked, in a letter to the editor of a local paper, on the similarities between the Montgomery struggle and Gandhi's crusade. The leaders of the boycott seized on this idea, and began to use Gandhi as an authority in their frequent appeals for restraint.

The opening to Gandhi was facilitated by two factors: King's propensity, largely because of his philosophical training, for large ideas and concepts; and the further fact that the movement was based on the solid rock of the Negro religious tradition. Early in the campaign, the leaders began to hold nightly mass meetings in Negro churches, using, consciously or unconsciously, Negro spirituals and the Negro religious idiom as morale builders. King's genius—and it was that, precisely—was not in the application of Gandhism to the Negro struggle but in the transmuting of Gandhism by welding it with the only thing that could give it relevance and force in the Negro community: the Negro church.

Nonviolence, as we have seen, was not a new idea in the ghetto. Asa Randolph pioneered in the use of the technique in the early forties, and CORE and other organizations institutionalized the technique in the late forties and the early fifties. By 1950, two Negro-Americans—Adam Clayton Powell in *Marching Blacks* and Howard Thurman in *Jesus and the Disinherited*—had written books applying Gandhian techniques to the Negro protest. (King read or re-read at least one of these books, *Jesus and the Disinherited*, in the early days of the boycott.) The Fellowship of Reconciliation, a predominantly white pacifist group, and CORE also had considerable experience with nonviolence and, soon after the boycott began, members of these groups, Bayard Rustin in particular, drifted into town with advice and patterned programs.

During the next few months, King plunged ever deeper into Gandhism. A trip to the land of Gandhi, in 1959, solidified his commitment to the cause. Even more decisive perhaps in the transformation of King was an apocalyptic vision. Stretched taut on the rack of himself, King came one night in 1956 to the end of his personal resources. The air was thick with doubts and very real dangers, and King, sitting dejected in the kitchen of his home, told God that he couldn't go any further alone. "I am here taking a stand for what I believe is right," he recalls telling God that midnight in January. "But now I am afraid. The people are looking to me for leadership, and if I stand before them without strength and courage, they too will falter. I am at the end of my powers. I have nothing left. I've come to the point where I can't face it alone." Into King's kitchen, or so it seemed to him anyway, came "the presence of the Divine," and he thought he heard the "quiet assurance of an inner voice, saying, 'Stand up for righteousness, stand up for truth. . . .'" After that experience, King says in his autobiography, *Stride Toward Freedom*, "my uncertainty disappeared. I was ready to face anything."

Building on the Gandhi tradition, learning not so much from words as from words fed by the blood of experience, King transformed himself and the Montgomery movement, giving men, women, and children a new vision of battle and a new vision of the possibilities of the Negro personality.

After Montgomery, the arena of action changed, moving from the courts to the streets, and the foci of action shifted, moving from Negro lawyers to the Negro masses. Another important shift was from the issue of school integration to public accommodation. The net result, and all of the results would not become apparent until much later, was a re-structuring of Negro leadership patterns.

As a result of his conversion in the church of fire, King came to radically different conclusions about the nature of the Negro struggle. A key concept in his new orientation was the idea of confrontation, the idea of bringing out into the open sub-merged evils, of *forcing* face-to-face meetings of man and man, of community and community, individually as in the refusal of a single individual to accept segregation, collectively as in the open challenge by a Negro community of the fiats and fears of the white community. The idea that nothing substantial would happen in the field of race relations if men and communities were not *forced* to face the evils they were trying to hide was stated with great eloquence by Randolph in the forties, but King carried it to a higher stage of development, making the "showdown situation" the central component of the Negro's new vision of battle. Like Randolph, King believed in negotiating from a position of strength. Like Randolph, he believed direct action indispensable for racial progress. Pressure, even conflict, he said, was an unfortunate but necessary element in social change. Abandoning the Negro leadership tradition, which shied away from conflict and considered direct appeals to the masses inflammatory, King called for a mobilization of all resources in the Negro community—"the no D's and the Ph.D's." He stressed, moreover, the responsibility of every individual to history in the making. Every individual, according to King, had a right, nay, a duty to break or ignore unjust laws.

With the formation of the Southern Christian Leadership Conference, King became an institution. Sixty Negro leaders, most of them preachers, from ten Southern states founded the organization at a two-day meeting at Ebenezer Baptist Church on January 10-11, 1957. The next month at a meeting in New Orleans the Southern Conference on Transportation and Nonviolent Integration became the Southern Christian Leadership Conference with King as president. In its formative years, the organization, as its first name indicated, was concerned primarily with transportation and voter registration. Some of the more theoretical sit-in students claimed later that the Montgomery idea was aborted before it reached full development. While there is some truth in this, it is surely true also that the foundations for the movement of the sixties was laid by King's first stumbling strides in the darkness of confrontation.

Future consequences apart, King's ideas had immediate effects. With the organization of the Southern Christian Leadership Conference and the diffusion of King's ideas through articulate strata of the Negro community, a sense of urgency penetrated Negro leaders. Lewis W. Jones noted this fact in an essay on the Tuskegee movement. "In the spring of 1957," he wrote, "strong sentiment developed among Tuskegee Negroes to 'do something about our situation.' Outspoken persons within and without [the Tuskegee Civic Association] talked about 'something' similar to the action taken in nearby Montgomery regarding the public transportation boycott." This feeling opened fissures in several Negro communities and prepared the way for the displacement of accommodating Negro leaders by activists. More significantly, young Negro preachers began to view themselves through the prism of the King image. The immediate consequences were a series of bus boycotts in Tallahassee, Atlanta and other communities. Tuskegee leaders, deciding against an uncritical duplication of the Montgomery idea, began a boycott of Tuskegee stores as a protest against the action of the state legislature which had excluded Negro voters from the city boundaries. As the decade of the fifties neared an end, a massive ballot-box confrontation began in Fayette County, Tennessee, where white men of power were trying to contain the "new Negro thrust" by tactics of intimidation and terror.

King contended that soft answers turned away wrath, but there was no confirmation of this theory in the Black Belt areas of the South. The period between 1955 and 1959 was punctuated by a series of violent incidents, by lynchings, murders, and the bombings of churches, synagogues, and schools. There were three lynchings in Mississippi in 1955. Two NAACP leaders, Rev. George W. Lee and Lamar Smith, were slain on May 13 and August 13, respectively, because they refused to take their names off voter registration lists. On August 28, Emmett Till, a fourteen-year-old Chicagoan who was vacationing in the South, was kidnapped and murdered by two white men near Money, Mississippi. This reign of terror, particularly the Till lynching of 1955 and the Mack Charles Parker lynching of 1959, had a sharp impact on the Negro mind, causing some leaders to call for federal occupation of Mississippi and other defiant areas of the South.

As the struggle widened and deepened in the South, the ghettos of the North came awake. The struggle in the North in this period was largely verbal, but it was no less important for all that. Enraged by the Till lynching and other atrocities, and the creeping misery of the masses in the wake of mounting unemployment, Northern Negroes began to move to new positions. This development was, in part, a result of the Southern revolt, but it grew out of different realities and it reflected a different perception of social reality. Negroes in the North already enjoyed many of the *de jure* privileges Negroes in the South were fighting and dying for. Although there were fair employment and public accommodations laws in many areas of the North, the Negro's *de facto* position in the North was bad and it was rapidly getting a great deal worse.

One other factor in the Northern world view should be stressed. Many Negroes, particularly intellectuals, had deep misgivings about the philosophy of love and nonviolence.

Though not necessarily violent, they insisted on their right to self-defense and scorned the idea of loving their oppressors.

If King did not convince intellectuals, he did, at least, stimulate them. And the intellectuals, thus stimulated, escalated the struggle to a higher plateau, hacking their way through the deep underbrush of myths that hid Negroes from themselves. As the fury rose in the South, Negro intellectuals found their voices and embarked on a perilous journey of self-naming, self-emancipation, and self-discovery. The revolt of Negro intellectuals, which began shortly after Montgomery and reached a red hot fury in the sixties, was an objective manifestation of the convulsive stirrings in the nerve ends of their inarticulate brothers. As cause and effect, the revolt of the intellectuals prepared the way for a new myth of challenge and renewal.

An event of major importance in the revolt of Negro intellectuals was the publication in Paris of a book called *Bourgeoisie Noir*. E. Franklin Frazier, the author of the book, was an eminent Negro sociologist who was on leave from his position as professor of sociology at Howard University. Frazier's book, later published in America as *Black Bourgeoisie*, was a scathing attack on the Negro leadership class which was composed, or so Frazier said, of "idle, overfed women" and "glamorous men," "running from the Baptist to the Congregationalist and the Bahai, trying to find some place where people don't know they're colored." Never before, Frazier said, had so few led so many so badly. Not only had the Negro leadership class failed to lead, Frazier said, but they were in full flight from the responsibilities of leadership. Frazier saw members of the group wallowing in materialism and a make-believe world, trying to escape reality, trying to escape themselves, trying, above all, to differentiate themselves from the Negro masses.

Black Bourgeoisie had an immediate and overwhelming impact. Negro youth and Negro intellectuals appropriated its ideas and used them as weapons to express their loathing of the timidity and caution of the Negro establishment. It can be said, I think, that *Black Bourgeoisie* weakened the foundations of the Negro establishment and prepared the way for its partial displacement by younger, bolder men who heard the sound of a different drummer.

What has not been noted often enough is the fact that Frazier's book attacked not only the Negro bourgeoisie but all bourgeoisie. This larger theme, though not stated, is implicit in the questions Frazier raised about the goals of Negro life. For if Negroes were not aiming for middle-class status within the confines of a middle-class civilization, if their most burning desire was not to join the hollow men in the suburbs, if they did not really intend to become good Rotary-minded, martini-drinking, barbecue-burning, convention-going, girl-chasing executives, then what, in God's name, did they want?

This question gave rise to thought and a series of writers' and artists' conferences organized around the query: Whither? Out of this creative ferment came a new breed of writers with a new frame of reference and a new sense of respect for themselves: men and women like Lorraine Hansberry, LeRoi Jones, John Killens, Frank London Brown, Hoyt Fuller, Ossie Davis, Miles Davis, Ruby Dee, Oscar Brown. Towering over this group was the wraith-like figure of James Baldwin who returned to the States in 1957 and began to turn out a series of provocative essays. The net effect of this germination period was the literary efflorescence of the late fifties and early sixties, an efflorescence that approached the Renaissance of the twenties. Equally important was the part this group played in focusing and sharpening Negro discontent. As artists and as human beings, members of the new literary generation were engaged. Their work and their lives vibrated with a new fire. The new Negro artists had a new relation to their past and to the Negro folk tradition. They did not look at themselves through the eyes of the white Other. In fact, they annihilated the white Other, denying the validity of his concepts, his categories, his definitions. Challenging the white man's images, challenging his *meaning*, they came at last to the heart of the matter, the question of values. By 1959, the new generation of artists had drunk to the full the white liquor of despair. By that time, according to Lorraine Hansberry, "the mood of Negro writers" approached "what can best be described as *crimson fury.*" Proof of that fact was a series of plays, books, poems, essays, and works of art that spoke to white America with an incandescent candor unprecedented in the history of America.

Almost parallel with the revolt of Negro intellectuals was the growth of Negro nationalism, which should not be confused with specific black nationalist groups. The mood is, in essence, an affirmation of Negro experience and Negro values. It is not necessarily a rejection of whiteness, but it is quite definitely an acceptance of blackness and all that that implies. Buoyed up by new ego-ideals, by a King, by a Kenyatta or Nkrumah, Negroes began in the late fifties to experience themselves in new ways.

An extraordinary phase of this development was the migration of modern jazz which has reflected, rather accurately, the tensions of Negro life. In the early forties, with the be-bop movement, jazz became opaque, discordant, menacing, reflecting the new anguish of the Negro spirit. In the early fifties, there was a new development. Jazz became cool, uninvolved, withdrawn. Now, in the wake of Montgomery and Ghana and Emmett Till, jazz became hard, hot, hostile. The climax of this development was the Soul movement of the late fifties which was a return, literally and figuratively, to roots.

The currents of the fifties, musical and otherwise, reinforced and sustained each other, the blue note of defiance of jazz, the revolt of Negro intellectuals, the *mystique* of Negro nationalism, and the myth of Montgomery all melding in a new ideology, an overarching social myth. This myth, which we shall call the Myth of the Black Man's Burden, was made up of many ripples and sub-myths, of a *mystique* of movement, of activism, of things happening, building to an apocalyptic climax. The myth gave Negroes a messianic sense of destiny and purpose, a new relation to time, to America, to themselves. The myth asserted:

1) That Negroes were a community of maligned *victims* waging, with the aid of a band of *rebels,* a righteous war for *freedom.*

2) That they were being *deprived* of their freedom by oppressors whose bad deeds and bad consciences had poisoned their minds and their dreams.

3) That it was necessary to wage the struggle to save not only the oppressed but the oppressors.

4) That the oppressed stood in a challenge relation to the oppressors who were *indebted* to the oppressed not only for services rendered and not paid for but for values invented and not acknowledged.

The central thread of this myth, whether expressed in the elegant language of the Harlem Writers' Workshop or the muscular language of Birmingham pool halls, was this: nice Negroes finish last. Dr. Kenneth B. Clark put it nicely, saying there was a feeling in the ghetto of "Oh, the hell with you polite Negroes. . . ."

The new ideology was an interwoven fabric of desire and despair welling up from the deeps of the ghetto and it released energies that put Negro leadership machinery under severe strain. The great surge of passion of modern jazz, "the great Negro cry" of writers and artists, the Negro nationalism of the North, and the Montgomery spirit of the South began to be clearly felt by Negro leaders, if not clearly seen, by 1956. By that time, the NAACP was under sharp fire by Southern governments who were trying to drive the organization out of the South. By that time also, unemployment was rife in the Negro community, Negro hate was spreading in the South, and the law of diminishing return was working in the courtroom. Here was a new situation that called for a new response.

What would established Negro leadership do?

What could Negro leaders do?

There was no clear answer to these questions. On the national level, there was confusion and doubt. Voices within and without the National Urban League and the NAACP called for new departures and a re-examination of basic premises. Militants within the Urban League formed an *ad hoc* group, the "Disturbed Committee of the Executive Secretaries Council," to fight for a more daring program. Edwin C. (Bill) Berry, who later became executive secretary of the Chicago Urban League, was chairman of the committee. He contended that the League had "played it so safe that we are well behind the safety zone."

Another warning came from John H. Johnson, publisher of *Ebony, Jet,* and *Negro Digest.* Speaking of the League on its golden anniversary, Johnson called for a confrontation with the dominant challenge of the age, the Negro masses.

"It is the responsibility of leadership to point out the hard and narrow path," he said. "But it is also the duty of leadership to travel that path, to set an example. People are no longer willing to follow the leader who says—Don't do as I do —Do as I say do.

"I believe the leadership of the future will find it necessary to remain in close and constant touch with the masses of people. Too many Negro leaders live too far from the scene of battle. Too many of us are isolated from the people we are supposed to be leading."

The NAACP just then was undergoing a similar crisis of conscience. The organization was in a state of transition, organizationally and programmatically. Walter White, the longtime secretary, died in 1955 and was succeeded by Roy Wilkins, a former newspaper editor (*Kansas City Call*) who joined the organization in 1931. It would be Wilkins' fate to preside over the NAACP in one of the most turbulent periods in its history. He was no sooner settled in his seat than the specter of King appeared on the horizon. Then, in triphammer blows, came the rout of litigation in the South, and a wave of lynchings and bombings. Finally, and most ominously, the South began in 1956 to strike at the roots of the organization, filing suits against Negro lawyers for "soliciting" civil rights suits and harassing state organizations by subpoenaing their membership lists.

To make things even more vexing, Negro activists chose this moment to attack the organization on its exposed left flank. Jimmy Hicks of the New York *Amsterdam News* said that neither Walter White nor his successor, Roy Wilkins, was a "true" Negro leader. Hicks charged that Wilkins was a "captive" of prominent whites on the NAACP board. Jackie Robinson, a member of the board, did not endorse Hicks's views, but he declared in no uncertain terms that the organization was not reaching the "little man." He was particularly disturbed, according to a 1958 interview, about "the failure on the part of the organization" to do an effective selling job.

In the center of the controversy, buffeted by critics of the left and right, was Roy Wilkins, who was born in St. Louis in 1901 and graduated from the University of Minnesota in 1923. Tall and thin, Wilkins was extremely able in the area he marked off for himself: administrative expertise and lobbying. He had come up through the NAACP bureaucracy and was, accordingly, a desk-oriented man who lacked King's charisma and Malcolm X's skills in mass organization. Wilkins' skills were the skills of the conference table and the committee room. He was not an overpowering speaker and he lacked color. Wilkins' base of power was the NAACP organization, militant members of the Negro middle class, and the white liberals of labor and church groups. Outside this group, he was relatively unknown.

What was Wilkins' program?

Wilkins' program was the NAACP's program which had not changed, really, since 1909. Negro interests, Wilkins believed, were best served by tactics of litigation and lobbying. He did not then, nor does he now, believe in the use of combat strategy (demonstrations, picketing, boycotting) as a primary tactic of struggle.

It looks simpler now than it did then. With the aid of hindsight, we can see clearly that events were foreclosing the possibilities of the leadership style Wilkins represented. The grain of history was moving in another direction, and Wilkins and the NAACP would have to move with the grain or lose the power to make history.

Could the NAACP change fast enough to keep abreast of the times?

Could it adapt itself to the new orientation of the Negro?

Wilkins has been criticized for his responses or lack of responses to the challenge of the age. There is, to be sure, a great deal to criticize, but most of the criticism should be directed not at Wilkins but at the idea he represented. In general, the limitations of Wilkins' responses grew out of the limitations of his style rather than fumbling. The task Wilkins faced in the late fifties was a formidable one, and he was not, by any means, a free agent. Above all else, the new NAACP secretary must be seen as a prisoner of the NAACP idea which had built-in limitations. By the late fifties, the NAACP structure was set in a rather rigid mould. Not only the national staff but major local branches were top-heavy with moderate types whose freedom of action was limited by internal and external ties to the status quo. It is by no means certain that a new secretary could have shifted the organization structure fast enough to meet the new challenge, even if he had wanted to. Still, when all allowances are made, this must be said: that it is the duty of leaders to lead and that the highest function of leadership, as John H. Johnson pointed out in his Urban League address, is to anticipate change. The failure of the entire leadership spectrum, Wilkins included, to anticipate change and to prepare for it was a failure of large proportions. Far more fateful and decisive was the failure of the entire Negro leadership class to relate itself in a meaningful way to the aspirations of the masses.

Wilkins admitted in the forties that the NAACP lacked skill in mass organization, but he said the organization knew it, and was doing something about it. What, if anything, the organization did is not clear. It is true that church and labor secretaries were appointed, but these acts did not even touch the fringes of the problem. By 1955, the NAACP's lack of skill in mass organization was, if anything, more obvious, and it was becoming more embarrassing day by day.

Although Wilkins denied the bill of particulars of NAACP critics, he moved quietly, in the late fifties, to reinforce his exposed flanks, appointing James Farmer, former director of CORE, program director. Farmer, who was born in 1920 in Marshall, Texas, was a stocky, pugnacious pacifist with a superb sense of strategy. After leaving CORE, he had served as a union organizer and propagandist. As CORE director and as a union organizer, Farmer had demonstrated a talent for drawing up long-range programs. His first act as NAACP program director was to draw up another blueprint, calling for an expanded program. The NAACP announced that Farmer had "prepared a tentative prospectus, essaying an analysis of some of the major problems confronting the Association and offering various preliminary long- and short-range program suggestions designed to meet these problems. No attempt was made to provide a blueprint or 'master plan,' but merely to take the first step toward development of coordinated program planning to meet the challenge of changing times." What this meant, if it meant anything, was that Farmer had indeed drawn up a blueprint for "changing times," and that the NAACP had decided not to change with the times.

When we pass from the national scene to the local branches, we find a similar leadership ferment. In Chicago, for example, the National Urban League chapter was closed down after a simmering controversy over the "radicalism" of the executive director. A committee, composed of white and Negro businessmen and professionals, reorganized the branch and hired a new executive director. In the same city, Negro businessmen and the Dawson political machine captured the NAACP branch and ousted the president, a militant Negro labor leader who was attacking the Negro and white power structures and calling for an opening to the masses.

As in other periods of internal strife and mass unrest, Negro leaders banded together in *ad hoc* coalitions. This was, in part, a banding together for warmth and comfort in a new and terrifying world, but it was also a quest for new methods and combinations of methods. The new era began on Tuesday, April 24, 1956, with the first of several "state of the race" conferences. Some seventy national leaders attended the Washington meeting which was called by Asa Philip Randolph. The conferees specifically rejected gradualism and attacked both political parties for a "do nothing" policy in the field of civil rights.

A more substantial token of coalition effectiveness was the 1957 Prayer Pilgrimage to Washington, a mass demonstration by some fifty thousand persons who gathered at the Lincoln Monument to protest the slow pace of desegregation. The use of the mass demonstration idea, the broad support of white liberals from labor and religious organizations, and the unprecedented cooperation of the entire spectrum of the Negro power structure: all this marked a new level of strategic awareness and strategic effectiveness. Among the leaders of the march were Asa Philip Randolph, Bayard Rustin, Roy Wilkins, and Martin Luther King, Jr. The mass demonstration idea was used again in 1958 and 1959 in the two youth marches on Washington organized by Rustin.

The climax of this period of groping and uncertainty was the Negro Summit Conference of 1958. The meeting, which was sponsored by the National Newspaper Publishers Association, attracted the largest gathering of Negro leaders in American history. More than four hundred leaders representing every major protest, church, and fraternal organization formally debated the state of the race on Monday and Tuesday, May 12-13, at the Raleigh Hotel in Washington.

What brought the decision-makers to Washington?

"Two million Negro children," the Summit Conference said, "are still attending segregated schools. Public officials, members of Congress, business, social and political leaders in the South have joined in open, massive, concerted resistance to the Supreme Court decision. They are attempting to nullify this decision by a manifesto, by new laws, by denial of registration and voting, by economic and physical intimidation, by propaganda, and by gerrymandering. We are denied equal employment opportunity in state after state, also in the State Department, the Defense Department, the Agriculture Deparment, the Justice Department, the Commerce Department and numerous commissions and bureaus of the national government. We are segregated and discriminated against in transportation, education, public accommodation, recreation and entertainment facilities. We are hampered unfairly in registering to vote or denied registration completely, intimidated in voting or denied the right to vote. We are denied equal justice under law, both civil and criminal."

Such were the grave truths of Negro life as Negro leaders saw them and wrote of them in 1958.

What was to be done?

In an opening address, President Dwight D. Eisenhower enraged almost everyone present with a call for "patience and forbearance." The strongest call for action came from Randolph who said Negroes faced a crisis of monstrous proportions.

"The Negro today," he said, "is not only NOT winning his fight for civil rights, but the South—with its doctrine of white supremacy, its White Citizens Council and its Ku Klux Klan—is pressing, if not winning, the war against the Negro's fight for freedom." Nor was that all. Northern newspapers, he said, were in retreat. Liberalism was timid and weak. There was a "corrosive spirit of despair and creeping paralysis of faith among Negroes." "We are now being nailed to the cross and going through the trial by fire."

Randolph called for a mobilization of all resources for a relevant response to the "counter-revolution" in the South. A "fetish," he said, was being made of "moderation." Negroes were depending too much on "outside forces." What was needed, he concluded, was pressure and more pressure. "We must renew the Negro's faith and power in himself."

This was eloquently said and fervently received, but eloquent words were not enough by themselves. What would Randolph and the assembled leaders do?

Not much. The Summit Conference decided finally to recommend a stepped-up campaign of political activity based on a massive voter registration campaign. The group also recommended a Presidential executive order barring bias in federally financed housing, continued support for Negro business, intensive efforts on the part of church and neighborhood groups to prevent juvenile delinquency, and additional pressure to force action on a civil rights bill.

The Summit Conference was important perhaps as a morale booster, but it accomplished very little of substance. One is tempted to say that it was not designed to accomplish anything. It was a ceremonial of the kind held from time to time by Negro men of power who feel vaguely that the *via media* is inadequate but cannot decide, singly or collectively, on a new departure. Nothing indicates more clearly the programmatic poverty of the Negro power structure on the eve of the cataclysm than the fact that it had nothing of value to say about mass action, passive resistance or boycotts three years after Montgomery.

The defalcation of established Negro leadership created a vacuum into which other, more daring, men sprang. Elijah Muhammad and his disciple, Malcolm X, were working just then with Jackie Robinson's "little man," and finding the experience profitable and stimulating. The lean years of the thirties and forties were over for the Black Muslims, who purchased a Jewish synagogue near the University of Chicago and sent messengers into the boiling ghettos of the North. Muhammad called for a total separation from the "white devils," and a surprisingly large number of Negroes flocked to his temples.

To the left of Muhammad, to the left of almost everyone in America, loomed the obscure bearded figure of Robert Williams, who called for defensive guerilla warfare and the formation of a string of rifle clubs. Williams' militancy led to his ouster as president of the Monroe, North Carolina, NAACP chapter and his indictment on a charge of kidnapping a white couple. Before fleeing to Cuba, Williams said that King's crusade was doomed to failure. "My only difference with Dr.

King," he wrote, "is that I believe in flexibility in the freedom struggle. This means that I believe in nonviolent tactics where feasible. . . . In civilized society the law serves as a deterrent against lawless forces that would destroy the democratic process. But where there is a breakdown of the law, the individual citizen has a right to protect his person, his family, his home, and his property. To me this is so simple and proper that it is self-evident."

Midway between Williams and Muhammad was restless Negro youth who also wanted to be heard. The most dramatic example of youthful impatience was the sit-in campaigns staged in 1958 by the youth council of the Oklahoma City NAACP branch. In a series of direct action thrusts, the youth succeeded in integrating several lunch counters in the downtown section.

Of words and acts of defiance, of prophets and dreamers and soothsayers, there was no lack, in the dying days of the fifties.

Which way to the promised land?

Separate from the "white devils," Elijah Muhammad said.

Demonstrate, said the youth of Oklahoma City.

Register and vote, said the Negro power structure.

Fight fire with fire, said Robert Williams.

And Martin Luther King?

As the fifties died, King was in a state of transit. He had resigned his position at Dexter Avenue Church and was preparing to move, on February 1, to Atlanta where he was going to devote all his time to the SCLC program of voter registration in the South. While King was moving, the Bastille of the Negro rebellion fell.

EPILOGUE

CONFRONTATION II

America Face to Face

THE Bastille of the Negro rebellion—a five-and-dime Bastille so peculiarly American—was about to fall.

It was Monday, February 1, 1960.

There was trouble that day in Algeria and Israel, but all was quiet in Greensboro, North Carolina, in the United States of America. It was 4:30 or thereabouts and shadows were gathering beneath the spreading branches of the trees on South Elm Street. There was a slight chill in the air, but it was pleasant and warm in the F. W. Woolworth store which was filled now with Negro and white shoppers wandering, bemused, down aisles piled high with bottles and boxes in bright reds, greens and blues. Among the shoppers were four Negro teen-agers: Ezell Blair, 17; Joseph McNeil, 17; David Richmond, 17; and Franklin McLain, 18. It was obvious to the casual viewer that the four neatly-dressed young men with the large textbooks were students at one of Greensboro's Negro colleges. The four students stopped here and there and whispered conspiratorially. But no one paid them any attention. No one remarked on their behavior at the notions counter where they bought several items and asked, politely, for receipts. All was bustle and movement and swirling fragments of conversation, and the quartet moved along on the tide of commerce. There was a great deal of activity at that hour at the lunch counter, which was reserved for the exclusive use of white patrons. Behind this counter, a Negro woman collected dirty dishes, brushed away fragments of meat and bread, and disappeared through a swinging door. The hand on the big store clock moved. It was now 4:45. At that precise moment, the four students appeared on the edge of the lunch counter section. They stood for a moment suspended in time, suspended in being. Then, squaring their shoulders and taking a deep breath, they leaped into history.

It was not a very large leap spatially; but psychologically the leap covered several centuries. The system of Negro subordination was—and is—founded on willing compliance, on the fact that most people of whatever race or group accommodate themselves to prevailing power realities. By walking across a few feet of open space and taking seats at the lunch counter, the four Negro students laid siege to the Bastille of white power, a great white prison in the mind.

This was not immediately apparent to the white waitress who seems to have believed that a mistake had been made. (It was not unusual for young students from the North to "forget" temporarily that they were in the South.) The waitress told the students that Negroes were not served there. The four young men told her she was mistaken. They had just been served at the notions counter and they had receipts to prove it.

Why couldn't they be served at the lunch counter?

This was a psychological question, and the waitress, perceiving it, retreated for reinforcements. Men came and argued with the youths. It was not their fault, really; they were businessmen—they could not change the mores of the South. The Negro youths did not seem sympathetic. They said they would remain until served. To emphasize this point, they opened books and began to study. Now came an incredible scene. A Negro woman, a dishwasher, was summoned from the kitchen; and two generations, two ways of life, two ways of being, confronted each other. The woman said the youths were only making things worse. "You are stupid, ignorant!" she said. "You are dumb! That's why we can't get anywhere today. You know you are supposed to eat at the other end." One of the young men said he was sorry she felt that way, but the strategy of her generation hadn't worked, and he was tired of waiting.

By now, a crowd had gathered. But, incredibly, no one did anything. The hands on the big clock moved, and everyone waited, tight with tension. The store closed an hour later without serving the four young men who vowed to return the next day.

Night fell on the Piedmont city of Greensboro, and everything went on as before. No one knew then that the confrontation was about to begin. No one knew then that the Bastille of the Negro rebellion was about to fall.

Remarkably, this fact did not communicate itself to Negro leadership. Lights did not burn late that night at NAACP headquarters in lower Manhattan. The CORE people went home early. There was no action that night at Martin Luther King's headquarters in Atlanta. Outwardly, the night of Monday, February 1, 1960, was idyllically serene. But beneath the surface, down deep in the minds of children, matters of consequence were unfolding. While America slept, four young men were making a decision in a dormitory at North Carolina A. and T. College that would change race relations forever.

Who were these young men?

Ezell Blair and David Richmond had lived in Greensboro all their lives. Franklin McLain was from Washington, D. C., and Joseph McNeil was from Wilmington, North Carolina. All were members of the college chapter of the NAACP, but all were scornful of the *via media* of the NAACP and the middle- and lower-middle-class groups it represented. The four youths had decided, late in 1959, that it was time for somebody to do something about the indignities suffered by Negro citizens in the downtown sections of Southern cities—something, that is, besides petitioning and protesting. By January, the four students had decided that *they* would do something. In late-night "bull sessions" in the dormitory, they formulated a plan, choosing a tactic, the sit-in, and a target, the Woolworth store on South Elm Street. The quartet said later that they chose a chain store because of its vulnerability to pressure by Northern demonstrators. They insisted then and later that they acted on their own, and that they had no familiarity with the sit-in successes of CORE and the NAACP youth councils of Oklahoma City, Oklahoma, and Wichita Falls, Kansas.

After the initial sit-in, the foursome decided to widen the struggle. On the night of February 1, they recruited reinforcements from militant layers of the student body. They also asked George Simkins, Jr., a dentist who headed the adult chapter of the Greensboro NAACP, if his organization would back them. Dr. Simkins immediately took a step that would have large implications later. Instead of contacting *his* organization, he got in touch with national leaders of CORE which had a great deal of experience in direct action campaigns. Both CORE and NAACP rushed staffers to the Piedmont area; but neither organization played a significant role in the first wave of assaults.

With a hastily-assembled group of irregulars, the four students renewed the struggle on Tuesday, February 2, and were again repulsed. They returned again the next day with an even larger group. By that time, the students had formed their own organization, the Student Executive Committee for Justice.

With the organization of this group and the engagement of the energies of a large part of the A. and T. student body, the struggle broadened and deepened. Woolworth's capitulated finally, but by that time the struggle had become Southwide, and demonstrators were picketing chain outlets in the North.

On February 8, sit-ins started in Durham and Winston-Salem. Three days later, the demonstrations leaped the borders of North Carolina, and took deep roots in Virginia. By the end of March, sit-ins had been staged in every Southern state except Mississippi, and more than one thousand Negro students had been arrested on charges of trespassing and disorderly conduct.

The basic tactic of this unprecedented student movement was the sit-in which speedily became a part of the American vocabulary. The technique had the virtue of simplicity and paralyzing effectiveness. A student would take a seat or request service at a "white" facility. If refused service, he remained seated. If struck or manhandled by hoodlums, he refused to retaliate. If ordered to move on by police officers, he politely refused. The code of conduct drawn up by Nashville college students characterized the entire movement:

> *Don't strike back or curse if abused.*
> *Don't laugh out.*
> *Don't hold conversations with floor workers.*
> *Don't block entrances to the store and aisles.*
> *Show yourself courteous and friendly at all times.*
> *Sit straight and always face the counter.*
> *Remember love and nonviolence.*
> *May God bless each of you.*

As the movement spread, techniques and targets changed. Attacks on lunch counter segregation shifted to community-wide assaults on segregated facilities in department stores, supermarkets, movies, and libraries. The basic sit-in technique was supplemented by picket lines and sit-in extensions: wade-ins, read-ins, kneel-ins, pray-ins. Even more important for the future of the Freedom movement was the mammoth mass march which was used for the first time on February 25 by students of Alabama State College in Montgomery. By April, there had been mass marches of from one to five thousand students on state capitols and downtown areas in Alabama, South Carolina, Georgia, and Louisiana.

There was a frenetic sense of movement about all this. The swirling ferment of bodies in motion, the uproarious scenes in stores and lunch counters, the unprovoked attacks by bullies and duck-billed hoodlums: all this engaged emotions deeper than the pit and hotter than the fiery furnace. The movement caught men up; it pulled them out of themselves, sending them in ever-increasing numbers into the white and watchful streets. This spring, so fateful for the future of race relations, saw long columns of teen-agers tramping the pavements of hundreds of Main Streets, singing freedom songs, waving placards, shouting defiance. This was something new in the history of race relations. Never before had so many Negroes been in the streets. Never before had Negroes demonstrated so much passion and perseverance. The demonstrators were beaten with chains, burned with matches and cigarette butts, and doused with acid. They were sentenced to chain gangs and confined in pitch-black cells on bread and water. Everything was tried—tear gas, billy clubs, smiles, pleas—but nothing stopped the long black lines that marched on and on, endlessly. It was not clear just yet where all this would lead, but children were marching, and hearts were marching with them.

This ferment, which shook the South to its foundations and set off social tremors that were felt in every part of the land, was the real turning point in the Negro-white dialogue. Montgomery created a revolutionary point of departure; Greensboro was rebellion itself. Montgomery was a reaction; Greensboro was an act. The *Zeitgeist,* in the person of a sullen bus driver, tracked down Montgomery; Greensboro, in the person of four Negro students, tracked down the *Zeitgeist* and bent it to its will. The difference, and the difference was enormous, was a difference in being. The students knew what they were about: they did not stumble into it. They knew what they wanted, and they knew what they intended to do to get it. The students were *conscious.* They were revolutionaries or, at least, rebels.

Who were these rebels?

They were children of *anomie,* of broken limits, broken expectations, broken hopes. Fruit of an uneasy past and seeds of troubled tomorrows, they were living links between the Renaissance and the Rebellion. Most of the students were between seventeen and twenty-one in 1960 which means that they were born between 1939 and 1943, the years of the Rehearsal and of Asa Philip Randolph's defiance. Born in a fateful break between two epochs, raised in a hot war and a cold war, these students had never known the white man when he reigned supreme. They were mere tots when Nehru became master of India and teen-agers when the black man's flag was raised in Ghana. The major events of their formative years were the Supreme Court decision of 1954, the Montgomery bus boycott of 1955-56, and the Little Rock confrontation of 1957. The students' ego-ideal was Martin Luther King, Jr. As Dr. Frederic Solomon and Dr. Jacob R. Fishman pointed out in their psychosocial study of the sit-in generation, King was the kind of man the students wished their fathers had been. When he talked, they heard themselves thinking out loud. According to a survey the author made for *Ebony* magazine, the students were also influenced by E. Franklin Frazier's attack on the Negro middle class.

The students were, for the most part, children of Frazier's *Black Bourgeoisie*. But a substantial number were sons and daughters of domestics, laborers, and blue-collar workers. Of whatever class, of whatever background, the students were committed. They were "obsessed," as one Negro college president observed, "with conviction and dedication." There was in them a latent sense of power, of what E. Pumpian-Mindlin called "omnipotentiality."

What moved these students was a profound dissatisfaction with the pace of desegregation. Until that moment, the strategic objective of Negro leadership was integration. What did the students want? They wanted *freedom*. The shift from integration to freedom was significant, spiritually and strategically. The students were not asking for a new departure; they were fighting against an unjust deprivation. Many of them, moreover, were thoroughly disillusioned by the standards and values of the middle-class society which many of the older Negro leaders had considered Canaan.

To a student, the rebels deplored traditional Negro leadership techniques. It seemed to them that Negro leadership was "timid," "acquiescent," and "accommodating." James Lawson, the young Methodist minister who played a leading role in the key Nashville movement, said: "This movement is not only against segregation. It's against Uncle Tom Negroes, against the NAACP's over-reliance on the courts; and against the futile middle-class technique of sending letters to the centers of power."

In a very real sense, Lawson and other Negro activists were in revolt against the white *and* Negro power structures. Joseph McNeil, one of the Greensboro four, said the sit-ins indicated that "youth of today are not pleased with the acquiescent leadership of the adults. . . . Old leaders follow the methods of Booker T. Washington. Most of us are in favor of W. E. B. Du Bois." Ezell Blair, another one of the original four, was also critical of the Negro power structure. "Some of the Negro leaders," he said, "are pretty good, but there are not enough of them. There are not enough who will stand up for principle." The significant words here and elsewhere are "stand up." The sit-in generation wanted men and women to stand up and face each other.

The young Negro rebels, in plain, were dissatisfied with the way adults had been running the world. They were in revolt not only against white people but against their parents and traditional Negro ego-models. A surprisingly large number of sit-in students were quite articulate about this, saying at mass meetings and in interviews that if their parents had acted, if they had dared to be men and women, no matter what the price, it would not have been necessary for them to go out into the streets to do the work of men and women. There was a story related with gusto by sit-in students that in a brief, illuminating flash seems to describe perfectly the tensions between the generations. A mother, weeping and moaning, confronted her daughter in the Tallahassee, Florida, jail. The mother offered to pay the girl's fine, but the girl declined, saying: "Mamma, I love you. But I'm not free. And I'm not free because your generation didn't act. But I want my children to be free. That's why I'll stay in jail."

In the searching rhetoric of student action, all idols and ego-models toppled. Not even Martin Luther King, Jr., escaped. The students honored King but they refused to accept his leadership *because they did not think he was radical enough.* Borrowing the concept of confrontation and the tactic of direct action from King, the students carried the struggle to a new level, adding mass action to direct action, adding, above all else, the fateful escalator principle. And what was the escalator principle? It was the idea that racial tensions must be raised to the highest pitch, that nothing, in fact, would happen if tension were not maintained at the highest octave. Central to the new orientation of the students was the idea of choice and responsibility. It was necessary, they said, to present communities with clear-cut choices between bias and some other highly-cherished value, civic peace, for example, or profits. Not until a community was faced with such a choice, they said, not until men had to choose once and for all between, say, dollar bills and bigotry, would a breakthrough occur. The theory did not suffer through implementation. In the period from February, 1960, to September, 1961, the sit-in movement affected twenty states and more than one hundred cities. During this period, according to the Southern Regional Council, one or more establishments in 108 Southern and Border States were desegregated as a result of sit-ins and demonstrations by some seventy thousand persons.

What this meant, strategically, was spelled out in a Nashville jail in the spring of the struggle. In this jail on a bright balmy day were scores of sit-in students awaiting trial on charges of disturbing the peace. John Lewis, an American Baptist Seminary student who later became national chairman of the Student Nonviolent Coordinating Committee, decided that the moment was appropriate for a sermon. He opened his Bible, peered through the bars at the guards and his fellow students, and announced his text: Matthew 10:34.

> Think not that I am come to send peace on earth: I came not to send peace, but a sword.

The cutting edge of student fervor reopened the Negro white dialogue and initiated the age of the triple confrontation: the confrontation between Negroes and Negroes, whites and whites, Negroes and whites.

The student rebels were mirrors reflecting the reality of American life; they were clocks telling America what time it was historically; they were bridges spanning the abyss between two mutually hostile and mutually hateful communities. By disturbing the peace, the rebels made America face the fact that there could be no peace between the oppressor and the oppressed. By widening the chasm between communities, the rebels forced America to face the fact that it had not created a single community. By saying "No," the rebels made America face the fact that millions of Americans—Negro and white— were saying "Yes" to oppression.

In the light of the student fire, Negro and white Americans saw themselves and knew themselves and they were undone by their mutual complicity in horror. It is a point of great significance that the student struggle and the Freedom movement that followed it was not a struggle between citizens within the state but a struggle between Negro citizens and the state. Two things, therefore, became clear almost immediately: 1) that there were two sharply separated communities in America, and that one of these communities was not represented, North or South, in the political (i.e., the decision-making) process; 2) that the state was not an independent arbiter between contending groups but an organization of white people exercising dominion over Negroes.

Men had always known this, but the absence of conflict had made it possible for them to evade the power realities of their lives. The student revolt revealed not only the anatomy but the soul of the state—and that soul was white.

As conflict spread, intensifying awareness, men and communities began to drop their masks. They began to look at each other. They did not, on this account, love each other any more. But love was—and is—irrelevant. What was required was a recognition of the law of reciprocity—a duty for a duty, an obligation for an obligation, a hate for a hate.

In the wake of the sit-ins, hundreds of white organizations were forced to admit for the first time that there were not and could not be "white" cities. For the first time, white communities were forced to confront Negro citizens not as wards but as serious social actors, not as suppliants but as citizens. Most significantly—and this is not noted often enough—the white South was forced to deal with the Negro as a man of power. What happened here—and it had an importance that transcended everything else—was that the Negro became real to others and this development forced the first real communication between Negro and white communities since the counter-revolution that ended Reconstruction. After the white terror of that age, an elaborate structure of evasion was invented, and this structure hid Negroes and whites from themselves. The student rebels laid siege to this structure which had been internalized by adult Negroes and whites whose bodies and minds had committed to memory rituals of evasion. The immediate result was the opening of a void in the center of race relations. The cake of custom began to crumble and raw reality began to push through the fissures. Consider, for example, the testimony of a white minister who attended negotiations between store executives and student rebels in a large Southern city. "There was a poignant moment at that meeting," he said. "The man speaking for the store managers accused the Negroes of breaking their truce. 'We made no truce,' they said. 'Those men you called in didn't speak for us.' The chairman and all the other white men were astonished. They looked at each other. 'If we're not dealing with leaders we can somewhat control,' they seemed to say, 'with whom are we dealing?'"

Here, again, was a psychological question that could not be answered with the categories and rituals of the old system of accommodation. What this meant, in practical terms, was that the problem was out in the open, and that somebody would have to do something about it.

Flowing with and out of this was a realization that the problem could not exist without the complicity of "the good people," without a collective shutting of eyes to flagrant defiance of the Constitution and the open oppression of millions of American citizens.

In a great upswelling of confession, America began to face that fact. A Southern governor, Le Roy Collins of Florida, went on a statewide television program to tell white citizens that it was "unfair and morally wrong" for a business to serve Negroes at one counter and deny them at another. And President Eisenhower, who had maintained an air of elegant neutrality, came close to committing himself on the moral issue.

In statements and sympathy demonstrations, white students and church leaders intensified the white man's dialogue with himself. Students at Wake Forest College moved from support of the sit-in demonstrations to an attack on their trustees for not admitting Negro students. The Board of Social and Economic Relations of the Methodist Church took note of the exposed flank of the white Christian church in a statement praising the demonstrators. "We confess with sorrow," the board said, "that as a denomination we have failed to live up to our own pronouncements. In no section of the land have we carried out the teachings of our Lord with respect to race."

Indisputably; but these were mere words, and there had been too many words already. What the students wanted was action, and that was precisely what they got from white students in the North and South. In the South, students at several colleges and universities joined Negroes on the firing line. In the North, the generation known until then as the "silent generation" came awake. At Yale, at Wisconsin, at California, at colleges and universities all over the nation, white students streamed from classrooms to teach. Melvin B. Freedman, coordinator of the Mellon Foundation Research Program at Vassar, said: "This is the first time that Vassar girls have picketed in twenty years."

Of similar tone and tenor, though more pointed, was the ferment in the Negro community. It began to dawn on men, dimly at first and then with every increasing clarity, that it takes two to oppress: someone to do the oppressing and someone to accept the oppression. Spurred on by the restlessness of youth, adults awoke with a start and scurried to get into step with the marching students. There was an increasing emphasis in the Negro community on "selective buying" (boycotts) and a new willingness to risk the defection of white moderates and liberals.

Significantly, there was a wave of confession in the Negro community that paralleled the wave of confession in the white community. Rev. Matthew McCollum, president of the Orangeburg, South Carolina, NAACP chapter, said: "We've been lying to the white man for years. 'Yassah, cap'n! Everything's all right.' We have to stop lying to him."

Confessing in action, students and militant Negro adults precipitated a sharp struggle in the ranks of the Negro leadership group. Since the Amenia Conference of 1916, Negro leadership had tacitly respected the "peculiar problems" of men subservient to the white power structure. It was known generally in the Negro community that certain Negro leaders were "accommodators" downtown and militants and moderates on their campuses and on the platforms of national conventions. Men, as I say, knew this. It was no secret; it was part of the game. In the rhetoric of the old leadership tradition, it was not considered good form to push men against the wall and expose their practical support of the status quo. It was not sporting; it simply was not done. But the students did it, creating embarrassing situations where men had to choose. Some college presidents, notably Stephen Wright of Fisk and Benjamin Mays of Morehouse, supported their students openly; but many decided, overtly and covertly, to support the system. Hundreds of students and scores of teachers were fired by Negro college presidents. The resulting furore created a grave leadership crisis. The Phelps-Stokes Fund and other organizations tried to close the breach between the young activists and accommodating Negro leadership. The fund sponsored several conferences at its Negro leadership retreat in Capahosic, Virginia, but the controversy was too deep to be papered over by words and the rituals of conferences.

The inability of national Negro leadership to come up with viable answers to the challenges of the new age created a vacuum into which new men and new organizations sprang. In this, the first period of the new age, there was a shift in the center of gravity in the Negro community: a shift from lower Manhattan to the Deep South, a shift from moderates to militants and from bureaucrats to agitators. National organizations, feeling the approaching storm, changed their sails, but they did not change fast enough to catch the prevailing wind.

On March 16, 1960, Roy Wilkins announced "an expanded racial defense policy," saying: "We have always used persuasion through various means of political and economic pressure, but now we're going to use it much more intensively than in the past because the membership has become restless over the slow pace of the civil rights proceedings." Other "established organizations" made similar pronouncements, but the words were not translated into action. Combat tactics (picketing, demonstrations, etc.) did not appeal to the NAACP and the National Urban League and their attempts to disguise this fact by verbiage were unconvincing. The NAACP and the Urban League, moreover, were confronted with a fact not a theory. The followers were in the streets marching, and the leaders had to get at the head of the line or retire to the galleries. Because the NAACP and the Urban League did not seize the banner thrust up by the first wave of sit-in students, the laurels of leadership passed to other men and other organizations with consequences that are still reverberating in the paneled offices of lower Manhattan.

A distinguishing feature of the first phase of the sit-in age was the mushroom growth of two organizations oriented to direct action. The first organization was CORE which was, as we have noted, founded in 1942. In the late forties and fifties, CORE played a significant role in the desegregation of downtown facilities in several Northern and Border State cities. But the organization failed to attract widespread support in the Negro community. By 1960, CORE consisted of a small number of whites, many of them pacifists, and an even smaller number of Negroes. The organization had profited from the Montgomery movement, but it was far from a going concern, having only two or three paid staffers and a small office in New York City. The sit-ins changed all that, giving CORE a wider field of action and a new sense of purpose. As we have seen, the organization was called into the sit-in struggle at the very beginning by an NAACP branch officer. Both the NAACP and CORE rushed staff people to the Piedmont area, but CORE got there first "with the mostest." And, as the conflict spread, CORE maintained its lead over the larger but bureaucracy-bound NAACP organization. Relevant here were matters of style as well as temperament. The CORE people were oriented to direct action. They talked the students' language; they shared the students' vision of battle. CORE, moreover, had an advantage in structure. It was organized to struggle not negotiate.

Within a short time, CORE staffers were organizing their

own sit-ins, sending "task forces" into South Carolina and Florida. The CORE concept of the "task force" (one or more persons specially trained to organize and activate local leadership) became a central feature of the organizational structures of the three organizations—CORE, SNCC, SCLC—that led the rebellion.

Feeling its increasing weight, CORE called its first director, James Farmer, from his job as program director of the NAACP. With Farmer as executive director, the organization became a formidable force in the rebellion. The Freedom Rides, organized by Farmer in 1961, revived the flagging force of the movement and carried it to a new stage of development.

Another man untroubled by Hamlet-like misgivings about direct action was Martin Luther King, Jr. King had been in and out of the spotlight since Montgomery. But in 1960, he, like Farmer, was a man looking for a mission. It can be said, in fact, that King was perhaps the chief beneficiary of the sit-in movement. Before the movement started, King was making vague noises about voter registration. Greensboro, which his image helped to create, created a new King with a new mandate. The students, as we have noted, borrowed the concept of confrontation from King and added mass to direct action. Now King lifted direct mass action from the students and carried it to a new level of effectiveness. King later became something of a specialist in creating and directing citywide confrontations between Negro and white communities.

King made another contribution to the developing struggle which may, in the long sight of history, turn out to be equally important. Believing that the force of student fury would dissipate for lack of a structure, he and his aides, principally Ella Baker, took the lead in calling a conference of student leaders. The conference met on April 17, 1960, on the campus of Shaw University in Raleigh, North Carolina. It was believed by many that the students would ally themselves with King's organization, the Southern Christian Leadership Conference. But the students chose instead to create a new structure, the Student Nonviolent Coordinating Committee. The drift of the conference can be gauged by the tough keynote speeches of King and James Lawson, the Methodist minister who played a key role in the Nashville movement which contributed a disproportionately large number of leaders to the struggle. There was, as Helen Fuller noted in the *New Republic,* a distinct difference between the speeches of Lawson and King. "Where King," she wrote, "is insistent on speaking in moral terms—actually changing the hearts of white and black segregationists

—Lawson talks knowledgeably of 'power structures' in the Negro and white communities, and, according to those who have observed him in operation, displays considerable hard-headed political calculation. He warned that students must expect expulsion, must organize financial support, and must think of 'an army of youth to carry on picketing.' " Lawson went on to attack the whole Negro leadership structure, placing particular emphasis on what he considered the failures of the NAACP. The young minister, who had served a year in jail as a conscientious objector during the Korean War and who later spent three years in India, spoke bitingly of the *Crisis*, the monthly publication of the NAACP, as the journal of the "black bourgeois club."

Lawson, King, and Ella Baker were among the first adult advisors of the student leaders who met later on the campus of Atlanta University and created the structure of the Student Nonviolent Coordinating Committee. This organization, a loose federation of students and young professional rebels, became the real cutting edge of the rebellion, establishing beachheads of resistance in Black Belt counties in Southwest Georgia and Mississippi and forcing adult leadership to take more militant postures by its penchant for forcing an issue. Among the leaders of the new organization were Negro students and ex-students like Marion Barry, Edward King, Jr., Charles McDew, Diane Nash, and John Lewis. James Forman, a dynamic young Chicago school-teacher, became executive secretary of the organization in 1961.

SNCC—insiders call it "Snick" as opposed to SCLC's "Slick" —was more a spiritual community than a formal organization. Composed for the most part of students and ex-students, Negro and white, who had adopted rebellion as a profession, SNCC was—and is—a revolutionary organization dedicated to the creation of "a new social order." SNCC workers wanted to transform American society. They were critical of the acts and values of the middle class. Detached from a society which they rejected, living on subsistence wages of ten to thirty dollars a week, scorning the ties of family and conventionality that stay the arms of the adjusted, the SNCC workers were free, spiritually and physically, and they intended to free America or die trying.

The missionary-tinged SNCC organization brought a revolutionary rhetoric and a revolutionary will to the struggle. More importantly, it made the first sustained effort, the black nationalists excepted, to organize the Negro masses. Borrowing the "task force" concept from CORE, SNCC sent workers (field secretaries) into backwoods areas to live with the people and to show them a new way of living and a new way of resisting. Field secretaries lived wherever they could find a bed. They shared the food, the dangers, and the privations of the people. Talking to the people in pool rooms, in kitchens, in cottonfields, in bars, they won their confidence and began the slow and painful process of developing "indigenous leadership." Day after day, they knocked on doors and urged Negroes in Black Belt counties to assert themselves, to organize, register, and vote. Many doors, in the beginning, were slammed in their faces. But the students kept coming back, and a man here and a woman there threw caution to the wind and invited them in. Slowly, painfully, dangerously, the SNCC contingent sowed the seeds of assertion and humanity, giving men, women, and children the courage to defy sheriffs, nightriders, and the organized power of the state. More than any other organization in the history of Negro protest, SNCC confronted the difficulty and the reality of mass organization. More than any other organization, SNCC put flesh on the stark, white bones of Ignazio Silone's brave words:

> I am convinced that it would be a waste of time to show a people of intimidated slaves a different manner of speaking, a different manner of gesticulating; but perhaps it would be worthwhile to show them a different way of living. No word and no gesture can be more persuasive than the life, and if necessary, the death, of a man who strives to be free . . . a man who shows what a man can be.

With the organization of SNCC and the revitalization of SCLC and CORE, the rebellion moved to a new stage of strategic effectiveness. These three organizations, the battering rams of the rebellion, were markedly different from the so-called established organizations. CORE, SNCC, and SCLC were action organizations, not membership organizations. One joined them not to vote or resolve but to fight. The "new orgs" also used direct action as a *primary tactic* of fighting. They believed in bargaining from strength. Indeed, according to the leading strategists of the "new orgs," anything less was not bargaining but begging. And whatever else the "new orgs" were, they were not beggars.

To be sure, the "new orgs" were far from perfect. CORE was primarily a Northern organization with shallow roots in the Negro community. SNCC was primarily a Southern organization which decided, *as a matter of strategy,* to violate all the rules of logic and war. Although it was a small, powerless group, it chose, as a matter of strategy, to fight a powerful, heavily entrenched enemy in his strongest positions: the Black Belt counties of the South. SNCC, moreover, decided, after an internal struggle that almost wrecked the organization, to place major emphasis on voter registration. This was a curious choice for an avowedly revolutionary organization. It is true, of course, that SNCC had more in mind than registering voters. What it wanted to do was to force a confrontation between federal authorities and the authorities of the lily-white governments in the South—to force, in other words, the federal government to face the implications of governments that were organized conspiracies in contempt of the peace and security of Negro men and women. One of the basic objectives was federal occupation or, at least, a federal presence in states like Mississippi and Alabama.

Similar problems of strategy and structure bedeviled King and SCLC. It was impossible for the rebellion to succeed without a national, mass-based movement headed by a charismatic leader. The only man who could have created such a movement in 1960 was Martin Luther King, Jr. But King decided against such a move, limiting himself, *as a matter of strategy,* to the South. Men close to him have suggested that he did not want to offend the NAACP and the Negro leadership structure by invading the North. Whatever the reason, King's decision to make SCLC a Southwide rather than a nationwide organization was a crucial turning point in the history of the rebellion. If King had attempted, as Randolph attempted in the forties, to create a national nonviolent movement, and if the SNCC students had chosen to mobilize the Negro masses in cities, North and South, where the terrain was more favorable to guerilla warfare, it is likely, indeed probable, that the rebellion would have taken a different and more favorable course. One fact that future historians will find incredible is that in the whole period from 1960 to 1964 *none of the major leaders of the rebellion led a major compaign in a major American city.*

Limitations of strategy and structure did not weigh heavily on men's minds in the bright morn of the rebellion. In the shot and smoke of battle, men did what they had to do and what they did seemed adequate to the hour. From the acts of different men and different organizations a loose structure of understanding rather than of thought-out strategy emerged. King became the great symbol of the rebellion and the master strategist of the mass confrontation. SNCC contributed the idea of the professional rebel, the idea of the man or woman or child who abandoned place and position to live with the people and to lift them where they were. CORE brought to the marriage of visions a long history of nonviolent direct action and a tough, to-the-wall posture. The grand outcome of all this was the Freedom movement, an ongoing development of mass marches, mass meetings and demonstrations, of struggles in the streets and men, women, and little children tramping stones and singing the *Marseillaise* of the rebellion, "We Shall Overcome."

We shall overcome, we shall overcome
We shall overcome some day,
Oh, deep in my heart, I do believe
We shall overcome some day.

The truth will make us free, the truth will make us free,
The truth will make us free some day,
Oh, deep in my heart I do believe
We shall overcome some day.

We shall live in peace, we shall live in peace,
We shall live in peace some day,
Oh, deep in my heart I do believe
We shall overcome some day.

We are not afraid, we are not afraid
We are not afraid today,
Oh, deep in my heart I do believe
We shall overcome some day.

The waves of dammed-up energy released by the Freedom movement created a circular reaction that escalated the racial problem to new plateaus of strife and contention. The movement forced a realignment in Negro leadership circles and this realignment intensified the triple confrontation which in turn forced a further realignment in the Negro community. This development unfolded in six waves, each succeeding wave of rebellious action going further than the last, each throwing up new problems and new leaders. The five waves were:

1) Sits-ins (February, 1960) to Freedom Ride I (May 4-15, 1961).
2) Freedom Ride II (May 17, 1961) to Birmingham demonstrations (April-May, 1963).

3) Birmingham riot (May 11-12, 1963) to March on Washington (August 28, 1963).
4) Birmingham church bombing (September 18, 1963) to second New York School Boycott (March 16, 1964).
5) Stall-in (April 23, 1964) to passage of Civil Rights Bill of 1964 (July 2, 1964).
6) Harlem Riots (July 18, 1964) to Selma-to-Montgomery March (March 21-25, 1965).

The first phase, from the sit-ins to the Freedom Rides, was a phase of groping and uncertainty. Seen whole, the sit-ins were a series of guerilla wars on local and widely-separated battlefields. The problems of this period—and these problems were never solved—were problems of methodology and structure.

How could the local fires be harnessed to a larger, national purpose?

What was the best way to fight?

What was the ideal structure?

CORE contributed an answer of sorts with the Freedom Rides which were, in essence, peripatetic sit-ins. On May 4, 1961, thirteen Negroes and whites left Washington, D. C., on two buses. Their announced purpose was to test compliance with federal court orders forbidding segregation on carriers and in supporting facilities (lunch counters, waiting rooms, etc.). From the beginning, however, the Freedom Rides had a larger purpose: to dramatize lack of compliance and to force America and the federal government to confront that fact.

Would the federal government protect the right of Negro and white citizens to travel peacefully and biracially on public highways?

Would—could—the federal government force local officials to obey national laws?

It was these questions that CORE raised with its organized sally into the South. The CORE protestants sought their answers in a manner similar to the sit-in. But there was a basic difference. As the Southern Regional Council pointed out:

> Characteristically, the sit-ins were demands by local residents that they share in the privileges of their communities. The persons who were asking for service did themselves want to use it. With only a few exceptions, the demonstrations were locally planned. The Freedom Ride, on the other hand, has started from the premise that all Americans have a right to demonstrate against discrimination in the South.

The rides began peacefully enough. There were scuffles in South Carolina, but the integrated riders encountered only minor problems in Virginia and Georgia. All this changed drastically in Alabama. Outside Anniston, Alabama, the bus with the first group of Freedom Riders was bombed and burned by segregationists. On Mother's Day, May 14, in Birmingham, Negro and white riders were savagely assaulted by a white mob. It proved difficult after this event to find a bus that would carry the Freedom Riders who abandoned the hazardous trip and flew to New Orleans.

At this point, the militant student cadre took over. The Nashville group, led by Diane Nash, a pretty Fisk coed who played a key role in structuring student discontent, insisted that the ride continue as scheduled—no matter what the price. A second group of riders which included James Lawson was hastily assembled and Freedom Ride II began. Several of the students were beaten in Montgomery which teetered for several hours on the edge of total social disorder. National Guard troops were called out, and Attorney General Robert F. Kennedy sent federal marshals to the city to help restore law and order. On May 24, Freedom Ride II continued with an improbable assembly consisting of three airplanes, two helicopters, and seventeen highway patrol cars. The riders arrived in Jackson, Mississippi, on the same day and were promptly arrested for entering a "white" waiting room.

Jackson, Mississippi, now became the vortex of a swirling national controversy. Negroes and whites of all ages and faiths converged on the city from all points. Most of them were arrested as soon as they "violated" local segregation laws which conflicted with long-standing orders of the federal court. Scores served prison sentences and hundreds were required to post bail. The financial drain almost broke CORE which was identified in the public mind with the Freedom Rides although SNCC, SCLC, and the NAACP also played a part.

The struggle continued in and around Jackson and several other Southern cities for a spell and then died down. Both sides—integrationists and segregationists—had suffered a defeat in this confrontation, and both sides withdrew as gracefully as possible to lick their wounds and think. The federal government had demonstrated (in Montgomery) that it would not tolerate massive and brutal defiance of federal court orders. But it demonstrated (in Jackson) that it would not act promptly and decisively to prevent legal defiance of federal courts. Robert F. Kennedy circumvented the problem by asking the Interstate Commerce Commission to issue regulations banning segregation in interstate bus transportation and terminal facilities. The commission later issued a "no segregation" order which was hailed as a great victory for the Freedom Rides. It was, in a manner of speaking, but the deeper question had not been touched, and both the integrationists and the segregationists knew it.

If the Freedom Rides did not solve the problem, they did, at least, throw glancing light on it, bringing America closer to a confrontation with itself. Liberal journals generally deplored the "provocative" tactics of the "extremists on both sides." Yet, there was, underneath this, a growing understanding of the urgency of the problem. Walter Lippmann noted:

> What has been a movement of gradual reform is showing unmistakable signs of turning into a movement of physical confrontation. . . .
>
> We are witnessing a non-violent rebellion . . . non-violent in that the agitators are unarmed and passive. This rebellion marks a lessening of hope and faith in the processes of the courts, of elections, of Congress, and of education. . . . It would be vain for anyone to expect that there can be a quick and easy end to the kind of courage and determination which has been shown in the bus rides and in the lunch counter sit-ins. No one should expect this kind of thing to disappear . . .

Another development of this period, the awakening of the masses in Northern ghettos, also gave men pause. This development presented a different face to America. Awakened by the same event—the sit-ins—Northern Negroes and Southern Negroes moved from the beginning in different directions. This was a function not of choice but of place. Northern Negroes faced larger problems and more subtle opponents. Almost all doors, in theory, were open to them, but almost all doors, in fact, were closed. And more: Northern white men were more skillful in explaining to themselves and to others why closed doors were, in theory, open. Because of the pervasive bad faith of Northerners, the Negro revolt in the North unfolded in a climate of desperation. One can, in fact, date the Northern revolt from an inarticulate spasm of despair: the United Nations "riot" of February 15, 1961. As Adlai Stevenson, America's UN Ambassador, was speaking, Negro demonstrators—American activists and African nationalists—created an uproar with a demonstration for Patrice Lumumba, the slain premier of the Congo. "Responsible" Negro leadership deplored the incident, but a surprisingly large number of

Negroes deplored not the demonstration but Ambassador Stevenson's speech and the whole drift of American policy in the Congo. When Ralph Bunche apologized for the behavior of the demonstrators, Lorraine Hansberry, the prize-winning playwright, apologized to Lumumba's widow for the behavior of "our" Mr. Bunche.

Commentators seeking the source of this new tone of uncompromising militancy found a new mood in big-city ghettos, a mood made up of equal parts of nationalism, hope, and despair. Negroes just then were feeling the cramp of repeated recessions and the day-by-day aggression of automation. There was, contrariwise, a new feeling of racial expansiveness in the ghetto and a new pride in blackness. This double movement, of dilation and distension, shook the minds of Negroes out of old furrows and prepared them for new postures. Significantly, it was during this period that mass media "discovered" Elijah Muhammad and his Nation of Islam (Black Muslim) movement.

While these events were unfolding in the North, the last embers of the Freedom Rides were glowering and flickering in the South. These embers, guerilla strikes by young activists in Monroe (North Carolina), McComb (Mississippi), and Albany (Georgia), precipitated local resistance movements that seeded the struggle of 1963-64. A Freedom Ride into Albany, Georgia, in December, 1962, and the infiltration tactics of SNCC laid the groundwork for a minor peak of the second phase, the Albany movement. The arrest of the Freedom Riders in Albany led to a local movement which attracted the attention of Martin Luther King, Jr., and his aides. On the invitation of the leaders of the local movement, King and his aides entered the area and organized the Freedom movement's first mass confrontation.

The Albany demonstrations, like the Freedom Rides, introduced a new concept to the movement. What King wanted to do in Albany was to bring the full resources of the Negro community to bear in an across-the-board attack on the *system* of color-caste. What he demanded was not only integrated facilities but *the recognition of the Negro community* (the hiring of Negro policemen, the creation of a biracial committee, etc.).

How did he intend to *force* recognition?

By an encounter, by a frontal attack on the system, by a series of direct action probes involving not tens or twenties but hundreds and, if possible, thousands.

The Negro community was prepared by a series of mass

meetings and nonviolent workshops. There then followed a series of mass marches on city hall, sit-ins at libraries and recreational outlets, and prayer vigils on downtown streets. King and some two thousand of his followers went to jail during the struggle which raged throughout the spring and summer of 1962. The arrest of King and several Northern clergymen and laymen who joined the struggle created a mood of national concern but did not appreciably affect the outcome. Laurie Pritchett, the chief of police of Albany, demoralized the demonstrators by "legal defiance," i.e., the prompt and, to the television viewer, "peaceful" arrests of demonstrators for illegal assembly, unlawful parades, and disturbing the peace.

Albany, by any standard, was a staggering and perhaps necessary defeat for the Freedom movement. The sit-ins and the Freedom Rides had given men an excessive confidence in the power of demonstrations which are, in truth, useful instruments if used in the right place and the right time within the right strategic framework.

Was Albany, a small city in a backwater of Georgia, the right place?

Were men using the right strategic framework?

Had the necessary planning preceded the demonstrations and were the demonstrations themselves informed by a strategic plan embracing structure, objectives, and tactics?

By raising these questions, Albany served a useful purpose. King and the young workers of SNCC gained valuable fighting experience in the Southwest Georgia city, and that experience would tell in the days ahead. Equally important perhaps, though no one remarked it at the time, was the backlash of Albany, the despair that seeped through the pores of the ghetto. This, too, was educational; and this, too, would tell in the days ahead.

During this same period, men were learning from whips in the North. Sentiment crystallized in the North in 1962 against *de facto* segregation in schools and housing and *de facto* discrimination in the employment market. Northern Negroes began in the early part of this period to file suits against local school systems. Direct action followed with sit-ins and picketing in Chicago and a brushfire boycott in Harlem. Demonstrators also staged wade-ins at a segregated Chicago beach and a series of sit-ins to protest off-campus bias in housing owned or controlled by the University of Chicago. Of greater importance were the first toddling steps of Northerners in the field of mass confrontation. In the summer of 1962, SNCC started an Albany-type campaign in Cairo, Illinois. The most dramatic indication of Northern discontent, however, came in Englewood, New Jersey. The indigenous Englewood movement, which started in 1961, used a variety of tactics (sit-ins at schools and municipal offices, boycotts, political pressure, litigation) in a long and frustrating effort to integrate the school system of the middle-class suburb.

Englewood, Cairo, Chicago, and Albany were important milestones on the road to Birmingham. Far more fateful and decisive, however, were events that happened not on streets but in the minds of men. The long-drawn-out defeat of Albany, the genteel evasions of Englewood, the neo-South defiance of Cairo, and the day-by-day defeats of rats, roaches, and *de facto* degradation fueled the fire of discontent and laid the groundwork for a national resistance movement.

During this whole period, a deep process of growth was taking place in the Negro masses. The perverted uses of the state by white men, North and South, horrified millions and fastened their gaze on the void in the center of race relations. A space opened in this period between black man and white state, between black man and white man, and that space widened in the fall of 1962 and the spring of 1963. Soul-racking incidents like the national crisis over integration at the University of Mississippi intensified the distinguishing feature of the second wave: the widening chasm between the Negro and white communities.

By using the army to squelch Governor Ross Barnett's attempt to prevent James Meredith from enrolling in the University of Mississippi, the federal government gave additional notice that there were limits to the defiance of court orders. But the government's response to church burnings in Southwest Georgia and shootings in Mississippi indicated again that there were limits to the government's ability to protect the rights of Negro citizens to peacefully assemble and organize for the redress of grievances. Hardly less revealing was the continued defiance, despite a federal presence, at the University of Mississippi. From the University of Mississippi, where racists were making his life miserable despite the presence of federal marshals, James Meredith threw dirt on the coffin of Negro hope. "Hearts have shown," he said, "that they do not intend to change."

The road to Birmingham was paved with such despairing cries. Some Negro artists and writers went off to Paris and Ghana saying the American Dream was a nightmare. Those who remained at home dug in for a tough, no-holds-barred fight.

Malcolm X, who was then the leading spokesman for the Black Muslims, played a leading role in focusing the new climate of national defiance. Mass media, having "discovered" black nationalism, thrust Malcolm forward as a leading spokesman of the Negro community. A dominant feature of this period, one that will prove interesting to future historians, was the Malcolm X TV commentary. Wherever one turned in this period, there was Malcolm X denouncing the "hypocrisy" of white and Negro leaders and calling for a Negro exodus to an unspecified place. It is hard, even in retrospect, to figure out what mass media thought they were doing by exposing Malcolm to a larger public and what Malcolm thought he was doing by taking advantage of this exposure. But there can be little doubt about what Malcolm did with the help of mass media. He educated the Negro masses, many of whom were not reached by the pamphlets and speeches of Negro leaders, giving them a new understanding of themselves and of the inequalities and deficiencies of their lives. The Black Muslim spokesman did not convince many Negroes that they should separate from white Americans. But most Negroes, some of whom were very, very conservative, believed—and believe—that Malcolm's indictment, as distinguished from his proposed solutions, was a true bill.

Another factor of immense importance was Malcolm's open challenge to established Negro leadership. He leaped, via television, over the heads of Negro leaders and appealed directly to the masses, thereby drawing them into the social arena and forcing establishing leadership to enter into a contest for their allegiance. Malcolm X, in sum, prepared the way for Martin Luther King's rebellion. Only time will tell if King, in turn, prepared the way of Malcolm X's successor.

Equally persuasive as a propagandist of revolt was James Baldwin whose essays opened new furrows for all Americans, Negro and white. The publication of Baldwin's essay, *The Fire Next Time,* in 1963 was a social act as important in its day and time as the publication of Du Bois' *The Souls of Black Folk* sixty years earlier.

Baldwin, like Malcolm, was a superb user of TV. But Baldwin was not a black nationalist. In fact, he had no patterned program of resistance. His message was simple, stark, eloquent: guilt, national atonement, and the wages of white sin.

By television and radio, by magazines and newspapers, the thoughts of Baldwin, Malcolm X and other Negro rebels penetrated the Negro masses, giving them a full consciousness of the horror of their position and a larger understanding of the mission history was offering them.

The war of words, the dialogue between God, Allah and the prophets, was a continuation at another level of the struggle in the streets. Men said in public in this period what was whispered in other periods within separate groups: that Negro and white Americans hated and feared each other and that things were going to get a great deal worse before they got better. Baldwin, Malcolm X and other speakers and writers of the period abandoned the dreary charts of sociologists and the polysyllabic rationalizations of the race relations professionals. By saying the unsayable, by asking the unaskable, they brought out into the open the gangrenous wounds of Negro and white Americans. In a word, they—Baldwin in particular—made truth fashionable, and truth proved embarrassing to several groups.

Under the twin impact of men's words and men's deeds, the liberal link, the only institutional bond between the Negro and white communities, began to unravel at the seams. Consider, for example, the action of the NAACP which began in 1960 to attack its traditional ally, organized labor. Herbert Hill, the labor secretary of the NAACP, opened the attack, charging several "liberal" unions with giving lip service to the cause while practicing discrimination themselves. Particularly annoying to Hill and others was the fact that "liberal" unions like the UAW-CIO and the ILGWU had few, if any, Negroes in the upper echelons of their administrative hierarchies.

A. Philip Randolph, the elder statesman of the cause, pushed the fight from within the ranks of organized labor. Randolph delivered a slashing attack on the Jim Crow practices of organized labor at the 1959 AFL-CIO convention in San Francisco. George Meany, the president of the union, said the attack was unjustified and asked Randolph: "Phil, who the hell made you the guardian of all the Negroes in America?" The AFL-CIO executive committee later censured Randolph for his strictures against bias in the labor movement. Undaunted, Randolph continued the fight, organizing, in 1961, the Negro American Labor Council, a loose federation of militant Negro labor leaders.

With the snapping of the liberal link, which is a major factor in moderating Negro discontent, the Negro and white communities drifted further and further apart and the road lay open for Birmingham and the dangers beyond.

The swirling current in the North amplified by the movement in the South carried the rebellion to the peak of Birmingham—which was to Albany what Greensboro was to Montgomery. Birmingham, in short, was a conscious act. It was chosen, not stumbled upon. It was *created* by men who knew exactly what they wanted and how much they would probably have to pay to get it. It was created, moreover, by men fresh from the debacle of Albany.

In the summer of 1962, King and his aides decided to launch a series of Albany-type demonstrations in Birmingham. Profiting from the mistake of Albany, they drew up a detailed battle plan and designated the forthcoming struggle "Project C." The "C" stood for confrontation.

Project Confrontation was scheduled for the fall of 1962, but it was postponed several times by negotiations with the white power structure. By January, 1963, however, King and his aides were convinced that a crisis was necessary for racial progress in the South. King's aide, the Rev. Wyatt Tee Walker, spoke for millions of Negro Americans who were seeking a relevant celebration of the one hundredth anniversary of the Emancipation Proclamation. "We've got to have a crisis to bargain with. To take a moderate approach hoping to get white help, doesn't work. They nail you to the cross, and it saps the enthusiasm of the followers. You've got to have a crisis."

So saying, Walker, King and other SCLC aides departed for Birmingham to create a crisis. It seemed for a spell that Birmingham would end in the same manner as Albany. But Birmingham was informed by a deeper strategic insight. The terrain of Birmingham, moreover, was more favorable to Negro resistance. Birmingham, unlike Albany, was a key industrial center, and men could not long remain indifferent to what happened there. Another element in the Birmingham equation was Eugene ("Bull") Connor, the commissioner of public safety who led the police and fire forces defending the status quo. Connor blundered into the hands of Negro demonstrators by using tactics (fire hoses and police dogs) that went beyond the "polite repression" America had become accustomed to.

The struggles on the streets of Birmingham in April and May of 1963 raised temperatures in America to a new high. When King and his aides smashed the white defense with a series of massive charges by thousands of school children, some of them no older than six or seven, the second wave of the rebellion came to a roaring climax. The agreement ending the demonstrations called for phased integration of business facilities, upgrading of Negro workers, and the creation of a bi-racial committee. This agreement, incidentally, confirmed a fact Americans had long evaded: broken community. The Birmingham agreement was in form and substance a political truce between two separate communities.

The third wave of the rebellion, a wave remarkably different in tone and texture, began almost immediately. A bombing counterattack by disgruntled segregationists wrecked the home of a Negro leader and damaged a Negro-owned motel, detonating a mass explosion by Birmingham adults, many of whom had held themselves aloof from the nonviolent demonstrations. The Birmingham riot of May 11-12 sent shock waves across the country and announced the entry of a hitherto uncommitted group, the so-called underclass, the permanently depressed strata of the Negro working class.

In the following weeks, Birmingham-type demonstrations spread across the country, engulfing community after community in wholesale strife. More significant was the beginning of mass confrontations in Chicago, Philadelphia, New York and other cities of the North. There was a new harshness in these confrontations, the result of the tapping of new layers of the Negro lower class and the emergence of bolder, more political (in the sense of power and community decision making) leaders.

Two events in June signalled the new departure. The June demonstrations in Cambridge, Maryland, degenerated into open warfare and the imposition of limited martial law. In this same period, there was a bloody brawl in Philadelphia where pickets protesting union bias used their bodies to stop work on construction projects. The leaders of these focal events, Gloria Hays Richardson of Cambridge and Attorney Cecil Moore of Philadelphia, were personifications of new social types. Though their bases of power were different, Gloria Richardson and Cecil Moore were stamped in the same mould. Moore, a big bluff lawyer, colorful and flamboyant, had converted the NAACP chapter in Philadelphia into an instrument of mass appeal. Gloria Richardson, a slim Howard graduate in her early forties, had performed the same feat in Cambridge, using laborers and unemployed workers on the executive committee of the SNCC-affiliated Cambridge Nonviolent Coordinating Committee. Although she was a descendant of one of the first families of the black elite, Gloria Richardson was, by her own account, "a radical, a revolutionary."

Both Gloria Richardson and Cecil Moore were tough, bare-knuckled fighters who gave no quarter and asked none. Instead of relying on a small group of elite nonviolent professionals, they appealed to the masses, stressing bread-and-butter issues like unemployment and the inequities of the American economic system.

The emergence of men and women made in the image of Cecil Moore and Gloria Richardson gave the third wave of the rebellion a new intensity. New tactics, tactics verging on open civil disobedience, were articulated and applied. In Savannah, Georgia, New York City, Chicago and other cities, men and woman lay down in the streets to stop traffic and used their bodies to halt work on construction sites.

The new tactics and the new leaders escalated the problems to a new height. In June and July, scores of communities teetered on the edge of miniature civil wars. Events at the NAACP convention in July underlined the new mood of desperation and defiance. At a July 4 NAACP rally, the audience booed Mayor Richard J. Daley, the powerful Democratic boss of Chicago, and Rev. J. H. Jackson, the conservative president of the National Baptist Convention.

The convention itself was punctuated by several rebuffs to other invited speakers, including James Meredith, who criticized the rebellious ardor of Negro youths. In the climax of what was essentially a confrontation between Negro militants and Negro activists, NAACP youths staged a mass march on the NAACP Board of Directors and demanded greater autonomy from adult NAACP chapters.

Shaken by the turbulence within the convention and the turbulence without, the NAACP moved again, verbally at any rate, calling for an intensified program of direct action and the modification of the NAACP structure by the creation of "task forces" and the recruitment of additional field secretaries.

The NAACP convention underlined a fact that was becoming more disquieting to the Kennedy Administration and "established" Negro leadership. The hard, cold fact in July of 1963 was that "established" Negro leadership was following not leading the rebellion. Birmingham had released forces that were accelerating events at an ever-dizzier pace. By July 4, the big black locomotive of Negro despair was lurching wildly through the night while fumbling hands searched frantically for the mechanism of control. To understand developments of this period we must hold one fact in the center of our minds: some of the hands were seeking the accelerator and some were seeking the brake. The various acts of federal, state, and local officials—the Kennedy civil rights bill, and executive orders of several state governors, etc.—were attempts on the part of constituted authority to brake the accelerating and leaderless train. So also were the new levels of commitment and concern expressed by the white liberals of labor and the white Christian church.

The most extraordinary facet of this effort to damp down and contain Negro discontent was the coalition movement organized by white liberals and national Negro leadership. During the months of May and June, white liberals and Negro leaders met in private homes and board rooms in New York City to find ways and means of keeping the rebellion from overflowing channels and becoming a revolution. The white liberals said frankly that they were concerned about the increasing willingness of Negroes to go it alone. They were alarmed, too, over the defiant mood of the Negro masses who were forcing "established" Negro leaders to take bolder and more militant postures to keep up with their competitors and with their followers. Above all else, white liberals wanted to relieve the intense pressure on the moderately militant Negro leaders of the NAACP and the National Urban League. Their dominant purposes were to detach militant and moderate Negro leaders from the Negro masses, to insulate them from the turbulence of the rebellion and to relieve them of the necessity of being responsive to the increasingly demanding Negro masses.

Set down thus, the liberal purpose seems cold, cynical, calculating. It was, in part, but it stemmed also from nobler motives: the general welfare, the fear of race riots, etc. James A. Wechsler of the *New York Post* was in or on the fringes of these conversations and his columns of that period make fascinating reading. Let us attend him. He is reporting (June 27, 1963) the series of meetings between white liberals and "established" Negro leadership.

> Fortunately it can be reported that there have been private, fruitful sessions among the top Negro chieftains with such key labor allies as Walter Reuther and such liberal leaders as Lloyd Garrison and Stephen Currier of the Taconic Foundation. In the mundane but serious matter of fund raising, a major accord has been reached and will be formally announced in a few days. A great, sustained effort to rally financial support for the equal rights drive is under way, and *the sometimes acrimonious competition for such support should be greatly reduced.*
>
> Equally important are the signs that general strategy

will be increasingly coordinated. This will not be a
monolithic movement; there will inevitably be some
difference of tone and timing. But there is apparently
growing agreement that, as the Congressional showdown approaches, any evidences of conflict within the
civil rights camp (*or any random exhibitionism designed to establish the superior militancy and virtue
of one group over others*) would play into the hands
of the segregationist battalions. [Emphasis supplied.]

What this meant, in plain English, was that "top Negro
chieftains" and "key labor allies" and "liberal leaders" were
searching frantically for a de-escalator. The biracial containment movement concentrated, as Wechsler noted, on two related points: 1) the creation of a coordinating council composed of moderate as well as militant and activist leadership;
and 2) the development of a financial umbrella that would
shield militants and moderates and constrain activists.

Among the leaders of this movement was Stephen Currier,
a wealthy young businessman and philanthropist, and Arnold
Aronson, a white reformer who had long moved on the edges
of Negro leadership circles. Currier succeeded in persuading
several major corporations and prominent businessmen to
donate several million dollars to Negro civil rights organizations. A spokesman for Currier denied that the money was
given to control the rebellion. What the donors wanted, according to the spokesman as reported by Reese Cleghorn in
the *New Republic,* was a better organized, more orderly rebellion.

To accomplish this purpose, a new organization, the Council
on United Civil Rights leadership, was established, with Currier and Whitney Young, executive director of the Urban
League, as co-directors. The new group consisted of SNCC,
SCLC, CORE and other organizations that were cool
(NAACP) or detached (Urban League) from the rebellion.
The coordinating structure consisted, therefore, of an unwieldy group of moderates and rebels whose voices check-
mated each other, a fact that was probably not lost on the organizers.

Under the banner of this organization and the March on
Washington group, Negro leaders stitched together a rebellion
directorate which has held regular meetings since the summer
of 1963. Characteristically, the Negro Summit Group has done
little since the March on Washington, although it has been
extraordinarily active in deciding that things should not be
done. The Negro Summit Group vetoed the proposed Christ-

mas boycott and the World's Fair Stall-in. It also called for a moratorium on demonstrations after the Harlem riots. CORE and SNCC dissented from some of these decisions, particularly the call for a moratorium on demonstrations.

The creation of a national directorate with a built-in brake of moderation was perhaps the turning point of the rebellion which limped now to the diversionary peak of the March on Washington. The March grew out of and was colored by the movement to contain and control the rebellion. On July 2, Arnold Aronson announced that he had issued a call for the first Negro Summit conference of the rebellion. Negro and white power holders met at the Hotel Roosevelt in New York at the height of the NAACP convention and decided that greater unity was needed. The Negro Summit Group later announced support of the March on Washington idea which A. Philip Randolph had suggested in early January. With the support of important segments of labor and the white Christian church, the Negro Summit Group succeeded in amassing some 250,000 people, about 60,000 of them white, in Washington, D. C., on August 28. The demonstration was designed to exhibit broad white and Negro support for "freedom and jobs" and passage of the Kennedy civil rights bill.

As a morale booster, the March was a stunning success. But as an exercise in leadership, it was something less than scintillating. The March was not coordinated with anything that preceded it or anything that followed it. It led nowhere and was not intended to lead anywhere. *It was not planned as an event within a coherent plan of action.* As a result, the March was a stimulating but detached and isolated episode.

The March on Washington, moreover, created a climate that men had to respond to or lose thrust. With the March, the rebellion became national. The March was an act near the peak. After that event, men had to decide whether to go up to the top of the mountain or to go back down to the valley of protest.

The fourth wave of the rebellion, beginning with the bombing of the Sixteenth Street Baptist Church in Birmingham, intensified the unsolved problems the March illuminated. The central problem of this period were problems of definition.

What, precisely, were Negro leaders doing?

What did they intend to do?

In the fall and winter of 1963, these questions beat like a fusillade on the minds of Negro leaders. This was a period of groping and uncertainty not unlike the period following the sit-in breakthrough. Birmingham was a breakthrough of similar dimension, and men again stumbled blindly in the dark trying to find their bearing. In this period also the center of gravity shifted again from the South to the North, and new cadres, principally the angry young men of World War II and the Korean War, entered the ranks, bringing with them the blind fire of a deeper discontent.

After the Birmingham bombing, Negroes of all ranks indicated a new willingness to embrace more radical tactics of action. From the fall of 1963 to the spring of 1964, "established" Negro leadership fought a rearguard action against Negro activists who tried, unsuccessfully, to push the rebellion into open civil disobedience. The central question of the hour was stated starkly by Wyatt Tee Walker, one of the best strategists of the movement, soon after the Birmingham bombing. "The question is," he said, "whether we want to continue local guerilla battles against discrimination and segregation or go to all-out war." Walker went on to ask in a speech to the SCLC convention: ". . . has the moment come in the development of the nonviolent revolution that we are forced [by delays and painfully slow results] . . . on some appointed day or some appointed hour literally [to] immobilize the nation until she acts on our pleas for justice and morality that have been too long denied. Is the day far-off that major transportation centers would be deluged with mass acts of civil disobedience; airports, train stations, bus terminals, the traffic of large cities, interstate commerce, would be halted by the bodies of witnesses nonviolently insisting on 'Freedom Now.' I supposed a nationwide work stoppage might attract enough attention to persuade someone to do something to get this monkey of segregation and discrimination off our backs, once, now and forever. Will it take one or all of these?"

James Baldwin, the writer, and some of the more militant SNCC activists said it would probably take all of these. Baldwin called for a nationwide campaign of civil disobedience. He said: "If we don't move now, literally move, sit down, stand, walk, don't go to work, don't pay the rent, if we don't do everything now in our power to change this country, this country will turn out to be in the position, let us say, of Spain, a country which is so tangled and so trapped and immobilized by its interior dissension that it can't do anything else."

Baldwin and a group of New York writers and artists (John O. Killens, Ruby Dee, Ossie Davis, Louis E. Lomax and others) later urged a total boycott of Christmas. They contended that

America had forfeited the right to hide behind Christian rituals. The proposal generated a great deal of interest, but the Negro Summit Group vetoed the plan.

Negro leaders also vetoed a more radical plan for a full-scale civil disobedience movement in the South. This plan was suggested by Diane Nash and some of the SNCC activists. The plan, as reported by Lawrence Still in *Jet* and Wallace Terry in the *Washington Post,* called for the recruitment of a civil rights army of twenty-five thousand and the launching of a total civil disobedience campaign (nonpayment of state and local taxes, work strikes, and the blockading of transportation facilities) in Alabama. The plan called for demonstrators to declare that "within our conscience" the Wallace government was "null and void."

By vetoing this and other new departures, Negro leadership elected to continue nonviolent guerilla warfare. The rebellion at this juncture was essentially a middle-class rebellion consisting, as Bayard Rustin put it, of focused demonstrations composed of "disciplined" demonstrators with a specific target and a specific objective. Even this was too radical for "established" Negro leaders who continued to oppose demonstrations as a primary tactic.

By the fall of 1964, demonstrations had reached what seemed to be a point of diminishing return. Southerners were easily crushing demonstrations by massive repression. Worse, demonstrations, North and South, had not succeeded in winning important victories. As a result, voices of moderation grew louder and the value of demonstrations was questioned by some of the more militant leaders. Bayard Rustin spoke disparagingly of demonstrations at the SNCC convention in Washington, D. C. Dr. John Morsell, administrator of the NAACP, emphasized that his organization was still committed to direct action but he warned of "several dangers." "It seems to us," he said, "and several other civil rights leaders, including the executives of CORE that some demonstrations have degenerated into a kind of gimmickery in which you try to outdo the last gimmick in outlandishness and sensationalism." The NAACP executive told *Jet* magazine that repetition was dulling the impact of demonstrations. "If every time you look up someone is marching past with placards—you don't pay much attention any more." What did Mr. Morsell propose? The position of the NAACP, he said, was that mass direct action should take the form of mass letter-writing, selective buying, or voter registration.

There was some truth in the widespread criticism of demonstrations, but it was not the whole truth. There was nothing wrong, really, with demonstrations. What was wrong was the use men were making of demonstrations. The problem, broadly stated, was that men were creating acts that were not joined to each other, acts that were not subordinated to a thought-out plan of action. What was lacking at this point was strategic planning and a structure capable of carrying out a long-range plan instead of a series of brilliant but nonetheless blundering steps in the dark.

By this time, too, demonstrations had become to the new Negro leadership what voter registration was to the old: something to do when no one knew quite what to do. Worse yet, some Negro leaders, some of them high in the national hierarchy, were openly calling demonstrations cathartics. According to these leaders, demonstrations were instruments for venting Negro despair. They were occasions for working off resentment—like wrestling matches. This view, more than anything else, doomed the demonstrations to futility.

The dialogue between Negro militants and Negro activists was essentially a dialogue over the use of demonstrations and that dialogue continued throughout the fall of 1963 and the spring of 1964. The Chicago school boycott of October 22 dramatized a new way of fighting which spread in 1964 to Harlem, Cincinnati, and other Northern cities, creating deep fissures within the Negro communities and between the Negro and white communities. There was a noticeable lack of white liberal and NAACP-Urban League support for the second round of boycotts in New York City and Chicago in the spring of 1964.

As the controversy spread, attitudes hardened on both sides of the racial line and within contending groups in the Negro and white communities. The generalized community-wide attacks on *de facto* school and housing segregation were followed by a "white backlash," a euphemism for the surfacing of latent bigotry. The surfacing of anti-Negro hysteria was clearly apparent in the low-income white groups, but it was not confined to this segment as the large number of votes received by Alabama Governor George Wallace in Northern Presidential primaries indicated.

The gathering battle lines within and between communities were shattered temporarily by the outpouring of national grief over the assassination of President Kennedy. But tension began to rise again soon after the period of national mourning. This development reinforced the fears of Negro leaders who favored "sha-sha" (hush-hush) tactics, but did not moderate the fervor of activists who struck out for higher ground. There were increasingly harsh confrontations in the spring of 1964 between Negroes and whites in Jacksonville and St. Augustine, Florida, Chester, Pennsylvania, and Atlanta, Georgia. There was also a widening of the circle of combatants. Rent strikes in Harlem and hunger marches in Chicago announced a new theme of a more basic despair.

Despite this activity, the movement as a whole was clearly in a state of crisis. By the spring of 1964, the Negro leadership group was in a state of complete disarray. No single group, nationally or locally, could command the allegiance of the masses, and what leadership there was, was in the hands of coalition groups like the Coordinating Council of Community Organizations of Chicago, the United Freedom movement of Cleveland, and the City-wide Committee for Integrated Schools of New York City. On the national level, there were continuing coalition conferences but a complete absence of direction and planning. Nationally and locally, there were deep cleavages within the coalition groups, and these cleavages widened under the impact of events.

Militants and moderates within the coalitions said the movement had gone as far as it could go as a Negro movement. It was necessary, Bayard Rustin said, for the rebellion to branch out in a search for alliances with white labor, the white Christian church, etc. Leaders thrown up by the fourth wave of the rebellion agreed with Rustin's analysis, but scorned his proposed solutions. The rebellion, they said, had gone as far as it could go as a rebellion. It would have to become a real revolution now, they said, or give up the pretense. A shadow coming before the event was the threat of a Brooklyn CORE chapter to "bring New York to a complete standstill through techniques of massive civil disobedience." This threat put flesh on the bones of the dispute which grew in fury in the spring and summer of 1964.

As a result of internal squabbles and the hard logic of events, there was still another reshuffling of the leadership group. The leaders of the third wave of the rebellion moved now to the right, or, rather, they stood still and the spectrum moved left. The grand outcome was the upsurge of a new cadre of leaders on the non-Communist left. Among the dominant voices of the new left wing of the movement were Rev. Milton Galamison, leader of the New York school boycotts; Lawrence Landry, leader of the Chicago school boycotts; Gloria Richardson, the Cambridge, Maryland activist; and Dick Gregory, the militant comedian. Another voice on the left was Malcolm X who had been suspended from the Black Muslims for equivocal remarks about the assassination of President Kennedy. Malcolm later resigned from the Black Muslims and announced his intentions of forming a mass-based black nationalist movement allied with the civil rights movement. Malcolm X, Gloria Richardson and others were instrumental in the founding of ACT, a militant organization of activists, most of them Northerners.

Two climactic events of this period joined the issue between the disputing leaders of the rebellion. Staging an internal revolt against the national leaders of CORE, two dissident CORE chapters lurched forward into an open civil disobedience. On Friday, March 6, the East River (New York City) chapter of CORE tied up rush-hour traffic by staging a sit-in on the Triborough Bridge. A month later on Wednesday, April 22, the Brooklyn chapter of CORE threatened to tie up traffic on expressways leading to the World's Fair. The threatened stall-in failed to materialize, but it created the most acrimonious debate since the beginning of the sit-in age. CORE later suspended the chapter. James Farmer said the threatened sit-in was not a "relevant" confrontation with the white power structure. The problem, however, was in the opposite direction. The stall-in was a real confrontation and the power structure knew it, though Farmer chose, probably for reasons of strategy, to deny it. The stall-in was war, a war, to be sure, without violence, but nonetheless war.

Of minor importance in itself, the stall-in was yet an event of far-reaching implications. The stall-in was a focal point which defined the rebellion, not intellectually but emotionally. What was striking in the stall-in was the fact that it did not leave Negro leadership a line of retreat. By refusing to accept the lead card of dissidents, Negro leadership was forced to confess to itself and to others that it was depending on a line of retreat. We are not concerned here with the rightness or wrongness of that decision. It is highly probable that Negro leadership was right and that Negroes were not ready for open revolt. But the admission of that fact in public by action or lack of action eroded the moral prestige of the leaders of the rebellion, opening a deep fault between them and the masses.

As the rebellion passed the turn of the stall-in and headed into the backstretch of "the long hot summer of 1964," the position of "established" Negro leadership became more untenable. In June and July, the Negro masses moved further to the left, changing again the real position of Negro leaders who again remained in the same place.

All the currents of the rebellion reached tidal wave proportions in the fifth wave which threatened to engulf all Americans. In the summer of 1964, the air turned sultry, darkening with thunderheads of unrest. The level of desperation in both the Negro and white communities began to rise and the chasm between the communities widened and deepened.

The mood of desperation in the Negro community in this summer was wild and unfocused. Preceding waves of rebellion had carried Negroes to a new peak of hope which the old leaders could not satisfy. Gains which would have seemed spectacular a few years before now seemed petty and paltry. Rebuffs which were taken in stride months before now became matters of monstrous importance. There were, at the same time, demands for an immediate and total solution of the real problems of the Negro masses, problems neither established Negro leadership nor the American political system was equipped to deal with.

If Negroes were growing more set in their anger, the fury of white folk was also mounting. The "white backlash" became ugly, acrid and neo-fascist in this summer. The struggles in the streets did not, as some have contended, "cause" the "white backlash." The "backlash" was already there, had always been there, lurking beneath the surface. The demonstrations made men—Negro and white men—face up to a problem they were trying to evade. The demonstrations pushed men—Negro and white men—to an increasingly desperate confrontation with themselves.

This was the real meaning of the "white backlash" which revealed the desperate dimensions of white fear and the lengths to which men were prepared to go to evade the implications of that fear in themselves and in others. As temperatures rose in this summer, more and more white people, some of them quite liberal, reminded Negroes of their real position, quasi-colonial status maintained by the naked force and power of a hostile majority.

The so-called white backlash found focus in the campaign of Senator Barry Goldwater for the Presidency. After voting against the civil rights bill, the Arizona senator captured the Republican Presidential nomination on a campaign that appealed to disgruntled racists and rightists. The Senator denied that he was a racist, but his campaign was based, implicitly and explicitly, on the organization and amplification of anti-Negro hysteria. There was also an undoubted neo-fascist undertone in the call for Negro repression by right-wing extrem-

ists who supported the Goldwater campaign. The practical
effort of all this, whatever the intentions, was the introduction
of racism into mainstream politics with incalculable results
for the future of the American idea.

Two series of events in this fateful summer reflected the
growing desperation in the minds of men—reflected the desperation and intensified it. The first high point was the "invasion" of Mississippi by hundreds of Negro and white civil
rights workers, most of them college students. After training in
centers in Ohio and other states, the young Americans entered
Mississippi to help members of SNCC and other civil rights
organizations. This campaign was designed to increase the
number of Negro registered voters in Mississippi and to focus
national attention on the flagrant defiance of the Constitution
by Mississippi officials.

The Mississippi Project, as it was called, was a widening of
long-standing efforts of civil rights organizations, principally
SNCC, to force America to confront the unpalatable fact that
Mississippi and entities like it did not have a republican form
of government as required by the Constitution.

Since the Freedom Rides, the Freedom movement had been
attempting, by every means possible, to bring about a confrontation of the federal government and defiant state officials.
The federal government, as we have seen, had intervened
when Southern defiance reached embarrassing dimensions, but
it had intervened sporadically, always avoiding the basic issue
of the open oppression of millions of American citizens by illegally constituted political entities.

The Mississippi Project was designed really to force the government's hand. Since the American government and the
American people had shown only scant interest in the brutal
repression of the rights of Negro Americans, SNCC and other
civil rights groups decided to commit hundreds of young white
Americans to the struggle. The brutal murder of three civil
rights workers—two whites and one Negro—and the beating,
intimidation, and harassment of scores of their colleagues pin-
pointed the problem and revolted large sections of the American populace. There were widespread demands for a federal
presence in Mississippi, but little of substance was done.

Civil rights groups, led by SNCC, later perfected organization of the Freedom Democrat party, an integrated political
group, which challenged the right of the lily-white Democratic
party to represent Mississippi at the Democratic national convention. After an acrimonious dispute, the convention devised
a compromise, recognizing the entire delegation of the lily-

white group and granting two at-large seats to the Freedom Democratic group. Both groups turned down the compromise. The lily-white group refused to sign a loyalty pledge and returned to Mississippi. The Freedom Democrats, despite fervent pleas from "practical" national leaders, scorned the "tokenism" of the two at-large seats.

The riot season of 1964 reflected on another level the mounting desperation of the period. The riots which began in Harlem on July 18 and leaped across the country (Rochester; Jersey City; Dixmoor, Illinois; Philadelphia) were, in essence, rebellions against white control. The chief targets of the rioters were symbols of white control (policemen) and symbols of white power (white-owned stores). The riots were largely street wars between Negroes and the predominantly white police forces that had been the main protagonists of the Negro rebellion since the first week of February, 1960. The riots followed the same pattern: an incident involving alleged police brutality, street fighting between Negroes and white policemen, the throwing of bottles, bricks, and Molotov cocktails, the smashing of plate-glass windows, and the looting of stores.

Two things emerged from this orchestration of desperation with alarming clarity: 1) the almost total alienation of the Negro masses, most of whom regard policemen as occupation soldiers of an unsympathetic colonial government; and 2) the almost complete lack of rapport between the Negro masses and "established" Negro leaders who were jeered, hooted, and abused by the street mobs.

The sixth phase of the rebellion, the phase beginning with the Harlem riots and ending with the Selma-to-Montgomery march, marked an intensification of the structural and ideological problems of the rebellion. The riot season of 1964, like the riot season of 1943, served to consolidate the position of moderates and militants. There were, at the same time, widespread attempts to silence Negro agitators and a general backlash in white-oriented media. The assassination of Malcolm X (February 21, 1965) before some five hundred of his followers in a Harlem meeting shattered the false calm and refocused the national spotlight on the troubled ghetto. Malcolm X had been formulating a new philosophy based on self-defense and self-assertion in closer alliance with the African freedom movement; and his death lent new urgency to the quest for fresh instruments and combinations of action in the Negro community. That new combinations of action were necessary was made clear by the Selma demonstrations which were initiated by the Student Nonviolent Coordinating Committee and carried to a climax by the charismatic artistry of Martin Luther King, Jr. The Selma voter rights drive began as a traditional Freedom movement campaign and ended as a massive thrust against white supremacy in the Black Belt areas of the South. When, on Sunday, March 7, 1965, Alabama state troopers and possemen crushed a Selma-to-Montgomery march with massive brutality, the Freedom movement lurched to a higher level of intensity. Thousands of whites—bishops, nuns, priests, ministers, rabbis, college students, labor leaders—flocked to Selma where one Negro and two whites were killed in action. Outraged by the brutalities of Selma, President Lyndon B. Johnson went before Congress and recommended the strongest voting rights bill since the Reconstruction era. The President later federalized the Alabama National Guard and sent elements of the U.S. Army to Alabama to protect Negro and white demonstrators who marched from Selma to Montgomery and held a large rally at the Alabama State Capitol.

Though nominally a victory, the Selma campaign reawakened Negroes to the reality of their lives and to the urgent necessity of freshness of thought and boldness of deed. Consider, for example, the actions of Martin Luther King, Jr., who immediately called for an economic boycott of Alabama and announced that he would soon mount Selma-type demonstrations in the big-city ghettos of the North. Consider further the actions of the NAACP which issued, in the wake of Selma, the most radical statement ever released by an "established" Negro organization. Roy Wilkins, the NAACP executive director, told white Americans that Negro Americans were "furious over the brutal attack by Alabama State Police on Sunday's [March 7] freedom march at Selma." Wilkins added:

"Like the citizens of Nazi-occupied France, Holland, Belgium, Denmark and Norway, Negroes must either submit to the heels of their oppressors or they must organize, underground if necessary, to protect themselves from the oppression of Gov. [George] Wallace and his storm troopers."

Not only Roy Wilkins, but millions of Negro Americans began to move to new positions in the wake of Selma. During and after the Selma demonstrations, there was a bitter behind-the-scenes struggle between Martin Luther King, Jr., and SNCC activists who believed King was too closely allied with the federal government and the labor and white church establishment. There was, at the same time, an intensification of the ideological struggle in the North where many intellectuals and activists adopted Malcolm X as a patron saint and called for a new policy of self-defense. The pressures from these groups and from the Negro underclass will increase rapidly in the next few months unless Americans make what they have not yet made, a relevant response to our deepest domestic crisis since the Civil War.

The confrontations on the streets of America in 1964-65 were signs unto America. More ominous yet were encounters in the winding streets of the mind. What the events of 1964-65 revealed was the depth of our problem and the irrelevancy of our techniques for containing the problem.

The Black Fury and the White Hysteria of 1964-65 were not isolated events. On the contrary, they characterized America down to its marrow. The riots, the demonstrations, the hysteria, and the widening chasms between communities and within communities: all were logical outgrowths of the conditions we have traced in this study.

Although the Negro rebellion is diffuse and somewhat chaotic, there is nonetheless an advancing order, reference points, a direction, and an orientation. The rebellion moves essentially on two axes: 1) toward the Negro masses, and 2) toward civil disobedience.

Faced with the implacable hostility of a powerful majority, Rebellion leaders have been obliged to use their resources to invent countermoves. But the increasing misery, psychological as well as material, of the Negro people has caused the countermoves to be always more radical, conceding more strongly each time to the just demands of the Negro masses. As a result, a movement which began as a middle-class revolt is rapidly approaching the status of a full-blown rebellion, if not revolution.

As I have said elsewhere, we approach now a land no American has traversed. The post-Harlem riot world is a world of contingent desperation in both the Negro and white communities. We are in a race here between white hysteria and Negro despair, between fascism and democracy, between America and America. The problems of the ages are stalking us like eerie footsteps approaching in an empty and deserted house.

Everything is at stake now, and we must dare now to risk everything or we shall surely lose everything. The events of 1965 told us, louder than a thousand trumpets, that we are two, and that we are heading for disaster if we do not soon become one. What is required now, above everything else, is the creation of a common American community. That community cannot be created until the law of reciprocity reigns between man and man. The abrogation of this law, for whatever reason, creates a condition of hate. It is unrealistic to expect Negroes to respect the laws and conventions of a unilaterally subjective white community that has no respect for their personality and prerogatives and rights. The truth of the matter is that the law of reciprocity works at either one level or another. A smile for a smile, a courtesy for a courtesy, an obligation for an obligation, a duty for a duty, a hate for a hate: this is the law of reciprocity, which is the only law that can make men more than strangers and less than enemies. Our present conundrum is a direct result of the breaching of the law of reciprocity and equivalence at the level of community; and we are heading for a disaster no man can stay if we do not make a massive attempt to reverse the energy-directions of Negro and white Americans.

To do this, we must make revolutionary changes at every level of our lives. We must, first of all, abandon our frames of reference, for our frames of reference—all our frames of reference—are vitiated by racist assumptions. We speak of the lack of responsible Negro leadership when the problem is the lack of responsible white leadership. We speak of Negro crime when the problem is white crime. We speak of Negro education when the problem is white education. Always, everywhere, we judge from white standards, assuming that Negroes are inferior white men or white men with black skins. Negroes are not white men with pigment in their skins; they are men, and neither we nor they can be saved unless we approach them as men.

There is no need really for us to continue to play the dreadful games of the professional race relationist: the game of education ("We must educate Negroes"), the game of appropriation ("We must improve the cultural standards of Negroes"), the game of technique ("It is a *very complicated* problem"). We are not now, nor have we ever been, playing those games. The game we are playing is racism. Negroes are not condemned in America because they lack education; they are condemned because they are Negroes. The truth of the matter is that neither Jesus Christ, nor Gandhi, nor Brooks Brothers, nor Yale, nor General Motors have been sufficiently persuasive in the ethic of the white man to make him treat Negroes as human beings.

We do not come up with the right answers to our problem because we seldom ask ourselves the right question. *There is no Negro problem in America; there has never been a Negro problem in America—the problem of race in America is a white problem.* To understand that problem and to control it, we must address ourselves to the fears and frailties of white people. We learn nothing really from a study of Harlem. To understand Harlem we must go not to Harlem but to the conscience of "good white people," and we must ask not what is Harlem but what have you made of Harlem. Why did you create it and why do you need it?

We spend a disproportionately large amount of time in America asking ourselves what can we do for Negroes. This is the wrong end of the problem. Nothing can be done for Negroes as long as they are treated like inferior beings. Once we face that truth, the problem becomes what it has always been. What can we do for white people? What can we do for teachers, policemen, mayors, bankers, realtors, social workers, labor leaders, businessmen, preachers? What can we do for the people who created and who sustain the Commonwealth of Absence, that America which exists as a negation of the Word.

And what can we do for the lambs—the ordinary people, the technically innocent, whose protective coating of status fright, greed, and numbness of heart let it all happen.

Prejudice in America is a deeply rooted part of the social structure, a defensive mechanism in the adjustment system of most white individuals, and an economic and political weapon in group conflicts. It is all these things and more, but most of all it is a series of little meannesses linked to petty considerations of status and snobbishness.

The real race problem in America is the problem of the white American. And that problem cannot be solved without a total re-examination of the foundations of our lives. In this re-examination, there must be no privileged areas. We must dare now to ask the unaskable. What do we really mean by miscegenation? Why do we fear it? As Myrdal suggested in the forties, it would be a distinct public service to bring these questions out into the open. What is involved really in the explosive fears that surround the white woman and the Negro male? Let us start there, for if we do not start here, in the heart of our fears, we shall not go anywhere.

If we are to avert a disaster here, there must be a massive re-education of white Americans. There must be, at the same time, a massive attack on the evidences of the mis-education of white Americans. A necessary prerequisite is the immediate cessation of segregation and discrimination and a massive program of national atonement for hundreds of years of soul-destroying oppression, a program that would involve *as a minimum requirement* the expenditure of billions of dollars and the engagement of the energies of all our citizens.

Anything less is a lie.

Anything less is deceit, fraud, silence.

This program should be spelled out in a series of federal, state, and local plans setting out in great detail phased approaches to integration in housing, employment and other areas. To be effective, these plans must be based on community-wide recognition, locally and nationally, that this problem can be solved and that it will be solved. Whatever difficulties, problems or sacrifices that might be connected with the implementation of these plans should be borne by those responsible for the outrages of segregation, not by its victims. Neither in law nor in logic are the robbed required to pay for the crimes of the robber.

The only thing that stands between America and integration is the decision to integrate. There are, to be sure, millions of unskilled workers and hundreds if not thousands of lily-white and all-Negro neighborhoods. But these are minor problems that could be solved tomorrow if we wanted to solve them. During World War II, we created an entire work force by on-the-job training, and we can do it again, whenever we want to. The same situation obtains in the field of education. We can cluster schools, Princeton Plan, or create school parks. The point here is that we can do any one of a number of things. All the techniques are available, but technique is not the problem, and any organization that wastes its time on technique is playing the oppressor's game. What is wanting, what has always been wanting here, is the will. And where there is a will there is a way to integrate.

The task of responsible Negro leadership is to force white Americans to face that fact by whatever means necessary short of offensive violence. Let us be absolutely clear about one thing. Negro leadership is also responsible for the plight of Negro Americans. As I have said before, it takes two to oppress: someone to oppress and someone to accept oppression. Nothing relieves a man of his responsibility in accepting degradation. The boundary of freedom is man's power to say "No!" and whoever refuses to say "No" involves himself tragically in his own degradation. It is unrealistic for Negro leaders to expect men associated in any way with oppression to take the lead in destroying oppression. It has never happened anywhere, and it will not happen here. The white man will not and cannot free the Negro. Negro leadership must dare to take the necessary steps that will free the oppressed and the oppressor.

Negroes cannot win in America until the masses are organized and mobilized for a sustained, to-the-end drive for full citizenship. A second prerequisite is a national structure, a single organization, capable of charting long-range strategy and carrying it out. This presupposes, of course, leaders who have severed all ties—emotional, economic and otherwise—to the status quo.

The alienation of the Negro masses from Negro leadership is based on a very sophisticated analysis of the programs and policies of so-called established leadership. The Negro masses know, better than some of their leaders, what time it is historically. They are not fooled. They know that nothing any "established" organization is *willing to do* is relevant to their total situation. They know, better than the sociologists and economists, that only a real nonviolent revolution, a revolution within and a revolution without, will change their plight.

America stands at a crossroad but so also does Negro leadership which must become real now or retreat to the old islands of petition and protest. A return to protest as usual would be unthinkable. It would doom millions of Negroes to apathy and social demoralization and would do more than anything else to create a condition that would lead inevitably to a terrifying explosion in the 1970's and 1980's. The road of relevance for Negro leadership and for America is a road forward into danger.

The Commonwealth of Absence has not only robbed Negro Americans of jobs and material things, but it has also robbed them of hope, reducing men and women to the level where despair in destroying courage destroys the credentials of manhood and humanity. To awaken the sleeping millions, to mobilize them and organize them, to give them hope and weapons to fight with, to show them how to fight and when to fight: this is the central challenge of Negro leadership, and it is a challenge no national organization, with the exception of SNCC and the black nationalist groups, has addressed itself to in a serious and sustained way. The organization of the Woodlawn community in Chicago by the Temporary Woodlawn Organization (TWO) is an example of what can be done. But the most relevant experience is the use of field secretaries and "task forces" by SNCC which has made impressive headway in mobilizing the masses and creating indigenous leadership in Black Belt counties in the South. Negro leaders cannot meet the challenge given them by history without transferring these and other techniques to the slums of the North.

There is a need also for a rehauling of the basic structures and programs of the NAACP and National Urban League. These organizations played important roles in creating a foundation for rebellion, but they have not been relevant to the total Negro situation since the great migration and the urbanization of the Negro folk. These focal events changed the Negro's relation to himself and to America, but the NAACP and the National Urban League did not change with the Negro. Instead, these organizations clung to the Talented Tenth idea of elites representing the masses from afar. As middle-class reform agencies with no roots in the Negro masses, these organizations play a certain role. But they are scarcely more relevant to the New World of Negro and white Americans than the model-T. In structure and in program, both organizations are equipped to fight on a battleground that was washed away by the waves of the Great Migration. The NAACP Legal Defense and Education Fund is an indispensable organization. But its incorporation as a separate agency in 1939 made the NAACP's search for a role more desperate and more urgent.

The NAACP and the National Urban League not only lack skill in mass organization; they also lack a vision of battle that includes the Negro masses. The time is long overdue for implementation of the "new" NAACP's program of 1935 (the creation of local branches that would be sustained instruments of education and action, and the organization of workers councils) and the Myrdal suggestions of the forties (the appointment of working-class members to local and national boards of the NAACP and NUL and the initiation of a sustained program of education and propaganda directed to the Negro masses). The problem here, however, is not a problem of technique. What is required is a turning, tactically and programmatically, from the Negro middle class and the white liberal colonies to the Negro masses.

The "new orgs"—SNCC, CORE, SCLC—are closer to the Negro masses, but they have not scratched the surface of the dominant challenge of Negro leadership. SNCC, SCLC, and CORE, as we have pointed out, are largely sectional organizations without broad national bases. The criterion here is not the usual middle-class criterion of membership. SNCC, CORE, and SCLC have proven beyond doubt that an organization can be effective with a small core of professional rebels reaching out to the Negro masses. What they have not proven, however, is that they can create national structures capable of a sustained national campaign. The "new orgs," moreover, have not yet solved the basic problems of the first wave of the rebellion. Too many men in too many places have been creating acts that were not joined to each other—building rooms, as it were, without a plan for a house. The rebellion cannot fulfill itself until it becomes more self-conscious, until it clarifies and defines its task, until it rises to a new level of awareness and struggle—until, in sum, it cuts the moorings of its fears and takes on society.

To paraphrase a schema of the Ecumenical Institute, we face a series of interlocking decisions here. We face, first of all, a national decision. The decision, quite bluntly, is that we must either give the Negro all now or take all. We must become a democracy or give way—the signs are all about us—to fascism. With the awakening of the Negroes to a full consciousness of their situation and their potential power, that decision cannot be long delayed. We either believe in white supremacy or democracy. There will be no peace, no love, no justice in America until we decide.

What is our deepest desire?

What do we really believe?

The white man must decide.

The Negro faces a similar decision. Freedom is not—cannot —be given. It must be claimed, taken. According to an old Spanish proverb, God said: "Take what you want and pay for it."

How much is freedom worth?

How much is the Negro willing to pay?

The Negro must decide.

The wheel of fate is turning, and a time is coming when all men will have to decide. There is no easy way out of our history and our dishonesty. The only choice we have left is between an orderly confrontation and a disorderly one. If we do not choose now to confront ourselves on the level of reciprocation, if we do not decide in an orderly way who we are and what gods we serve, we and we alone will be responsible for the bitter harvest we have already sown.

Let there be no mistake about the nature of the larger decision before us. The decision we face now is a decision about America. America is not out there; it is in here—in the mind. We create it every day from images engraved on our hearts. We have slums because of the slums in our minds. The Mississippis and the Harlems are there, because we want Mississippis and Harlems, because we need Mississippis and Harlems, because Mississippis and Harlems are logical extensions of our dreaming and our desiring.

Is the Commonwealth of Absence, the Commonwealth of Mississippis and Harlems, the real America?

This is the larger question we are called upon to decide. There are no visible signs *out there* of the Commonwealth of Silence that was promised, that was written, and that never was. That America has never existed, except in our minds, and even the image is fading away. If we do not stand up now and create the America that was dreamed, if we do not begin to flesh out the words of the creed, the Commonwealth of Silence will come to a definite and apocalyptic end.

Which America will prevail?

Who are we?

In the name of the dead and the unborn, what place is this?
The reader must decide.

BIBLIOGRAPHY

Allport, Gordon W., and Kramer, Bernard M. "Some Roots of Prejudice," *Journal of Psychology*, July, 1946.

Aptheker, Herbert (ed.). *A Documentary History of the Negro People in the United States*. New York, 1951.

Baldwin, James. *Notes of a Native Son*. Boston, 1955.

——. *Nobody Knows My Name*. New York, 1961.

——. *The Fire Next Time*. New York, 1963.

Ballagh, James C. *White Servitude in the Colony of Virginia*. Baltimore, 1895.

Bauer, Raymond, and Bauer, Alice. "Day to Day Resistance to Slavery," *Journal of Negro History*, October, 1942.

Bell, Howard H. "Expressions of Negro Militancy in the North, 1840-60," *Journal of Negro History*, January, 1960.

Bennett, Lerone, Jr. *Before the Mayflower: A History of the Negro in America, 1619-1964*. Chicago, 1964.

——. *The Negro Mood*. Chicago, 1964.

——. *What Manner of Man*. Chicago, 1964.

——. "The March," in *The Day They Marched*, ed. Doris Saunders. Chicago, 1963.

——. "The Revolt of Negro Youth," *Ebony*, May, 1960.

——. "What Sit-downs Mean to America," *ibid.*, June, 1960.

Bird, Robert S. *Ten Negroes*. New York, 1963. Pamphlet reprinted from *New York Herald Tribune*.

Bond, Horace Mann. "Social and Economic Forces in Alabama Reconstruction," *Journal of Negro History*, July, 1938.

Bontemps, Arna, and Conroy, Jack. *They Seek a City*. New York, 1945.

Botkins, B. A. (ed.). *Lay My Burden Down*. Chicago, 1945.

Broderick, Francis L. *W. E. B. Du Bois: Negro Leader in a Time of Crisis*. Stanford, 1959.

Brown, Sterling A. *et al* (eds.). *The Negro Caravan*. New York, 1941.

Bryce, James. *The American Commonwealth*. New York, 1912.

Buck, Paul H. *The Road to Reunion*. Boston, 1937.

Buckmaster, Henrietta. *Let My People Go*. New York, 1941.

Bunche, Ralph J. "A Brief and Tentative Analysis of Negro Leadership." Unpublished manuscript prepared for Carnegie-Myrdal Study, 1940.

——. "Memorandum on the Conceptions and Ideologies of the Negro Problem," *ibid*.

——. "Programs, Ideologies, Tactics, and Achievements of Negro Betterment and Interracial Organizations," *ibid*.

Butcher, Margaret Just. *The Negro in American Culture*. New York, 1956.

Cantril, Hadley. *The Psychology of Social Movements*. New York, 1941.

Cash, Wilbur J. *The Mind of the South*. New York, 1941.

Chicago Commission on Race Relations. *The Negro in Chicago*. Chicago, 1922.

Cleghorn, Reese. "The Angels Are White," *New Republic*, August 17, 1963.

Coleman, James S. *Community Conflict*. Glencoe, 1957.

Congress of Racial Equality. *Cracking the Color Line*. Pamphlet, n.d.

Cothran, Tilman C., and Phillips, William, Jr. "Negro Leadership in a Crisis Situation," *Phylon*, Second Quarter, 1961.

Cox, Oliver C. "The Programs of Negro Civil Rights Organizations," *Journal of Negro Education*, Summer, 1951.

Crisis. "The Negro and Non-Resistance," June, 1924.

——. "A Symposium on Segregation," March, 1934.

Cronon, Edmund D. *Black Moses: The Story of Marcus Garvey*. Madison, 1955.

Davidson, Basil. *Black Mother*. Boston, 1961.

Davie, Maurice R. *Negroes in American Society*. New York, 1949.

De Santis, Vincent P. "The Republican Party and the Southern Negro, 1877-1897," *Journal of Negro History*, April, 1960.

Detweiler, Frederick G. *The Negro Press in the United States*. Chicago, 1922.

Donnan, Elizabeth (ed.). *Documents Illustrative of the History of the Slave Trade to America*. 4 vols. Washington, 1930-35.

Douglass, Frederick. *The Life and Times of Frederick Douglass*. Hartford, 1881.

——. *My Bondage and My Freedom*. New York, 1855.

Drake, St. Clair, and Cayton, Horace R. *Black Metropolis*. New York, 1945.

Du Bois, W. E. B. *The Philadelphia Negro*. Philadelphia, 1899.

——. *The Souls of Black Folk*. Chicago, 1903.

——. *Black Reconstruction*. New York, 1935.

——. *Dusk of Dawn*. New York, 1940.

——. "N. A. A. C. P. and Segregation," *Crisis*, February, 1934.

Dufty, William. "A. Philip Randolph," *New York Post*, December 28, 1959-January 3, 1960.

Dumond, Dwight L. *Antislavery*. Ann Arbor, 1961.

Durden, Robert F. "The Prostrate State Revisited: James S. Pike and South Carolina Reconstruction," *Journal of Negro History*, April, 1954.

Ebony. "Special Issue in Commemoration of the 100th Anniversary of the Emancipation Proclamation," September, 1963.

Elkins, Stanley M. *Slavery: A Problem in American Institutional and Intellectual Life*. Chicago, 1959.

Embree, Edwin. *13 Against the Odds*. New York, 1944.

Farmer, James. "Memorandum to A. J. Muste on Provisional Plans for Brotherhood Mobilization." Unpublished manuscript prepared for Congress of Racial Equality organizational committee, February 19, 1942. (Mimeographed.)

Filler, Louis. *The Crusade Against Slavery*. New York, 1960.

Foner, Phillip S. (ed.). *The Life and Writings of Frederick Douglass*. 4 vols. New York, 1950.

Franklin, John Hope. *From Slavery to Freedom*. New York, 1947.

———. *Reconstruction*. Chicago, 1961.

Frazier, E. Franklin. *The Negro Family in the United States*. Chicago, 1939.

———. *Black Bourgeoisie*. Glencoe, 1957.

———. *The Negro in the United States*. New York, 1957.

Fuller, Helen. "Southern Students Take Over," *New Republic*, May 2, 1960.

Garfinkel, Herbert. *When Negroes March*. Glencoe, 1959.

Gosnell, Harold F. *Negro Politicians: The Rise of Negro Politics in Chicago*. Chicago, 1935.

Grady, Henry. *The New South, and Other Addresses*. New York, 1904.

Greenberg, Jack. *Race Relations and American Law*. New York, 1959.

Guzman, Jessie P. (ed.). *Negro Year Book*. Tuskegee, 1947, 1952.

Heberle, Rudolf. *Social Movements*. New York, 1951.

Herskovits, Melville J. *The Myth of the Negro's Past*. New York, 1941.

Hirshon, Stanley P. *Farewell to the Bloody Shirt*. Bloomington, 1962.

Hook, Sidney. *The Hero in History*. New York, 1943.

Hughes, Langston. *Fight for Freedom: The Story of the NAACP*. New York, 1962.

Hunter, Floyd. *Community Power Structure: A Study of Decision Makers*. Chapel Hill, 1954.

Isaacs, Harold R. *The New World of Negro Americans*. New York, 1963.

Jack, Homer A. "Journey of Reconciliation," *Common Ground*, August, 1947.

Johnson, Charles S. *Patterns of Negro Segregation*. New York, 1943.

Johnson, Guy B. "Negro Racial Movements and Leadership in the United States," *American Journal of Sociology*, July, 1937.

Johnson, James Weldon. *Black Manhattan*. New York, 1930.

———. *Along This Way*. New York, 1933.

———. *Negro Americans, What Now?* New York, 1934.

Johnston, James Hugo. "Race Relations in Virginia and Miscegenation in the South, 1776-1860." Unpublished Ph.D. dissertation, University of Chicago, 1937.

Kahn, E. J., Jr. "Walter White," *New Yorker*, August 31 and September 4, 1948.

Kardiner, Abram, and Ovesey, Lionel. *The Mark of Oppression*. New York, 1951.

Kesselman, Louis C. *The Social Politics of FEPC*. Chapel Hill, 1948.

Key, V. O., Jr. *Politics, Parties, and Pressure Groups.* New York, 1942.

——. *Southern Politics in State and Nation.* New York, 1949.

Killian, Lewis M., and Smith, Charles V. "Negro Protest Leaders in a Southern Community," *Social Forces,* March, 1960.

King, Martin Luther, Jr. *Stride Toward Freedom.* New York, 1958.

——. *Why We Can't Wait.* New York, 1964.

——. "Our Struggle," *Liberation,* April, 1956.

Konvitz, Milton R. *The Constitution and Civil Rights.* New York, 1947.

Lee, Carleton L. "Patterns of Leadership in Race Relations: A Study of Leadership Among Negro Americans." Unpublished Ph.D. dissertation, University of Chicago, 1951.

Lerner, Max. *America as a Civilization.* New York, 1957.

Lewis, Roscoe E. "The Role of Pressure Groups in Maintaining Morale Among Negroes," *Journal of Negro Education,* Summer, 1943.

Lincoln, C. Eric. *The Black Muslims in America.* Boston, 1961.

Litwack, Leon F. *North of Slavery.* Chicago, 1961.

Locke, Alain. *The New Negro.* New York, 1925.

Logan, Rayford. *The Negro in American Life and Thought: The Nadir, 1877-1901.* New York, 1954.

—— (ed.). *What the Negro Wants.* Chapel Hill, 1944.

Loggins, Vernon. *The Negro Author.* New York, 1931.

Lomax, Louis E. *The Negro Revolt.* New York, 1962.

——. *When the Word Is Given.* New York, 1964.

Lynch, John Roy. *The Facts of Reconstruction.* New York, 1913.

McCormac, E. I. *White Servitude in Maryland.* Baltimore, 1904.

McWilliams, Carey. *Brothers Under the Skin.* Boston, 1943.

Mangum, Charles S., Jr. *The Legal Status of the Negro.* Chapel Hill, 1940.

Marshall, Allan. "A. Philip Randolph: Dean of Negro Leaders," *Ebony,* November, 1958.

Marshall, Thurgood. "An Evaluation of Recent Efforts to Achieve Racial Integration in Education Through Resorts to the Courts," *Journal of Negro Education,* Summer, 1952.

Mays, Benjamin E., and Nicholson, J. W. *The Negro's Church.* New York, 1932.

Meier, August. "Negro Protest Movements and Organizations," *Journal of Negro Education,* Fall, 1963.

Meredith, James. "I Can't Fight Alone," *Look,* April 9, 1963.

Merriam, Charles E. *Political Power.* New York, 1934.

Meyer, Martin. "Bayard Rustin: Lone Wolf of Civil Rights," *Saturday Evening Post,* July 11, 1964.

Miller, Kelly. *Race Adjustment.* New York, 1908.

Miller, Loren. "Farewell to Liberals," *Nation,* October 20, 1962.

Montagu, F. Ashley. *Man's Most Dangerous Myth: The Fallacy of Race.* New York, 1945.

Murray, Florence (ed.). *The Negro Handbook.* New York, 1942, 1944, 1946-47, 1949.

Myrdal, Gunnar. *An American Dilemma.* New York, 1943.

National Association for the Advancement of Colored People. *An Appeal to the World: A Statement on the Denial of Human Rights to Minorities in the United States of America and an Appeal to the United Nations for Redress.* New York, 1947.

——. *Annual Reports,* also Press Service for current items.

Negro Digest. "Roundtable: Is Civil Disobedience Practical to Win Full Rights for Negroes?" March, 1943.

Neustadt, Richard E. *Presidential Power.* New York, 1960.

Newsweek. "Crisis in the Making: U.S. Negroes Tussle with Issue of Resisting a Draft Law Because of Racial Segregation," June 7, 1948.

——. "Negro in America," July 29, 1963.

Nordhoff, Charles. *The Cotton States in the Spring and Summer of 1875.* New York, 1876.

Olmstead, Frederick Law. *The Cotton Kingdom,* ed. Arthur Schlesinger. New York, 1953.

Ottley, Roi. *Black Odyssey.* New York, 1948.

Ovington, Mary White. *The Walls Came Tumblin' Down.* New York, 1947.

——. *How the National Association for the Advancement of Colored People Began.* New York, 1914. Pamphlet.

Park, Robert E. *Race and Culture.* Glencoe, 1950.

Peck, James. *Freedom Ride.* New York, 1962.

Pierce, Chester M., and West, Louis W. "Six Years of Sit-ins: Psychodynamic Causes and Effects." Paper presented to 12th annual meeting of American Psychiatric Association, Los Angeles, California, May 7, 1964.

Powdermaker, Hortense. "The Channeling of Negro Aggression by the Cultural Process," *American Journal of Sociology,* May, 1943.

Powell, Adam Clayton, Jr. *Marching Blacks.* New York, 1945.

President's Committee on Civil Rights. *To Secure These Rights.* Washington, 1947.

Puttkammer, Charles W., and Worthy, Ruth. "William Monroe Trotter, 1872-1934," *Journal of Negro History,* October, 1958.

Quarles, Benjamin. *Frederick Douglass.* Washington, 1948.

Raab, Earl (ed.). *American Race Relations Today.* New York, 1962.

Randolph, A. Philip. "Why Should We March?" *Survey Graphic,* November, 1942.

Record, Wilson. *The Negro and the Communist Party.* Chapel Hill, 1951.

Reddick, Lawrence D. *Crusader Without Violence.* New York, 1959.

Redding, J. Saunders. *They Came In Chains.* New York, 1950.

Reid, Ira De A. "Negro Movements and Messiahs, 1900-1949," *Phylon,* Fourth Quarter, 1949.

Reuter, E. B. (ed.). *Race and Cultural Contacts.* New York, 1934.

Riddleberger, Patrick W. "The Radical's Abandonment of the Negro During Reconstruction," *Journal of Negro History,* April, 1960.

Rose, Arnold M. *The Negro's Morale.* Minneapolis, 1949.

Roucek, Joseph C. "Minority-Majority Relations in Their Power Aspects," *Phylon,* First Quarter, 1956.

Ruchames, Louis. *Race, Jobs, & Politics: The Story of FEPC.* New York, 1953.

Rudwick, Elliot M. "The Niagara Movement," *Journal of Negro History,* July, 1957.

———. "The National Negro Committee Conference of 1909," *Phylon,* Fourth Quarter, 1958.

———. "Du Bois versus Garvey: Race Propagandists at War," *Journal of Negro Education,* Fall, 1959.

———. "Race Leadership Struggle: Background of the Boston Riot of 1903," *ibid.,* Winter, 1962.

Samuels, Gertrude. "Five Angry Men Speak Their Minds," *New York Times Magazine,* May 17, 1964.

Schuyler, George S., and Johns, Vere E. "To Boycott or Not to Boycott," *Crisis,* September, 1934.

Scott, Emmett J., and Stowe, Lyman Beecher. *Booker T. Washington.* New York, 1916.

Silberman, Charles E. *Crisis in Black and White.* New York, 1963.

Simpson, George E., and Yinger, J. Milton. *Racial and Cultural Minorities.* New York, 1953.

Smith, Lillian. "Negroes in Gray Flannel Suits," *Progressive,* February, 1956.

Solomon, Frederic, and Fishman, Jacob R. "Youth and Social Action: A Psychosocial Study." Paper read before Conference on Youth, Nonviolence and Social Change, Howard University, November 5, 1963.

Southern Regional Council. *The Student Protest Movement, Winter, 1960.* Atlanta, 1960. Special Report.

———. *The Freedom Ride.* Atlanta, 1961. Special Report.

Spero, Sterling D., and Harris, Abram L. *The Black Worker.* New York, 1931.

Stampp, Kenneth M. *The Peculiar Institution.* New York, 1956.

Still, Lawrence. "Should Negroes Stop Demonstrating for Civil Rights," *Jet,* October 24, 1963.

Student Nonviolent Coordinating Committee. *This Is SNCC.* Mimeographed, n.d.

Thompson, Daniel C. *The Negro Leadership Class.* Englewood Cliffs, 1963.

Thompson, Edgar T. (ed.). *Race Relations and the Race Problem.* Durham, 1939.

Thurman, Howard. *Jesus and the Disinherited.* New York, 1949.

Time. "U.S. Negro, 1953," May 11, 1953.

U.S. Commission on Civil Rights, *1961 Commission on Civil Rights Report.* 5 vols. Washington, D.C.

———. *The 50 States Report.* Washington, 1961.

———. *Civil Rights '63.* Washington, 1963.

U.S. Department of Labor. *The Economic Situation of Negroes in the United States.* Washington, 1962.

Walker, Jack L. "The Functions of Disunity: Negro Leadership in a Southern City," *Journal of Negro Education,* Summer, 1963.

Washington, Booker T. *Up from Slavery.* New York, 1901.

Washington, Booker T., and Du Bois, W. E. B., *et al. The Negro Problem.* New York, 1903.

Weaver, Robert C. *The Negro Ghetto.* New York, 1948.

Westin, Alan F. (ed.). *Freedom Now!* New York, 1964.

——. "Ride-In!" *American Heritage,* August, 1962.

Wharton, Vernon Lane. *The Negro in Mississippi, 1865-1890.* Chapel Hill, 1947.

White, Walter. *A Man Called White.* New York, 1948.

——. *How Far the Promised Land.* New York, 1955.

——. "Passing of Southern Liberals," *Chicago Defender,* December 12 and December 19, 1942.

Williams, Robert F. *Negroes with Guns.* New York, 1962.

Wilson, James Q. *Negro Politics: The Search for Leadership.* Glencoe, 1960.

Wolfe, Bernard. "Uncle Remus and the Malevolent Rabbit," *Commentary,* July, 1949.

Woodson, Carter G. *A Century of Negro Migration.* Washington, 1918.

——. *The Mis-Education of the Negro.* Washington, 1934.

——. *The History of the Negro Church.* Washington, 1945.

——. *The Negro in Our History.* Washington, 1947.

—— (ed.). *Negro Orators and Their Orations.* Washington, 1925.

—— (ed.). *The Mind of the Negro as Reflected in Letters Written During the Crisis, 1800-1860.* Washington, 1926.

Woodward, C. Vann. *Origins of the New South, 1877-1913.* Baton Rouge, 1951.

——. *The Strange Career of Jim Crow.* New York, 1957.

Work, Monroe N. (ed.). *Negro Year Book.* Tuskegee, 1914-15, 1918-19, 1925-26.

Wright, Richard. *Native Son.* New York, 1940.

——. *Black Boy.* New York, 1945.

Zander, James W. "The Nonviolent Resistance Movement Against Segregation," *American Journal of Sociology,* March, 1963.

Zinn, Howard. *SNCC: The New Abolitionists.* Boston, 1964.

PERIODICALS

Crisis Magazine	*New York Times*
Ebony Magazine	*Newsweek*
Jet Magazine	*Time* Magazine
Negro Digest	

INDEX